ARTISANS AND COOPERATIVES

ARTISANS AND COOPERATIVES

DEVELOPING ALTERNATE TRADE FOR THE GLOBAL ECONOMY

Edited by
KIMBERLY M. GRIMES AND B. LYNNE MILGRAM

Postscript by
JUNE NASH

THE UNIVERSITY OF ARIZONA PRESS
TUCSON

FIRST PRINTING
The University of Arizona Press

LIBRARY OF CONGRESS CATALOGING-IN-PUBLICATION DATA
ARTISANS AND COOPERATIVES: DEVELOPING ALTERNATIVE TRADE FOR THE GLOBAL
ECONOMY / EDITED BY KIMBERLY M. GRIMES AND B. LYNNE MILGRAM; POSTSCRIPT
BY JUNE NASH.
P. CM.
INCLUDES BIBLIOGRAPHICAL REFERENCES AND INDEX.
ISBN 0-8165-2051-8—ISBN 0-8165-2088-7
1. HANDICRAFT INDUSTRIES. 2. PRODUCER COOPERATIVES. 3. APPLIED
ANTHROPOLOGY. 4. ARTISANS. I. GRIMES, KIMBERLY M., 1961– II. MILGRAM,
B. LYNNE (BARBARA LYNNE), 1948– III. TITLE.
HD9999.H362 A78 2000
306.3´68—DC21
00-008226

BRITISH LIBRARY CATALOGUING-IN-PUBLICATION DATA
A CATALOGUE RECORD FOR THIS BOOK IS AVAILABLE FROM THE BRITISH LIBRARY.

TO THE ARTISANS
AND TO THE MASTERY
AND SURVIVAL OF THEIR CRAFTS

CONTENTS

1.

INTRODUCTION

FACING THE CHALLENGES OF ARTISAN PRODUCTION
IN THE GLOBAL MARKET
KIMBERLY M. GRIMES AND B. LYNNE MILGRAM

2.

DEMOCRATIZING INTERNATIONAL PRODUCTION AND TRADE

NORTH AMERICAN ALTERNATIVE TRADING ORGANIZATIONS
KIMBERLY M. GRIMES

3.

BUILDING ON LOCAL STRENGTHS

NEPALESE FAIR TRADE TEXTILES
RACHEL MACHENRY

4.

"THAT THEY BE IN THE MIDDLE, LORD"

WOMEN, WEAVING, AND CULTURAL SURVIVAL IN HIGHLAND
CHIAPAS, MEXICO
CHRISTINE E. EBER

5.

THE INTERNATIONAL CRAFT MARKET

A DOUBLE-EDGED SWORD FOR GUATEMALAN MAYA WOMEN
MARTHA LYND

6.

OF WOMEN, HOPE, AND ANGELS

FAIR TRADE AND ARTISAN PRODUCTION IN A SQUATTER
SETTLEMENT IN GUATEMALA CITY
BRENDA ROSENBAUM

ARTISANS AND COOPERATIVES

KIMBERLY M. GRIMES AND
B. LYNNE MILGRAM

1. INTRODUCTION

FACING THE CHALLENGES OF ARTISAN
PRODUCTION IN THE GLOBAL MARKET

As we enter the twenty-first century, the commercialization of artisan production continues to expand as the world market for craft objects grows.[1] Improved transportation and communication systems enable once remote artisan groups to reach ever wider regional and even global markets. Rural industries, such as craft production, are becoming more prominent and integral components of a community's economic activities. Increasingly, artisans integrate craft production and trade with their subsistence activities, such as farming, herding, hunting, and trapping. In response to the global demand for crafts, artisans combine their production of weavings, wood carvings, metalwork, and baskets made for local use and trade with work targeted for sale to regional, national, and international tourist markets. Through a variety of channels, artisans build on their historical practices of selling local crafts to neighboring villages to secure products not locally available. This edited volume focuses on the political, economic, and cultural issues of artisan production—including craft making as an expressive vehicle of ethnic, political, and gender identity; the accommodation of craft traditions in the global market; and the emerging role of the anthropologist as a proactive agent for artisan groups.

The following chapters address the interplay between subsistence activities and craft production to argue for the advocacy of individual artisans in deciding the nature of their participation in the world market system. By focusing on the interaction between crafts, domestic, and subsistence activities, both in individual and in cooperative contexts, the authors here demonstrate how different types of work are tied into household and extrahousehold strategies and into occupational mobility. The essays illustrate that markets and craft production for commercial sale have been integral parts of rural economies and that households and villages were never self-sufficient producers isolated from market relationships.[2]

The authors demonstrate that it is essential to incorporate a more comprehensive account of the historical and contemporary roles of nonsubsistence activities, such as handicrafts, into studies of rural change. The artisans discussed here are making the transition from producing crafts for use and trade at the household, community, and regional levels to producing items for sale to national and international buyers. While negotiating their economic and political positions in this new arena, they find themselves struggling with their need for cash income and with their resistance to the loss of autonomy and control in the production and marketing processes. By focusing on the specific dynamics of contemporary craft production and trade, the essays dispute the image of rural economies as composed simply of subsistence-oriented activities and highlight the active role artisans take to secure their place in regional-to-national-to-global market systems.

Although the commercial trade in crafts relies on the larger market for certain inputs and for sales, the extent of its dependence on capitalist market systems varies greatly in different contexts. The authors explore the nature of the interdependence between indigenous and Western capitalist economic forms as well as the agency of artisans in shaping the path of this articulation. Culturally diverse indigenous people's responses to Westernization and capitalism range from accommodation to resistance to rejection. In these case studies, we see evidence of all three. Recognizing the great diversity in how capitalism has expanded throughout the world, Marcus and Fischer (1986) suggest, "These processes are more complex than the dominant paradigms seem able to represent them, and thus one obvious course is for political economy to rebuild understandings of macrolevel systems from the bottom up" (80). The authors here illustrate how the changing dynamics of craft production are differentially manifested by artisans and artisan groups at particular historical moments. A strength of the volume is its in-depth ethnographic analyses, which strive toward more comprehensive accounts of such change in rural areas.

Artisan families and small traders, while still working at the household level, are able to accumulate and extract capital. Although family members provide the core of nonwage workers, nonfamily help is enlisted when required through the direct payment of wages and through a system of obligations rooted in reciprocal labor exchanges. Similarly those individuals working in craft cooperatives are often members of the same family or participate in the same community organizations. Seeing craft production and trade as embedded in the economic, social, and cultural environment in which it operates can highlight the combination of opportunities and constraints that determine the circumstances and relations of production and the parameters of individuals' socioeconomic mobility (Roseberry 1988, 172). Taking into account the cultural as well as the material aspects of craft production for the global market, the case studies consider how gender, power, and class relations crosscut transformations in the small commodity labor process with the current changes in rural economies. To deal with shifting spheres of power, individuals develop different political strategies that change according to the historically and socially situated conditions of production and its application. Artisans explain that they seek to make their enterprises financially successful at the regional, national, and global levels while retaining control of their operations, regardless of how small or local they may be.

Although in many instances small producers depend on larger national or global markets to sell their products, these artisans and traders do not necessarily have to adopt the norms of capitalist relations to operate in these markets (Lockwood 1993, 157–58). As Margaret Rodman (1987) maintains, simple commodity production rooted in family and community ties may indeed "persist indefinitely" alongside capitalist practices without being swallowed by them (716). To understand this multifaceted nature of small-scale artisan production, the essays in this volume emphasize both the internal dynamics of production practices and the external market conditions that producers face, while situating artisans at the intersection of the historical processes in which they participate. The authors adopt an actor-oriented perspective to trace the ways in which individual artisans and artisan groups work to ameliorate the detrimental effects of their participation in new markets. Grimes, Lynd, MacHenry, and Rosenbaum show how artisan groups have established alternative production and marketing systems with national and international partners to provide a more democratic and equitable basis of exchange. The result can be a strengthening of ethnic identity and political position.

Eber, Lynd, MacHenry, Milgram, M'Closkey, and Rosenbaum also address how artisan production is changing gender roles and everyday practices as we face the mass incorporation of women into the international labor force. Whereas research has shown that multinational factory work seldom provides the independence or security many young women seek, these authors describe how local craft production can lead to more self-reliance and independence for women, even though at times the risks can be high.

Since the 1970s, feminist scholars have combined Marxist and feminist approaches to demonstrate the value of women's activities in different arenas of action and, indeed, to try to dissolve the bifurcation between the reproductive and productive spheres. The question of how expanding markets and the introduction of new technology have affected women's positions and their access to resources has been widely used as an analytical tool for understanding the shifts in the relations of production and trade with the commoditization of rural economies.[3] We cannot assume that the advent of capitalist forces automatically marginalizes women's positions (although this is often the case), and we must guard against the hegemony of the Western construct that dictates a public/private dichotomy that assumes a priori the subordination of women. For example, in communities such as in northern Luzon (Milgram, this volume) or in Chiapas, Mexico (Eber, this volume), the dichotomy between public and private spheres is in most instances nonexistent.[4] The precedent for a high degree of gender equality, as seen by women's active roles in productive work outside the home and by the sharing of household tasks, demonstrates that all arenas of work can be valued. Often, women as well as men may move freely into commercial craft production when new economic opportunities arise.[5]

Women of different ages and of different indigenous social standings experience social change in different ways. Women do not comprise a homogeneous group; gender is crosscut by relations of class, race, and ethnicity (di Leonardo 1991, Gallin and Ferguson 1991, Moore 1988).[6] Their own statuses as well as their families' statuses and their control over economic resources vary within the context of their differing roles. Milgram, for example, shows how in northern Luzon, where seniority is based on age rather than gender, land ownership and tenancy remain open to men and women, conferring social prestige and a degree of power on both. As evidenced in the commercialization crafts described in these essays, class differences can either restrict or ease access to resources and to distribution networks, or as Eber, Grimes, Lynd, MacHenry, and Rosenbaum demonstrate, artisans can work together to promote relative economic equality.[7]

The essays in the volume also examine the avenues craft producers may pursue to take up producer-trader status. Operating individually or in a cooperative context, craft producers and traders mobilize and use whatever resources are at their disposal to realize their goals. These resources can include not only finances but also social capital in the form of access to individuals in influential positions; social networks and obligations; and cultural capital, such as access to important information and symbols. The entrepreneurs documented here, both men and women, operate according to the constraints and standards that prevail within their groups, while incorporating new or alternative patterns of business to achieve their ends.

The studies here document how small producers often market or trade crafts in addition to producing them, thus highlighting the need for a more flexible definition of entrepreneurial activities in which entrepreneurship is regarded as one aspect of continuous variation in production and marketing processes (Cook 1986, 54; Nafziger 1978, 25–26). In the case studies presented, craft entrepreneurs engage in productive activities as well as in managerial or supervisory roles. Entrepreneurs add physical value to the products they sell: artisans finish wood carvings (e.g., Causey); weavers sew woven yardage into functional products such as rugs (e.g., Cohen, MacHenry) or clothing and personal accessories (e.g., Eber, Lynd, MacHenry, Milgram) or household items (e.g., Rosenbaum). In changing economies, artisans combine the daily management of a business and the creative decisions of the entrepreneur. Implicit in this premise, the authors argue, is a fluidity in which today's craft entrepreneur may have been yesterday's craft producer, just as today's trader may be tomorrow's artisan (Cook and Binford 1990, 31).

With the growing market for crafts from developing regions, transformations in local production practices commonly occur in order for artisans to meet the demands of their new consumers. As production becomes increasingly linked to international capital, artisans have to make decisions about the design and style of the objects they produce. What physical features of the artifact are integral to its meanings and functions—and hence must remain part of the final product—and what features does the maker feel are dispensable? The case studies in this volume repeatedly consider such questions as they outline how artisans strive to develop products that successfully mediate between "traditional" standards and consumer expectations. Grimes, Lynd, MacHenry, and Milgram focus on the degree of autonomy and control artisans are able to maintain over their aesthetic decisions as they work to meet the changing tastes of North American and European buyers. Rosenbaum's study of artisans living in a squatter settlement provides an important counterexample of producer groups who do not grapple with this issue and why.

Most artisan groups desire to preserve local values through their production. They are not working solely to market products but also to sustain deeply held beliefs about their social relations and their relationships to the environment. The ingenuity of artisans to accomplish such goals is remarkable. Craft production has played an important role in cultural revitalization movements, as seen in Eber's chapter.

Given the embeddedness of objects in cultural systems, artisans do, however, adapt their products to meet shifting consumer tastes as they have done in the past. In examining the production of indigenous crafts of Middle America, Nash (1993a) discusses the relationship between producing and consuming communities because the culture of production and the culture of consumption are increasingly not the same. She argues that although production processes and the surface features of craft objects may speak of continuity, they more often hide roots that have repeatedly responded to change (1993a, 2, 6). The character of the products resulting from the relationship between producer and consumer, then, should not be regarded as controlled by external market forces or by unchanging local persistence but as tempered by the selective adoption and adaptation of external elements.[8] When a handcrafted object is sold in a commoditized transaction in domestic tourist or export markets, although it may be altered slightly in design, for example, it remains a symbol of the culture in which it is produced (see Nash 1993a, 12; Causey, Eber, Lynd, Milgram, M'Closkey, and Rosenbaum, this volume). Through this approach, the authors contribute to the ongoing discussion on issues of "authenticity" and tradition (see, e.g., Jules-Rosette 1986, Phillips and Steiner 1999, Picton 1995).

Indigenous artisans do not inevitably lose their autonomy when producing for foreign markets. Often, makers decide to retain those aesthetic elements of style that uphold local standards of design yet will still earn good economic returns (Stephen 1996, 383). However, when production grows to include a substantial tourist-export component, the market may become fragmented, affording artisans control in some areas but not in others.[9] M'Closkey, for example, shows how the appropriation of Navajo weavers' designs has not only eliminated their control over their designs but has undermined their entire weaving economy and the cultural meanings embedded in the weavings. Cohen shows how growth in tourist-export market for weavings made by the Zapotec in Santa Ana, Mexico, has yet to improve incomes due to the competition and control maintained by the neighboring Zapotec.

The "legitimacy" of crafts hinges on the circumstances of their production as they are made using traditional craft techniques in indigenous village settings (Nash 1993a, 12; Stephen 1996, 393). Whether crafts are made for local use or for tourist and foreign markets, they continue to reproduce indigenous concepts of ethnic identity even as some of their characteristics, such as colors and patterns, may change in the negotiation between makers and consumers. Indeed, the international market for crafts is built on an elite consumer ideology that contrasts manufactured, mass-produced, modern objects with handmade, authentic, local crafts (Stephen 1996, 382). Artisans maneuver to retain elements of so-called traditional design while fashioning products for global markets.

Research on crafts also documents how the development of craft cooperatives, initiated by both local and outside interests, affects the social relations of production and the character of the crafts produced.[10] Ehlers (1993) and Rosenbaum and Goldin (1997), for example, demonstrate how the entire production of many of the Maya weaving cooperatives in highland Guatemalan villages is exported to the fashion markets of the United States and Europe. Although the design of the fabrics is based on "traditional" patterns, these authors question how much autonomy weavers in these cases maintain as they are positioned between "volatile" markets and the "faddish" tastes of their northern consumers (Ehlers 1993, 183).

The incorporation of craft and art traditions in the world market during the second half of the twentieth century marked a time in which goods were no longer consumed just as necessities but as luxuries that accomodate the ever-changing wants, tastes, and styles of modern consumer culture. The authors of this volume question whether this change must necessarily lead to a decline in the quality and a loss in the meanings of crafts and art or whether artisans can strengthen their ethnic and political positions by means of alternative markets. Grimes, Eber, Lynd, MacHenry, Milgram, and Rosenbaum discuss alternative markets for artisan groups—including alternative trading organizations, collective work organizations, nongovernmental organizations (NGOs), and other community groups and individual practices that support the continuity of cultural traditions. Cohen and M'Closkey discuss their roles in organizing a community museum and a traveling museum exhibition, respectively, designed to highlight not only the skill and time involved in weaving but, more importantly, the meanings woven into the fabrics and the cultural contexts in which they are produced.

The authors also examine how they have expanded their activities from conducting scholarly research to using their positions in first world contexts to benefit directly the producer groups with whom they work. As advisors, consultants, curators, and marketers of art and craft products, the authors have applied their knowledge and research to address problems producer groups face in the global marketplace. They explore the changes in artisans' livelihoods and in their communities that have resulted from their actions. They also address strategies for enhancing the producer groups' working and living conditions and for resisting the debasement of their craft traditions. Although most of the authors have been successful in achieving their goals, Causey provides a cautionary note highlighting the difficulties an anthropologist faces when expanding his or her role from a scholarly position to one of advocacy.

In the late twentieth century, the gap between the living standards of the rich and those of the poor grew rapidly within and among countries. As the spread of transnational corporations and the concentration of wealth in the hands of a few increase this inequality, the exploitation of the earth's resources (human resources as well as environmental) is unsustainable. The artisans in this book reveal, however, that this trajectory can be modified so that people can have the opportunity to develop their talents and capacities more fully. Some of their strategies have yet to achieve the desired outcomes, and others have been more successful in obtaining positive results, yet all continue to strive to meet the challenges of daily survival and to build a better future for themselves, their families, and their communities.

NOTES

[1] Artisans or craft producers have been generally defined here to include a wide variety of individuals—weavers, wood-carvers, sewers, basket makers, potters, lace makers, and so forth.

[2] Cook (1984) has argued that scholars of rural, agricultural societies have repeatedly "agrarianised the countryside" in their research by failing to recognize the crucial role played by nonfarm work in a household's subsistence activities and the potential of artisans to build on this precedent (14; also Cook and Binford 1990, 39). Past scholarship postulates that rural cultivators are trapped in "endemic poverty" and rely only on income from farming for their livelihood and that agricultural practices are bogged down by ancient cultivation methods and "ingrained traditionalism" (Jensen 1987, 12).

[3] See, for examples, Deere and León de Leal 1981, Leacock 1981, Lockwood 1993, Mies 1982, Nash and Fernandez-Kelly 1983, Stephen 1996, and Tice 1995.

[4] See also Karim 1995 and Van Esterik 1995.

[5] See also Bacdayan 1977, Cherneff 1982, and Jefremovas 1994.

[6] Gailey (1987) argues that "Gender relations rarely are abstracted from other aspects of one's social identity in kinship societies. People exercise claims to specific relatives' labor or products, and work efforts may be organized on a relationship basis" (9).

[7] Recent studies on women's contemporary craft production specifically address the extent to which women's class membership affects whether they gain or lose economic control when the market for their production shifts from a local-regional to a national-export forum. Ehlers (1990), for example, maintains that within a climate of rapid economic expansion in a highland Guatemalan town, it is middle-class, urban, and educated women who are able to take advantage of the diversity of productive opportunities available with modernization to build strong family businesses in commercial weaving. For the Kuna of Panama, on the other hand, the establishment of women's self-managed craft cooperatives for the production of *molas* (appliqué panels sewn into blouses, pillows, purses, and so forth) has buffered the development of class differences within communities despite the fact that women's production is directly involved in the global capitalist economy (Tice 1995, 180).

[8] Other recent studies of craft production agree that producing objects geared toward external consumer tastes, in many cases, continues as an interactive process between consumers and producers. See, for examples, Stephen 1996, Jules-Rosette 1986, Baizerman 1987, and Picton 1995.

[9] Stephen (1996) outlines how the strong influence that foreign importers have had on Zapotec textile design since the 1970s has resulted in the emergence of a four-tiered market (383–84). Producers respond with specially designed, one-of-a-kind tapestries on the high end and with more quickly produced, functional items on the lower end. For many of the unique tapestries, the design is submitted from an outside source, leaving artisans in variable states of control over the aesthetic design details in the final product.

[10] See, for examples, Ehlers 1993, García Canclini 1993, Jules-Rosette 1986, Stromberg-Pellizi 1993, and Tice 1995.

KIMBERLY M. GRIMES

2. DEMOCRATIZING INTERNATIONAL PRODUCTION AND TRADE

North American Alternative Trading Organizations

> In this postmodern world of amalgamated cultures and the search for identity
> through consumerism, the strange alliance of a politically conscious consuming
> elite and culturally rooted producing communities may continue to generate new
> and beautiful forms and textures in artisan products.
> —*June Nash*, Crafts in the World Market

In search of Andean musical instruments in the early 1990s, I walked into a store a friend had recommended. The shop sold a wide variety of Latin American crafts, backstrap loom-woven clothing, and organically produced nuts and dried fruits. While waiting to make my purchase, I picked up the shop's mail-order catalog and discovered in it not only pictures of the products for sale but also photos and stories about the people who had made the goods. The catalog discussed the impoverished conditions in which millions of Latin Americans live and stated that by purchasing the products offered, one could directly help artisans and farmers to break the cycle of poverty and build economically and environmentally sustainable communities. Under the company's logo on the front cover, it stated its mission: "a non-profit organization benefitting artisan and agricultural cooperatives in Latin America."[1]

As an anthropologist working in the mountains of southern Mexico, where poverty is a fact of life for most people but especially for semisubsistence farmers and for people who produce handmade crafts for a living, I wondered if the company's claims were in fact true—if purchasing a basket here could directly improve the artisan's life there. I was skeptical at first, knowing how some businesses who claim to be "green" do so as a marketing strategy and in reality do very little for the environment or, at best, have contradictory practices.[2]

I discovered that this particular organization was part of a group of import businesses and retail stores called alternative trade organizations (ATOs). Like mainstream commercial importers, ATOs sell goods produced in other countries in the North American market. Unlike commercial importers, however, ATOs do not try to pay the lowest price for products. Rather, they work with the artisans and farmers to establish a fair price appropriate to local economies. Their goal is to benefit producers with whom they work socially, economically, and culturally—not to maximize shareholders' profits. They work to ensure safe and healthy working conditions and to see that the producers have a voice in production and export processes. To express their values of social and economic justice, ATOs in North America united under a new name, the Fair Trade Federation (FTF), in 1992.[3]

In this chapter, I discuss the development of the alternative trade system in North America and examine how this system has created and fostered more democratic and equitable international exchange. Alternative trade rejects most of the norms of capitalist relations and allows artisans an active role in making decisions pertaining to production and trade. I examine the social, economic, and cultural consequences of the artisan—fair trade alliance and highlight some of the problems artisans and retail organizations face as they work together in the global marketplace.

HISTORY OF ALTERNATIVE TRADE

The FTF is a trade association of retailers, wholesalers, and producer organizations whose mission is to expand the alternative trade market in North America.[4] The term *alternative trade* signifies an equitable and just partnership between marketers in the United States, Canada, Europe, Australia, and Japan and disadvantaged artisans and farmers in third world communities throughout the world.

The alternative trade movement in North America originated in the late 1940s and early 1950s with the founding of Mennonite- and Brethren-affiliated businesses. These church organizations began marketing products from artisan groups worldwide through their congregations, who established the first network of fair trade stores, organized local fund-raisers, and, later, produced a retail mail-order catalog. Their motive was driven by their beliefs in Christian solidarity and social justice. By marketing quality handmade crafts, the church groups strove to increase producer families' incomes by paying a fair wage for their work and to create a direct link between producers and consumers through the crafts and stories of artisans' lifeways.

Over the next twenty-some years, these groups slowly expanded their marketing efforts and sales, but they still reached a limited audience. In the 1970s, other fair trade stores arose, but not until the next decade would the movement receive more widespread attention. In the late 1970s and early 1980s, the four largest nonreligious fair trade organizations developed and grew. These include Equal Exchange, a fair trade coffee company; Pueblo to People, a retail and wholesale operation marketing products from Latin American cooperatives; Bridgehead, an affiliate of Oxfam Canada; and Marketplace, a catalog company featuring women's clothing and housewares from India.[5] The number of smaller retail stores continued to grow throughout the 1980s.

In addition, during the 1980s, each of these separate but like-minded fair traders in the United States and Canada established annual conferences to discuss marketing and consumer education strategies and to host representatives from producer groups, who in turn would bring samples of their work for a trade show. They began a newsletter to facilitate communication between conferences. At the 1992 conference, participants voted to formalize the organization. Two years later, a board of directors was elected and the following year an executive director hired. By 1995, fair trade sales in the United States totaled more than twenty million dollars. As of January 1998, the FTF had eighty-five trade members and was supported by sixty-four friend or allied members.[6]

Seven principles underlie the FTF's mission: the payment of fair wages to artisans and farmers; the guarantee of employment advancement; environmentally sustainable production practices; public accountability; the creation of long-term trade relationships; the assurance of safe and healthy working conditions; and the advancement of technical and financial assistance from the North American marketers to the producer groups whenever possible. When discussing reasons for starting a fair trade business, individual members of the FTF reiterate these principles and emphasize their opposition to current dominant production and trade practices.[7] As the *SERRV International 1998–1999 Catalog* states, "When you purchase a handcraft from SERRV International, you become part of a global partnership of justice and hope. Your purchase brings dignity and needed income to people in the developing world. In exchange, you receive a handmade, high quality product at an affordable price" (SERRV International 1999).

WHY ALTERNATIVE TRADE

People involved in fair trade believe that optimizing profits to the detriment of workers and the environment is unethical. They maintain that businesses must champion human rights, highlight labor issues, ensure sustainable environmental practices, promote economic justice, and work to preserve culturally embedded craft traditions. In the mid-1990s, the media gave significant attention to the worldwide problems of sweatshops, unfair labor practices, and child labor. In the spring of 1996, when Kathie Lee Gifford tearfully admitted on her television morning show her lack of knowledge about the appalling working conditions and the young ages of the girls sewing her name-brand clothes in a Honduran factory, she set off a chain reaction in the press. Campaigns against Nike, Disney, and Wal-Mart for using sweatshop labor became "hot stories." Many consumers have responded to this information by now considering the social conditions in which a product is made.[8]

Across the United States, students on dozens of university campuses have organized to protest against sweatshop labor. They have produced and distributed signs, leaflets, flyers, manuals, and other products to educate fellow students and the public about sweatshop labor and corporate exploitation.[9] Sit-ins and demonstrations have resulted in some university officials signing an antisweatshop policy for their campuses. At other schools, officials have promised to review the labor practices of companies that make their university clothing and other goods. Individual college groups have united to form two national organizations, the United Students Against Sweatshops, and the Student Alliance to Reform Corporations, protesting on the steps of the U.S. Department of Labor, the World Bank, and the World Trade Organization. They are demanding an end to corporate-controlled monitoring systems and any trade deals that do not include strict labor and environmental standards.

Some members of the FTF have played key roles in exposing corporations whose business practices further impoverish and threaten the health of workers, their families, and their communities while maximizing corporate profits. For example, Global Exchange, a nonprofit organization in San Francisco, began the campaign against Nike in 1996 after the severe repression of workers in Indonesia who were struggling to win the right to organize in U.S. production factories. As the cofounder of the organization, Kevin Danaher states, "Fair trade activists understand that although the key participants in global trade are producers and consumers, the dominant commercial trading system gives almost no control of the process to these two key groups."[10] Global Exchange's Corporate Accountability Program pressures U.S. companies working overseas to improve their labor and environmental practices by implementing, with outside monitoring, corporate codes of conduct that respect international labor and environmental standards.[11]

With the heightened media interest, FTF members began a consumer education campaign that focuses on the principles of fair trade and on how fairly traded products are an alternative to those produced by sweatshop and child labor.[12] During 1997, the federation's national office received more than forty requests per week for information on fair trade. However, as a young organization, the FTF suffers from a lack of staff and resources to respond to the numerous media opportunities. Although it has produced "Action Guides" and the "Conscious Consumer" booklet for consumers as well as press releases for its members, and has developed strategic alliances with like-minded organizations—such as Co-op America, Witness for Peace, International Labor Rights Fund, and Public Citizen, to name a few—the lack of funding has hindered it from reaching all of its targeted markets.

The North American FTF has had the benefit of communicating with members of the larger and more experienced alternative trade movement in Europe. Even though Europe has a smaller population, it has more than three thousand fair trade retail stores and fairly traded products stocked in thirteen thousand commercial shops and thirty supermarket chains.[13] The volume of fair trade retail sales in Europe is eight times that in North America.[14] European fair traders have developed three fair trade seals to help consumers identify fairly traded commodities—such as coffee, honey, cocoa, tea, orange juice, and sugar. Eleven of the large ATOs that comprise the European Federation of Alternative Trade (EFAT) have annual sales of approximately 150 million dollars; they receive some financial support from the European Union (Littrell and Dickson 1997, 351).

Although fair trade retail sales worldwide are substantial, a comparison of these sales and those of the world's largest trading companies reveals how small a share fair trade holds on the global scale. An examination of the major commodities entering world trade in the 1980s shows that only fifteen multinationals market 70 to 90 percent of the world's production. Moreover, for most commodities, only three to six of these giant corporations dominate almost the entire market (Brown 1993, 50–51). For example, three coffee companies alone have sales exceeding fifty billion dollars in 1980 (Brown 1993, 10). The trend for further concentration of wealth and power in the commodity markets seems imminent.

With the beginnings of international commodity agreements following World War II (such as the General Agreements on Tariffs and Trade) and the creation of global financial institutions (the International Monetary Fund and the World Bank), corporations from the richer industrial nations have continued to increase their share of global profitability at the expense of third world peoples, whose countries spiral downward, burdened by international debt (George 1988). This is a bitter irony because the original goal of the commodity agreements and the financial institutions was to increase third world countries' export earnings from their primary commodities.[15]

A new international economic agreement is currently under discussion at the Organization for Economic Cooperation and Development (OECD), comprised of the world's twenty-nine richest countries. The Multilateral Agreement on Investment (MAI) would "virtually eliminate restrictions on international investments; prevent governments from instituting policies aimed at strengthening local economies; allow multinational corporations to sue governments for impeding those corporations' 'right' to make a profit at the expense of communities and the environment; and force governments to respond to economic pressures by abolishing worker protections, public-safety regulations, and measures protecting the environment" (Roth 1997, 25). If signed, this ultraliberal agreement will be a formidable steamroller crushing social and environmental standards related to production and working conditions. Local citizens and their national governments will have no recourse to defend themselves against the damage caused by transnational companies (Barlow and Clarke 1998).

Agreements like the MAI will further multinationals' sphere of global economic control and intensify the inequality of incomes. Poor third world populations will be hardest hit because "the poorer the country the smaller the share of national income that goes to the poorest groups in society" (Brown 1993, 117).[16] Since the 1970s, the percentage of national income distributed to the poorest populations in all countries has been decreasing (Brown 1993, 117). The poor are excluded from discussions about issues and decisions that directly affect their lives. The majority of poor women are even more disenfranchised because patriarchal structures and practices within nations and local communities further magnify their exclusion and silence. The result is greater impoverishment for women and children.

As third world peoples, especially women, look to strengthen their positions at home and in the world market, and as many citizens around the globe become increasingly concerned about the rights of workers and the environment, the importance of fair trade organizations is highlighted. Alternative trade is still small, but whereas the annual growth of world trade has been declining, the fair trade network has been expanding rapidly (Brown 1993, 156–57). Fair traders help people embark on their own path of independent development rather than remain dependent on exploitative relationships with capitalist enterprises or on the charity of aid-relief organizations.

FAIR TRADE BUSINESSES IN NORTH AMERICA

In North America, the gross sales of fair trade businesses—including nonprofit, not-for-profit, and for-profit enterprises—range from several thousand to several million dollars. Although the size and type of organizations and their volume of sales vary, the commitment to providing an alternative market for world artisans makes each business's contribution to the fair trade movement important.

The oldest and largest fair trade businesses are the two religious organizations who began fifty years ago: Ten Thousand Villages (Mennonite) and SERRV International (Church of the Brethren). SERRV has two hundred small retail shops and a retail catalog that thousands of churches use to sell handicrafts from SERRV International's network of craft producers in forty developing regions, including Africa, Asia, Latin America, and economically depressed regions of the United States. Their sales totaled $4,992,000 in 1997, out of which SERRV International returned close to $2,000,000 to the artisans.[17] The organization educates consumers by describing the lifeways of particular artisan groups and their countries, highlighting artisans' new products and providing general information on fair trade issues in its catalog and in a monthly newsletter, *Partnerships.* At its headquarters in New Windsor, Maryland, it produces educational and marketing videos, and hosts an annual international festival. SERRV International and Ten Thousand Villages (whose sales equaled more than six million dollars in 1996) together are responsible for about half the volume of alternative trade in North America.[18]

Most of the wholesaler/retailer organizations' sales range in hundreds of thousands of dollars. Ganesh Himal Trading Company, located in Spokane, Washington, is representative of these organizations. Founded in the 1980s and growing slowly but steadily in the 1990s, Ganesh Himal gross sales ranged between $250,000 and $350,000 in the mid-1990s. The wife and husband team began the business in 1984 after meeting Tibetan refugees in Nepal who requested the couple's help in marketing products in the United States.[19] Over the past fourteen years, Ganesh Himal has made long-term commitments with several producer groups. It pays a higher price for high-quality products with the goals of increasing incomes, building a sense of pride in the production process, and offering security by ordering large quantities of goods every two months. The producer groups have thus been able to invest in their homes and family members' educations. Ganesh Himal also gives annual donations to the Dhukuti Girl-Child

Education Fund, supports three Tibetan refugees, and raises funds for disaster relief, such as the one thousand dollars for Nepalese in the Dhading District whose crops and homes were wiped out by monsoons and mud slides in 1997. In the United States, the owners are the codirectors of the Tibetan Rights campaign in Washington state, and they donate money and merchandise to shelters for women and teenagers.

New technology in mass-communication systems has opened up new possibilities for fair trade. Peoplink, the first on-line fair trade organization, equips artisans worldwide with digital cameras and computers, which enable them to capture color images of their lives and work; document their histories, legends, and productive processes; and send this culturally rich information via the Internet to consumers, who can purchase their crafts via the Web. The founder, Dan Salcedo, began Peoplink in 1996 because he wanted to build a global network of grassroots groups to showcase the richness of their cultures while selling their traditional crafts. By selling on the Web (as opposed to mail-order catalogs or retail stores), a consumer can click on to more information about the products, the artisans, and their communities. In addition to the electronic catalog, Peoplink also has a WeCare fund-raising program for schools, churches, and nonprofit organizations, an educational curricula of on-line cultural resources for schools, and a global gallery featuring exhibitions of one-of-a-kind works of art.

Although most fair trade in North America deals with handmade crafts and clothing, a few organizations deal in food products. Cultural Survival and Conservation International (CI), for example, support sustainable income-generating projects for groups living in rainforests. The Conservation Enterprise Department of CI markets nontimber forest and agroforestry products (coffee, cocoa, nuts, tree oils, and plant fibers) and marine products that are managed and harvested in ecologically friendly ways. They also provide technical and financial assistance. Several other fair trade companies work with coffee farmers.[20] Equal Exchange is by far the largest, comprising approximately 90 percent of the North American fair trade coffee market. Founded in 1986 in Massachusetts, Equal Exchange's mission is to foster mutually beneficial relationships with coffee farmers in Latin America and coffee consumers in the United States and Canada.[21] Equal Exchange guarantees a fixed price for coffee beans and provides coffee farmers with advance payments so that they can avoid borrowing money at high interest rates. In 1997, the gross sales of the company equaled more than four and a half million dollars.

Small retail businesses may not have the volume of sales that larger ones handle, but they form the heart of the fair trade movement. Retail stores comprise the largest sector of membership in the FTF. It is the growing number of voices working together to educate the general public about fair trade that helps spread its message. As a store owner stated, "I have always hated listening to people brag about how little they paid for something in Mexico, especially handmade things. Now with my own shop, I hope to make some kind of positive difference in the world."

My husband and I opened a nonprofit fair trade retail store in 1996. We had two main reasons for opting to retail goods. First, more fair trade retail stores are needed if fair trade is to sell the large amounts of goods artisans produce and to support the growing numbers of artisan groups in fair trade. Second, the store itself is an effective way to educate the general public about peoples' lifeways and how the global economy operates. We not only sell goods, we tell stories—stories about peoples and cultures around the world through photographs, information tags and flyers, and, most importantly, one-to-one conversations. In our store, like in many others, we have a consumer information section filled with books and material on community development projects—such as those by Heiffer International or Oxfam—and on current legislation dealing with international production and trade issues. We show videos so that the artisans can speak for themselves and North Americans can see how people in other countries live, work, and enjoy life.

In 1997 (our second year in business), our gross sales totaled close to $100,000, of which approximately 30 percent went back to the artisans for the goods. After expenses, we had another $4,500 in revenue that we gave to communities for development projects. One project provided disaster relief for an artisan cooperative in Kenya whose workshop and living quarters were washed away by El Niño rains. Since 1996, we have provided funding for a local ecology group in Oaxaca, Mexico, to set up a recycling center.[22]

Our store is similar to other fair trade retail shops. Owners are committed to making a connection between themselves, artisans, and consumers. Although attentive to cash flow, sales, and other matters of business, fair trade retailers state that if it were just a business, they would not be doing it. As one retailer commented, "I started working with poor women craft producers in Haiti in 1981. It changed my life and my outlook on what is important in life." Another retailer summed up most fair traders' feelings when he said, "I have always been interested in helping people help themselves and feel fair trade is a great avenue in which to accomplish this."

PROBLEMS FAIR TRADERS AND ARTISANS FACE

Although the fair trade movement is growing, several hurdles must be overcome if it is to make a significant impact in changing the way global production and trade are conducted. In a time when neoliberalism is destroying social, ethnic, and political consciousness under the guise of "freedom," fair trade plays an important role in preserving and promoting cultural traditions and the diversity of identities in this world of increasing globalization. Discussing the impact of free trade agreements on Mexican identity, García Canclini (1996) points out that we must question the focus on free trade and economic yields when this type of trade "drowns multiculturalism or subordinates diverse identities to a single identity that only one of these imagines the other should be" (155).

The FTF's director, board of directors, and general membership are currently working on five key problem areas to improve the alternative trade market in North America: the lack of direct access for many artisan groups to fair trade outlets; the lack of technical skills needed to compete globally; the lack of North American consumer demand; the lack of a fair trade label or seal to distinguish fair trade products; and the lack of retail outlets. The problems are clearly interrelated, and advancements in any one of them will feed back to the others.

Page-Reeves's (1998) research on the handknit sweater industry in Bolivia provides an example of how these problems affect the dynamics of production and export for artisan groups. Fair trade organizations are the main clients for many of the grassroots Bolivian knitting groups, but because of a lack of demand, they cannot absorb the growing production capacity of the producers. The fair trade retail price, in this case, exceeds the commercial price of Bolivian sweaters retailed by importers who pay miserable wages to the knitters.[23] Concerned about creating dependency, a fair trade organization limits its purchasing to up to 30 percent of the production of any one group, but the Bolivian knitters, as well as other groups, have limited skills to access other clients. They have become dependent on particular fair trade businesses, even though fair traders strive to help producers become more independent by teaching them how to do export and international trade. Most producers want to work exclusively in the alternative trade market because they receive higher prices and are treated with dignity and justice. This trend will strengthen as neoliberal policies and practices expand in the world market.

On the marketing side, fair traders have witnessed the demise of one of the
oldest and largest fair trade organizations, Pueblo to People, and of several smaller
ones in the past few years. Pueblo to People grew quickly, with annual sales in the
millions, yet ultimately went bankrupt. Two of the problems fair traders face are a lack
of marketing information and, more importantly, a limited consumer base educated in
fair trade practices and principles. Organizations want to raise artisans' revenues, yet
often consumers are unwilling to pay a fair price for certain products because they are
uneducated as to the time, work, and money invested to make these goods (see Eber,
this volume). Pueblo to People, for example, purchased sweaters from the Bolivian
knitting groups just mentioned. It paid a fair price for the sweaters but was unable to
sell the quantity purchased because it could not reach enough consumers who could
appreciate the quality of the work. A problem many fair traders share is a lack of business skills and connections because most enter the business world driven by concerns
of social justice and by a rejection of the dominant system in which profits, not people,
are put first.

Even with these seemingly insurmountable problems that fair trade producers and marketers face, fair trade does provide a viable alternative to current mainstream commercial production and trade. As Madeley (1996) states, "Trade could offer a way out of poverty, but only if it democratized. . . . The South today needs a new
development stimulus. Producer co-operation, more South-South trade and alternative trade, against a background of genuine participation, could be a powerful combination that helps countries, battered by an unjust international trading system, to take
the initiative in developing a more just system that helps to provide that new stimulus"
(176–77).

Nonexploitative relationships built through fair trade offer a way for groups
to defend themselves from the increasing social fragmentation of artisan and small farmer
communities in the global economy. Because the artisan groups working in fair trade
are democratically organized, sharing in decision-making processes and revenues, they
avoid the downward spiral in quality and revenue caused by exploitation and unfair
competition.[24] With globalization, the lifeways of producers are changing throughout
the world, but the striking difference between fair trade and mainstream production is
that with fair trade at least more voices are heard.

Producer groups already involved in fair trade remark how it allows them to
reinforce their social identities as artisans and as members of particular ethnic groups

(as seen in Lynd's, MacHenry's, and Rosenbaum's chapters, this volume). For some, this reinforcement has also led to a strengthening of their political positions in the national arena. For example, by exporting directly to the international fair trade market, indigenous groups—such as the Satere, Yanomami, Karaja, and Wai-Wai in the Amazon rainforest—earn money in hard currencies (U.S. and European). Generating export dollars, they now have another much needed means to defend themselves against encroaching ranchers and other nonindigenous developers.[25]

The benefits for women in fair trade, for the most part, have been multifold. Approximately 80 percent of the artisan cooperatives with whom North American fair traders work are women-run cooperatives. Not only do these women have opportunities to generate much needed cash revenue for themselves and their families, they are empowered as central players in making decisions and in gaining access to information and microcredit. They have used revenues to establish health clinics, education funds, child care, and other services in their communities.[26] Many women have learned how to export goods, combining production and trade, and increasing their entrepreneurial skills and choices.

FAIR TRADE IN THE TWENTY-FIRST CENTURY

Fair trade businesses have grown quickly at a time when small businesses in general struggle to survive. In part, this growth is a reaction to the current media focus on sweatshops and to the development of socially conscious consumers who seek out products made in environmentally and socially sustainable ways. The late twentieth century has been a time of dramatic change in Western consumption patterns. No longer is shopping just for acquiring basic necessities. In contemporary Euro-American societies, shopping now ranks as the number two leisure activity, following television watching, as people search for their wants, desires, and images in the maze of tastes and styles offered by modern consumer culture (Lury 1996). By connecting the consumer with the producer and thus creating a fabric of community, fair trade stores fill a void people experience in the mindnumbing superstores and commercial malls. As the consumer culture grows, the question remains whether grassroots collectives and fair traders with their alternative system will be able to strengthen their influence in the politics of production and consumption.

NOTES

1 The shop was Pueblo to People located in Houston, Texas.

2 See *Co-op America Quarterly,* a publication of Co-op America (1612 K Street NW, #600, Washington, D.C. 20006) or their website (www.coopamerica.org) for updates on businesses making false "green" claims.

3 The FTF's address is FTF, P.O. Box 698, Kirksville, MO 63501 (ftfok@fairtradefederation.com). See also the website www.fairtradefederation.com. The current executive director is Cheryl Musch.

4 Information on the FTF and its history comes from a grant entitled "Creating a Consumer Demand for Fair Trade Products," written in 1996 by then—FTF director Mimi Stephens and board members Nina Smith and Laura Brown.

5 Equal Exchange (www.equalexchange.com) is located at 250 Revere St., Canton, MA 02021. Marketplace: Handwork of India is located at 1455 Ashland Ave., Evanston, IL 60201. Bridgehead (www.web.net/~bridgehead/) is located at 99–880 Wellington St., Ottawa, Ontario, Canada KIR6K7. In 1997, Pueblo to People went out of business; some of the reasons why are discussed further in the essay.

6 Several of FTF's trade members have a network of stores. For example, in 1997, Ten Thousand Villages (the Mennonite-based ATO) had 120 retail shops and supplied goods to another 133 shops. SERRV International operates 200 retail shops. Other smaller fair traders may own one or two stores and have a mail-order catalog. The exact number of stores selling fairly traded goods in North America is currently undocumented because there are shops that carry fairly traded goods mixed with other products. There are also people who in essence are doing fair trade on their own but have yet to join the FTF (see Rosenbaum, this volume, note 1).

7 In 1998, I sent a questionnaire to all trade members in the FTF, 80 percent of whom responded. One of the questions I asked was, "What motivated you to start a fair trade business?"

8 See, for example, "The Shame of Sweatshops," *Consumer Reports,* August (1999): 18–20.

9 For example, at Duke University, students made antisweatshop coloring books, and at University of Wisconsin, they made "Disparage Reebok" T-shirts. At Earlham, they produced caps with "No on the FLA" across the front, referring to the Fair Labor Association created by Clinton, which allows corporations to voluntarily enact codes of conduct—a weak and ineffective measure to appease citizens' demand for antisweatshop legislation and labor standards in trade agreements.

10 Global Exchange 1996 newsletter. A nonprofit operation, Global Exchange (www.globalexchange.org) has two fair trade stores—one in San Francisco and the other in Berkeley—and sponsors human rights campaigns, reality tours, and lecture series. It produces a variety of educational resources on international production and trade issues. Its main office is located at 2017 Mission St., #303, San Francisco, CA 94110 (info@globalexchange.org).

11 See note 10.

12 The campaign was funded in part by the Ford Foundation.

13 Reported in the FTF grant (see note 4). Brown (1993) notes that "every major town in Britain has at least one supplier of products from this alternative system and the big cities have several" (157).

14 According to research conducted by Millennium Communications, a communications firm based in Washington, D.C., the main reason for larger volume of fair trade sales in Europe is the result of a more educated consumer base. Europeans tend to be more aware of international issues, have a better knowledge of world geography, and understand how their consumer choices affect the lives of people in other countries.

[15] See Brown (1993, 87–92) for more information on international commodity agreements.

[16] "In many Third World countries including Brazil, India, Mexico, Malaysia and Peru, the poorest 40 per cent of households received less than 10 per cent of the total income. By contrast, in the developed industrial countries the poorest 40 per cent receive at least 20 per cent of combined income" (Brown 1993, 117).

[17] Out of the final retail price, 43 percent is the cost of the goods, of which approximately 6 percent goes to shipping and 37 percent to the artisans.

[18] For more information on Ten Thousand Villages, formerly called Self Help Crafts of the World, see Littrell and Dickson (1997, 345–50).

[19] As co-owner Denise Atwood stated, "We felt that marketing their products would provide them money directly, enabling producers to improve their lives and educate their children. We also felt trade was a good vehicle for educating the American public about issues relating to refugees and the third world" (from the questionnaire cited in note 7).

[20] Other fair trade coffee companies include Aztec Harvest (part of Sustainable Harvest) in Emeryville, California; Just Us in Wolfville, Nova Scotia; Alternative Grounds in Toronto; and Headwaters Coffee in Minneapolis. Bridgehead distributes Equal Exchange's coffee in Canada.

[21] Latin American countries include Mexico, El Salvador, Nicaragua, Costa Rica, Colombia, and Peru.

[22] For the origins of the ecology group, see Grimes (1998, 50–51).

[23] More often the retail price will be about the same or even lower than the commercial price because fair trade eliminates a chain of middlemen and passes back the savings to the producers.

[24] See, for example, Milgram (this volume), who discusses these problems with regard to craft producers in the Philippines.

[25] See Hecht and Cockburn (1990) for other ways indigenous peoples in the Amazon have defended their rights to land and life.

[26] See, for examples, Lynd, MacHenry, and Rosenbaum (this volume).

RACHEL MACHENRY

3. BUILDING ON LOCAL STRENGTHS
NEPALESE FAIR TRADE TEXTILES

Over the past five years, I have worked in Nepal with small-scale producers and cooperative groups that are seeking Western markets for their textile products.[1] I have observed how women artisans negotiate change as they adapt their craft products to meet market demands and how they try to improve broader social conditions for group members. I have also actively participated in bringing about some of these changes by providing information about North American tastes and suggesting possible uses for artisans' textiles. Traditional Nepalese textiles are not well known outside of South Asia. Although they do not boast the intricate weaving techniques and brilliant color work of many of the Central and South American textiles discussed elsewhere in this volume (e.g., Lynd), they represent a long and continuous thread of indigenous material culture and encompass the knowledge of a broad range of techniques—some of which include spinning, weaving, felting, embroidery, and knitting using a variety of local materials such as wool, yak hair, silk, *pashmina*, Himalayan nettle fiber, hemp, *vimal* (the inner bark of the *Grewia oppositfolia* tree), and brown cotton.

This chapter focuses on small-scale textile cooperatives in the Kathmandu and Pokhara Valleys that operate within a fair trade framework.[2] With expanding outlets for local crafts, women artisans are developing textile products for export by using local materials and skills. However, a number of problems have emerged as artisans work to build successful businesses. I examine these difficulties, many of which are rooted in the harsh conditions Nepalese face in daily life. Artisan groups are often hampered by a lack of access to resources such as water and firewood, difficulties in obtaining raw materials, and limited means of communication and transportation. In my work with women's cooperatives, I became more aware of the detrimental ecological effects of production and learned of the various approaches the cooperatives have taken to deal with these problems. I examine how co-ops seek to address challenging social problems, such as the pressures facing young women, and discuss how cooperatives have taken action on such issues by providing viable employment alternatives. Finally, this chapter analyzes how cooperatives have both succeeded and failed in adapting their textile production to the demands of the Western market.

My approach has been informed by contemporary feminist scholarship in anthropology, ecology, and development studies. The female producers' needs, knowledge, skills, and economic and social situations are the central points around which my work revolves. In countless fields, homes, and workshops, I have learned far more than I have ever taught. Farmers, craftspeople, and social activists have generously shared their knowledge with me, explaining details about the growing of hemp, the finer points of backstrap weaving, and the lifeways of women in Nepal.

Current feminist critiques of mainstream development reveal the deeply entrenched patriarchal framework on which much development practice has been based and how this privileges certain worldviews over others. To further women's interests, it is necessary to incorporate issues such as representation, agency, indigenous knowledge, and political action in development programs (Parpart 1995, 221). As Kabeer (1994) points out, "women's lives across the globe appear to straddle more dimensions and activities than those of men" (xi). The diversity of women's experiences can be understood by recognizing their interconnected productive and reproductive roles. In addition, ecological destruction disproportionately affects women, particularly women in the developing world because they are forced to travel farther to obtain resources, such as firewood and potable water, or because they experience the effects of pollution and erosion on their agricultural lands (Mies and Shiva 1993, 70). This chapter also highlights the validity and importance of locally based, indigenous knowledge and skills to maintain self-provisioning, sustainable communities that value women's expertise (see also Appleton 1995, 10; Papanek 1995, 223, 113).

SETTING

In Nepal, as in other parts of South Asia, social and economic changes are occurring as the region grapples with the forces of modernization and political change. Nepal is one of the world's poorest countries. It is extremely diverse both geographically and culturally. The country encompasses the spectacular landscape of the Himalayas as well as the middle mountains (one thousand to three thousand meters) and the fertile, low plains of the Terai. Centuries of migration by both Tibeto-Burman and Indo-Aryan groups into Nepal have resulted in a rich and complex ethnic mix of peoples who mainly practice a form of Hinduism heavily influenced by Buddhism. Rural people often live in mountain valley communities whose isolation contributes to preserving cultural differences. There are more than thirty distinct ethnic groups in this small country, each with its own language, religious beliefs, and cultural practices. Nepal remains largely agricultural and nonindustrialized, but population pressures, deforestation, and soil erosion have reduced available arable land, especially in the middle mountains. The

subsequent migration of rural farm families in search of work is indicative of a shift in
the country's economy as both male and female farmers seek alternatives to subsistence agriculture. Few employment options are available to rural, low-caste people living in the hills. Men may leave home to work as drivers, agricultural laborers, or road
builders in India or as trekking guides in Nepal. They may also send money back to
their families while serving in the Indian army or in the British army.[3] Women earn
cash as seasonal agricultural workers, road builders, domestic servants, or hotel workers in the Kathmandu hotel industry. More recently, young Nepalese girls have traveled
south to work as prostitutes in India. Craft production offers an alternative to these
limited, exploitative, and often dangerous employment possibilities. Crafts made for
household and local use, particularly textiles, have always formed an integral part of
women's subsistence livelihood strategies. Currently, these craft skills provide a supple-
mentary source of cash income for both rural and urban low-caste women through
locally initiated cooperatives that produce crafts for export. In fact, handicrafts now
comprise Nepal's largest export sector (Pye 1988, 37).

Craft cooperatives are part of a broader picture of social and political activ-
ism that encompasses antipoverty groups, women's groups, environmental groups, and
anti-child-servitude groups, all operating at a grassroots level in agitating for change.
Before 1989–90, these groups generally worked within the context of the democracy
movement. After the shift to a more democratic form of government in 1990, activists
continued to press for reforms, focusing their efforts on children, women, low-caste
peoples, and other marginalized members of society. This environment has fostered
the growth of local, community-based structures. In contrast to regions where the idea
of gender equity is already part of local culture (e.g., the Phillippines, as discussed by
Milgram, this volume), women's underprivileged position is culturally maintained in
Nepal. Cooperatives thus provide important sites for women's voices to be heard.

I first started working with producers in Nepal in 1993 as a knitwear designer for a small, Canadian company. Every year I travel to Nepal to oversee sample
production, maintain quality control, teach new skills, and solve technical and production problems. The knitwear is produced by Himalayan Knitworks, a family-run business established as an income-generating project for women in 1985 with support from
British and Norwegian development programs. Today, it is a successful export production company employing more than two hundred women in fair trade working conditions. During the time I have worked with this company, I have learned about the difficulties knitters encounter in obtaining raw materials and in dyeing yarns, the limitations

that agricultural seasons and family responsibilities impose on the amount of time they are able to devote to craft production, the difficulties in transporting supplies and finished pieces to and from makers in isolated communities, and the challenges in dealing with more than two hundred home-based artisans without the use of telephones. I have also been deeply impressed with the high level of skill and expertise of the knitters and over time have come to realize the important role this employment plays in the women's lives.

Through independent investigations on these working trips, I have discovered a range of business initiatives developing in relation to textile production. Some were government supported; some were cooperatives established by activists in response to social conditions; others operated within the private business sector. In 1997 and 1998, my research focused on locally initiated cooperative groups engaged in textile production in the Kathmandu and Pokhara Valleys, both located in the heavily farmed middle mountains of Nepal. I discovered that although many of these groups share the production difficulties faced by the knitwear company, they also provide low-caste women with opportunities to effect social change and achieve economic advancement not usually available to them in Nepalese society. I focus on two of the various groups I have studied: the Association for Craft Producers of Nepal (ACPN) and the Dupgyal Community Carpet Cooperative.

The ACPN is a nonprofit association that provides services to more than eight hundred low-caste women craft producers living in farming communities and in urban areas in the Kathmandu Valley. The association purchases crafts produced by artisan groups living in geographically isolated areas of the country; these crafts are transported to the center by foot and by road. The artisans come from a variety of ethnic groups, including Rai, Gurang, Tamang, Chetri, and Newar. Rural producers living in the middle mountains around Kathmandu are involved in subsistence agricultural activity and depend largely on growing rice, corn, and millet, supplemented by forest products, vegetable crops, and some livestock.

The second organization I examine, the Dupgyal Cooperative, is located in western Nepal and was established by Tibetan refugees living around the town of Pokhara in order to provide support to their five-thousand-member community. Unlike the Hindu Nepalese living in the surrounding Pokhara Valley, the refugees are Tibetan Buddhists and place a high value on maintaining their culture, language, and religion in exile. However, their craft enterprise has brought employment to some eight hundred local Nepalese women, largely Rai farmers and a small number of urban Newar women, who spin the carpet wool in their homes. Another one hundred Nepalese women travel by foot and by public transport to work as weavers in the cooperative's weaving center. Artisans involved in both of these initiatives balance their craft production activities with child rearing, domestic responsibilities, and, in the case of rural producers, agricultural work.[4]

CRAFT PRODUCTION THROUGH COOPERATIVES

Craft producer groups are organized on a variety of structures that vary from formally registered cooperatives to loosely organized associations of relatives and neighbors. No matter how formally or loosely organized, they all deal with common concerns: ensuring a fair return on work, support for members, safe working conditions, availability of pooled or purchased raw materials, and access to viable markets. They also function as a crucial link between the capitalist Western market and local socioeconomic structures that are based on family and community ties and on ethnic affiliation or geographic location. In addition, craft producer groups often provide community support in the form of loans, accident and emergency funds, educational opportunities, and health care.

To illustrate the workings of cooperatives and to analyze their activities, I draw on my experiences with the ACPN and the Dupgyal Cooperative. These organizations represent two very different structural models, yet both address economic and social issues affecting marginalized women craft producers.

The ACPN was established by a group of activists in 1983 in response to the lack of economic opportunities available to low-caste women. The organization represents both rural and urban low-caste producers, many of whom work in loosely affiliated cooperative groups. An additional one hundred producers are based in the organization's center in Kathmandu, which also houses the administrative and organizational functions of the association. Each of the skill areas, such as embroidery or block printing, is headed by a female unit supervisor who organizes production, distributes materials to women working in their homes, and oversees quality control. From the center, women can learn new skills, obtain high-quality raw materials, and deliver finished products for which they are paid immediately. They have access to a producer's benefit program that includes services such as a savings and loan system, retirement fund, bonus program, girl-child education fund, health services, peer counseling, legal counseling, and a fair price shop. Through connections with alternative trading organizations (ATOs),[5] ACPN deals with buyers, obtains orders, and handles the export of the craft products to Western markets.

Other Nepalese artisan organizations may provide some of these services, such as credit or export advice, but do not offer members such a wide range of services. In its intent to provide support, technology, and marketing and managerial skills in an integrated manner, ACPN is unique. Its holistic structure allows producers to shoulder less direct risk of losing money because the organization assumes responsibility for marketing and can be somewhat flexible in response to the ever-changing demands of Western consumer tastes. However, because the producers are not directly responsible for marketing their craft products, misunderstandings can arise. For example, when I was working in Nepal in 1998, the demand for certain textile products fell off sharply because of rapid changes in the demands of the Western market. The artisans confronted the management committee for an explanation, fearing that they were being treated unfairly or cheated of their orders. The management committee, comprised of both low-caste artisans and high-caste managers, struggled to explain the situation. The result was that producers became more involved in order taking and in bookkeeping to ensure continuing fairness and transparency in ACPN's management practices.

The association produces a range of craft products using a wide variety of locally specific materials and techniques, but the largest sector is textile production. The materials and techniques that are employed strongly identify the products as Nepalese, but traditional uses may be altered to meet market demand. For example, textiles traditionally used for shawls may be redesigned as tablecloths, runners, or mats. The association produces items whose retail prices range from three U.S. dollars for an appliquéd potholder to three hundred for a handspun and handknit sweater. Indeed, since 1991, high-end knitwear has been their most successful export product.[6] The handknit line was developed in cooperation with the two American designers-owners of Tara Handknits. Comprised of intricate designs drawn from Nepalese art and architecture, the knitwear is produced by highly skilled handknitters for sale as fair trade products in the U.S. boutique and gift market. At the same time, ACPN continues to market products that have less outside design input and that are made by geographically isolated rural artisans. In this way, it services a wide range of artisans in various parts of the country.

Unlike ACPN, the Dupgyal Community Carpet Cooperative in western Nepal is not a workers' cooperative. It represents an unusual partnership between two distinct communities living in the area around the town of Pokhara in the Pokhara Valley.

More than five thousand Tibetan refugees are housed in four camps built on land donated by the Nepalese government. Tibetans are not permitted to own land or hold Nepalese citizenship, so the refugees have turned to a variety of community-based enterprises, such as crafts, to earn cash income. Their involvement in commercial craft production and trade has benefitted not only the Tibetans but also the local Nepalese community.

The most successful initiative is a carpet-weaving cooperative established in 1965 that generates the majority of the community's income. The cooperative's carpet exports currently help support a broad range of social programs—including day care, schools, an orphanage, a center for the elderly, a medical center, the Gompa (Buddhist temple and monastery), and a community insurance fund for illness or accident. As a result of this collective approach, social services (especially education opportunities) within the refugee camps far exceed those available to most Nepalese citizens. A total of about one thousand people are employed in carpet making. Women who do the spinning and weaving are principally Nepalese. Although these Nepalese artisans do not have a say in the running of the cooperative because the cooperative is for the Tibetan community, they do benefit from working within what is essentially a fair cottage-industry structure. The rate of pay is high compared to the pay for other forms of work locally available to women, and paid apprenticeships may be provided if the women are not already weavers.[7] Working hours are flexible and arranged to coordinate with women's multiple household, agricultural, and child-rearing responsibilities. The spinners work in their own homes, but the weavers work in the cooperative's weaving center, where safe working conditions include adequate light and air as well as fixed hours of work. Child care, bus fare, and food are also provided. It is one of the most attractive jobs available to women in the Pokhara area.[8]

Weavers' skills are in full use with the volume of carpets they need to produce. The cooperative's primary market is in Germany. Because German consumers do not seem to seek the Tibetan-style carpets with strongly colored designs and motifs depicting Buddhist themes, the cooperative's production largely consists of pastel-colored carpets based on nineteenth-century German wallpaper designs. When asked if artisans feel uncomfortable in producing such derivative designs, the cooperative leader explained that they will always continue to produce small numbers of Tibetan-style carpets for ceremonial and household use, but that they place the economic needs of the community and their weavers first. He commented that "our carpet factory will produce whatever will sell." In later conversations, community leaders admitted their hopes that carpets with Tibetan- and Nepalese-based designs, which have more significance to their makers, will become desirable to Western consumers (see Causey, this volume). Carpets are a costly luxury product, but Dupgyal enjoyed a steady income from this production and good relationships with buyers until 1993–94, when sales declined sharply due to international media coverage of child labor in the carpet industry and the harmful ecological effects of dye waste—both issues of special concern to German consumers (which I discuss further below). This loss in sales has led the cooperative to try to broaden their export market to include North America and Britain. They have experienced difficulty in obtaining information about the tastes of these potential customers. It was in this capacity that I worked with the community, developing carpet designs that had some connection with local textile traditions yet would be compatible with the tastes of the high end of the North American or British market.

Although these two organizations have different structures and aims, the artisans involved in both are members of low-caste groups and share a common desire for economic and political changes that would improve their lives. Because ACPN strives to involve women from all of the main ethnic groups in Nepal,[9] often social barriers break down as the women find themselves working together across boundaries usually maintained by class, caste, and ethnicity. They may discover that they share similar reasons for being in the cooperative. The money they earn contributes to household subsistence needs or may be directed toward their children's education and health care. Women report a marked improvement in their access to food. "Now we can eat more than one meal a day" is a common response when asked in what ways cooperative work has improved their lives. In some cases, a woman's income provides sole support for herself and her children after, for example, the death or abandonment of a spouse. Having independent income may also provide the opportunity for a woman to leave an abusive situation.

In addition to these important economic contributions, a woman's move into paid work often creates subtle and not so subtle shifts in power relationships defined by both gender and caste. Women report an increase in their physical mobility and confidence outside of the household as they move more freely between workshop or producers' centers and home (Peiris 1997, 45; Kabeer 1994, 255). Many of the women, for example, now freely use public transport or feel confident in walking to and from the producers' center—both activities that they previously would not have undertaken. However, they may also therefore face criticism from family members or other villagers who frown on their forwardness and immodesty. Sometimes this censure may cause their husbands or fathers to forbid them to work in the cooperative.[10] On the other hand, women speak of an increased sense of self-worth and confidence in relations with family members and in dealings with upper-caste people. Some weavers in the villages now feel they can bargain with higher-caste business people who have exploited them in the past. Other women report an improvement in their status in the family and a greater sense of their own value through their contributions to the household (Mazumdar 1989, 33).

At the Dupgyal Cooperative, most of the spinners and weavers are women from Rai farm families. Although farms in the lush Pokhara Valley are relatively prosperous, many households still cannot meet their daily subsistence needs as access to land is becoming more limited. Health care and education are still out of reach for most farm families, so cash income from crafts may be the only way a Nepalese woman and her family can gain these services. For the Tibetans, income generated by the cooperative means that their community's many social programs continue to be viable and self-supporting. However, some local Nepalese may resent the fact that the Tibetans enjoy "special privileges" that have allowed the community to flourish and have brought benefits that these Nepalese citizens envy. A common comment from some Nepalese workers is that Tibetans should "go back where they came from."

Because Pokhara is the starting point for Annapurna treks, tourism has had considerable impact on what was until the early 1980s a rather isolated area of the country. A new, paved road currently connects Pokhara to Kathmandu, enabling fleets of minibuses to arrive every evening with fresh loads of Western trekkers. The town is beautifully situated on the edge of a lake with the Annapurna mountain range rising behind it, making it a popular holiday destination for Indian tourists. For most visitors, Pokhara is an overnight stop at the beginning and end of their Himalayan trekking adventure. Most of the tourists are not interested in lugging a Tibetan carpet back to Kathmandu and will save the buying of gifts until they are back in the capital. For Dupgyal, the main benefit from the tourist influx has been the new road, which means that finished carpets can be easily transported by truck to Kathmandu and then to Calcutta for shipping—a change crucial for the success of the cooperative's venture.

In my research into artisan groups, I have found that an important factor contributing to groups' longevity and success is their ability to meet export deadlines. The structure of both Dupgyal and the ACPN is flexible. They can accommodate varying production demands and order deadlines by drawing on a pool of skilled craftspeople who feel a sense of involvement in the co-ops and enjoy the direct benefits of the organization. The groups are also able to monitor quality and consistency, either through a head weaver at the carpet workshop or through unit leaders in the ACPN. For both groups, social benefits and production aims tend to reinforce one another and help to ensure their success.

CHALLENGES FACING CO-OPS

The cooperatives face the same challenges that the Nepalese face in daily life. In many areas of the country, infrastructure has not kept pace with increased population rates, migration, and changing conditions. Access to fuel and water is often limited and costly. Most of the country does not have access to electricity, and other fuel, such as wood, is scarce due to deforestation.[11] Obtaining water can also be difficult, especially in mountainous rural areas, where women must carry water long distances. Availability of raw materials—whether unprocessed fiber, commercially produced yarn, or dyestuffs—is undependable. When importing these materials from India, Nepalese producers lack the economic power and control to ensure timely delivery and good-quality materials. Many producers complain that they are sold adulterated dyestuffs or are overcharged by middlemen. They feel powerless to rectify matters (see also Milgram, this volume). Finally, both transportation and communication networks in rural areas are dependent largely on foot travel, although truck transport, fax, telephone, and e-mail are currently available in urban areas.

Cooperatives have met these challenges by evolving and adapting their strategies to meet new demands. One approach they have chosen is to retain locally based technology whenever possible. For example, all of the wool spinning for the Dupgyal cooperative's carpet production is carried out on hand-operated wheels. Other groups make use of hand-cranked bobbin winders, backstrap looms, treadle sewing machines, and hand- or foot-operated fiber processors. However, human-powered machinery cannot always meet production needs; sometimes other forms are required. Because fuel resources are limited, increased dependence on firewood may be impractical in areas where there is no natural woodland or where there has been deforestation. Several groups are considering solar power, which is widely used for domestic water heating and has been recently developed for solar cookers and medical refrigeration units in India. Extension of this existing technology for use in closed dye units would also minimize water wastage, so it is a possibility worth investigating (Papanek 1995, 43).

Difficulties in accessing raw materials have been dealt with in a variety of ways. For example, several small cooperative networks have banded together to form a trade federation, which has enabled them to place bulk orders for dyes, yarns, and other materials from India, thus helping to reduce the cost and giving them access to better-quality materials. Through this federation, they have sought out technical advice on safer dyeing methods and have shared knowledge of botanical dyeing techniques, which they are collectively developing for use. Another group has incorporated the growing and processing of plant fibers, including hemp and nettle, into their production activities in order to ensure dependable access to raw materials and to broaden the base of participation among rural farm women.

The transportation of crafts from rural producers' homes to collection points is difficult in a country with few roads and where foot porters carry most goods over high mountain trails. Thus, meeting Western market deadlines is problematic. Unlike many other craft networks based in the Kathmandu Valley, ACPN has worked with rural artisans in areas not serviced by roads. The crafts are transported down to the center using the foot-porter system in the hills and then transferred to truck transport where there are roads. This willingness to encompass already existing systems has meant that isolated artisans who might not otherwise have access to markets are able to sell their work.

All of the locally based organizations I researched are also structured to allow craft production to fit around women's wide and varied responsibilities—including agricultural work, provision of fuel and water, food preparation and preservation, household work, child rearing, and religious activities. As noted earlier, working hours for craft production remain flexible in most cases. Women take on more or less work in their own homes or in a producers' center according to other demands on their time and their need for income. The Dupgyal workshop is an exception, instituting hours of work as 7:00 to 11:00 A.M. and 12:00 to 4:00 P.M. However, these set hours serve more to differentiate the cooperative from exploitative, commercial workshops, where weavers may be required to work twelve- or fourteen-hour days. Weavers at Dupgyal still set their own schedules within the allotted work times.

ENVIRONMENTAL ACTION

Artisan groups are involved with protecting and conserving natural resources while maintaining control over these resources at a local level. Because female artisans are often also farmers, they experience directly the consequences of land loss and overuse. Land ownership, the basis of a family's wealth, passes through the male head of household and is divided among his sons. It is rare for a woman to own land, although women are the primary agriculturists. The demands on smaller and smaller plots of land to feed an ever-increasing number of people have contributed to soil exhaustion. In the Kathmandu Valley, women have also witnessed the effects of severe air pollution and water contamination on the land and on their families' health. Although they are aware of the pollutants in the environment, they generally do not see themselves as being in a position to bring about change. Constrained by both gender and low-caste status, they feel powerless. However, through their involvement in cooperative groups, they are beginning to voice their ecological concerns and incorporate them into the structure of production. At ACPN, a number of ecological initiatives include, most significantly, an improved filtration system for disposing of dye waste and the introduction of less environmentally harmful water-based inks for textile printing. Other cooperatives are also striving to reduce the ecological impact of their production.

Other aspects of textile production can have additional detrimental effects on the environment. In the first stages of production, overuse of the land for growing cash crops, such as white cotton, depletes nutrients in the soil. In some areas of South Asia, the use of pesticides has been introduced to protect cash crops. The disastrous effects of these chemicals on both the people who use them and the environment are well documented.[12] However, the most ecologically hazardous aspects of cloth making are the softening, dyeing, and printing processes, which depend heavily on scarce water resources and create liquid waste that is potentially hazardous to crops, livestock, and people.

Impetus for environmentally sustainable practices comes both from artisans and from some Western buyers, especially those buyers in the fair trade movement. Most farmer-artisans minimize waste out of necessity; everything is utilized by means of reintegrating excess plant fiber, composting, and using the full loom widths of cloth (Rahnema 1997, 111–29). Specific environmental concerns are of special importance to women as farmers growing raw materials, as artisans producing textiles, and as mothers caring for their families' health. As farmers, they worry about the effects of deforestation and soil depletion on their lands from repeated and intensive cultivation of crops. They have become interested in growing crops such as hemp, whose cultivation imparts many ecological benefits to the land and the environment.

The serious health and environmental consequences of dumping untreated dye wastewater into rivers or onto agricultural land have received extensive media coverage, especially in Europe. Some European countries, such as Germany, have enacted laws requiring the application of environmental labels on textile products to assure the consumer that ecologically safe processes were used in the manufacture of those products.[13] Water contamination is perhaps the most pressing ecological issue to Nepalese women. One solution recently introduced with great success at ACPN is the closed system for dyeing, which reduces the quantity and toxicity of effluents. Instead of dumping liquid dye waste directly into common water sources or onto people's lands, the waste is passed through a skimmer, an aeration basin, and a gravel-sand-charcoal filter to separate the solid waste from the water. Although the sludge must still be stored and dumped, it is more manageable than liquid waste. Members of ACPN are able to clean their wastewater completely. They hope to interest other craft groups in building such a closed system or in contracting out the dye facility. However, because the unit requires both capital to build and fuel to maintain, it remains too expensive for many village-level producers. The lack of facilities for the safe treatment of dye waste is a pressing problem for most of the producers with whom I have worked, one that they know they must tackle soon.

Another aspect of production that creates potentially harmful waste is the softening of finished cloth. Hemp, nettle, and other plant fibers benefit from softening—a softer hand is especially desirable to the Western consumer. Although local treatments, such as wood ash, are still used instead of costly and toxic imported chemical softeners, another process under consideration by some groups is the use of biosofteners. The latter are natural enzymes that when applied to the finished cloth, soften cellulose fibers by breaking them down slightly and produce no harmful waste. These enzymes may also have applications to plant fiber extraction, a process that can put excessive demands on scarce firewood sources. However, further investigation is needed into the long-term environmental effects of these enzymes before they are used (J. Dunsmore 1997, 37).

RESPONSE TO SOCIAL CONCERNS

As discussed by Grimes (this volume), one of the main goals of the fair trade movement is to ensure fair and safe conditions for workers. This includes no tolerance for bonded, slave, and child labor. Women represent a low-wage labor force and are heavily employed in all areas of commercial textile and garment production, but children under the legal age of employment provide an even less protected and cheaper source of labor.[14] Child labor in the commercial textile industry in South Asia—and particularly in the carpet industry in Pakistan, India, and Nepal—has received much media coverage in the West. Although this practice may be perceived to be more widespread than its actual prevalence, children do continue to be employed in some areas of the rug-weaving industry. Most of these child weavers are boys who are often in a position of debt bondage to the carpet workshop owners. Mohan, a seven-year-old former weaver from Bihar, India, describes a life of harsh treatment, loneliness, and hunger. Cut off from his family and denied access to education, he was often required to work up to seventeen hours a day and given very little food. In the long term, widespread child labor can be problematic for local economies, causing wages for working adults to fall to the same level as those paid to children. The continued employment of children, in turn, becomes essential to families' economic survival.

The particular pressures facing female children employed in the industry are less publicized than child labor in general. Away from the protective structure of their families, girls are especially vulnerable as workers and are much more likely than boys to suffer sexual abuse in their place of work. Furthermore, in Nepal, working in the carpet industry is seen by some activists as a factor in girls moving into prostitution (Pradhan 1993, 29). Girls may also travel directly from their villages to join family members working in brothels in India or to find employment there as domestic servants (Ghimere 1994, 6). Although the exact nature of the work is often intentionally left unclear, it is indicative of both the low status of female children and the desperate need for cash income that poor parents are willing to send their daughters to work in India.

The textile cooperatives I researched are helping to solve some of the difficulties facing poor, marginalized women in securing paid work and are thereby indirectly addressing the complex problem of child labor. These cooperatives follow fair trade guidelines to provide a fair monetary return for women's work and strive to ensure safe working conditions in contrast to the exploitative alternatives often available. They also demonstrate an awareness of the particular pressures on girls. Many activists within the cooperatives see education as essential in giving girls control over their lives.[15] At ACPN, the girl-child education fund enables poor women to send their daughters to school. The association also provides the women with peer literacy groups. At Dupgyal, the Tibetans put all the working mothers' children in school, regardless of gender. It is often the case that once women earn a cash income, they spend it on their children's education. However, some still prefer to educate their sons rather than their daughters.

In 1995 in the Kathmandu Valley, a textile project called Eco-Himal was established in direct response to the perceived threat of prostitution facing young girls. Eco-Himal also addresses other problems, such as the lack of economic opportunities for low-caste women as well as environmental degradation and the subsequent hardships it creates for farm women. The group is led by the five Pradhan brothers, a high-caste, activist Newar family concerned with the social and environmental problems facing farm families in the valley. They have identified certain factors that encourage poor families to send their daughters away to work, including their lack of understanding of what kind of employment is being offered to their daughters, low value placed on girls, and the need for cash income.

In response to these findings, Eco-Himal has set up training programs in hemp processing coupled with literacy classes for women and girls. When the participants return to their villages, they teach other women how to work with Eco-Himal and how to grow, process, and weave hemp. Earning cash income gives them a higher status both in their families and in their communities. Their newly acquired literacy skills are of use to the entire village. By focusing on a combination of education and skills training, the project provides one alternative for young girls seeking employment. The Eco-Himal project has been successful in gaining members and intensifying hemp culture in the valley, thus providing an ecologically sustainable cash crop for women. However, they have been less successful in developing products suitable for export, which in the long run may result in producing more hemp fiber than can be sold.

DEVELOPING TEXTILES WITH INPUT FROM BOTH ARTISANS AND AN OUTSIDE FACILITATOR

Besides working with the Dupgyal carpet weavers to develop more culturally relevant designs, I have been involved in developing uses for hemp weaving. Fiber hemp has many ecological advantages for Nepalese farmers. It grows quickly and easily between rotations of other crops. Its cultivation does not deplete the soil as do other fiber crops, such as cotton; rather, farmers use it to reinvigorate the soil. It is also useful as a means of soil retention in deforested, overgrazed, and eroded areas. Women are usually responsible for harvesting and processing the fiber and for producing yardage on backstrap looms in their homes. Coarsely spun hemp is used locally for a wide range of utility textiles, such as bags, ropes, mats, and nets. Finer, smoother cloth is made into coats, wrapped skirts, and other clothing. In the West, there is an increased interest in hemp fiber due to its ecological benefits. However, there is little market for plain-woven cloth, especially because Nepalese hemp weaving tends to be weighty and thick—in contrast to Thai hemp weaving, which is crisp and light, and therefore more attractive to the Western buyer. These products may eventually compete for sale within the same market, so I sought to heighten the design quality of the Nepalese cloth. Partnering with the weavers and using local dye techniques, I experimented with resist dyeing to make the hemp cloth distinctive and suitable for a variety of products from accessories to household textiles. I also carried out experimentation on other locally produced cloth, such as nettle, pashmina, raw silk, vimal, and brown cotton.

My role as a designer-coordinator working with artisans has been difficult to define. I try to bridge a gap between the makers and the market, but this raises questions of responsibility. How much change is acceptable in the design, color, and eventual use of a piece of cloth? Where does a designer stop along the spectrum between the two cultures, between the needs of the makers and the wishes of the consumers? Ultimately, the craftspeople need viable markets in which to sell their crafts in order to survive. To do this, the craft product must be marketable. However, it must still be firmly embedded in local textile forms and not be a debased interpretation that has lost its cultural connection. It cannot lose its perceived "authenticity." To serve the needs of both the makers and the buyers, the product must have the right balance of traditional techniques and contemporary function. For example, weavers may be accustomed to producing lengths of fabric for saris, sarong-style skirts, or shawls. Such lengths have no specific use for the Western consumer. However, the same materials, techniques, and skill can be directed to the making of cloth with clear Western-oriented functions. Saris may become bedcovers and shawls scarves. Because South Asian clothing is largely draped, wrapped, and tied, and South Asian homes often consist of a few multipurpose rooms with very few furnishings, such uses for textiles are foreign to the local craftspeople. It is difficult for the women to comprehend cultures with such excesses of resources that people can afford to fill their homes with nonessential items. In order to develop and produce the textiles, the makers need to understand the utility of such items and to have specific information, such as appropriate dimensions for bedcovers or scarves.

In my discussions with various crafts groups, I found a lack of information about market demands in the West to be a major stumbling block to the development of suitable products (see also Causey, this volume). The success of an artisan group depends on the economic viability of its textile products, but costly risks that necessitate excess capital and resources are often not possible. Such groups cannot afford the economic or social costs of a trial-and-error method; they are, moreover, physically and culturally removed from the eventual market for their textiles.

It is also important to consider that Nepalese textiles ultimately will be sold in competition with crafts from other countries. Finding ways for these textiles to be differentiated from those also available in Western markets is important. This may be as simple as using particular colors or making an object slightly larger or smaller in order to make it stand out. The expertise of an outside facilitator can provide craftspeople with this much needed information about the demands of the marketplace and how this information can be applied to textile products. A facilitator can link fabric to product; assess materials, skills, and techniques; and minimize risks by providing accurate market information.[16]

Certain products, however, are better suited than others to cooperative production for export. Clothing, which is often suggested as an ideal vehicle for using handmade textiles, can be a poor choice. The rapid and erratic changes in Western fashions and the regional specificity of market demands necessitate constant and substantial outside intervention in order to make the garments marketable. Competition from cheaply made garments often produced in factories located in the same regions as the cooperative makes it unlikely that artisans would be able to charge enough to receive a fair return on their input.[17] It can be more effective to keep products close to their original forms so that continued outside intervention is not essential and so that women can maintain a greater degree of control over adapting the cloth to new uses (see Morris 1996). Textiles for household furnishings have more constant design parameters and generally require minimal cutting and sewing, thereby reducing the wastage of precious handwoven or stitched fabric. Some accessories, such as scarves and bags, involve little wastage and are quite consistent in shape and size from year to year. Furthermore, it is important that the craftspeople are not competing on the basis of low-cost labor at the low end of the market. Producers do not benefit by being in competition with industrially produced goods or with cheap sources of labor. In order to give appropriate value to women's work, it is important to ensure a fair return by selling at the higher end of the market. To do this, the design must have an appropriate function, and the quality of the product must be high.

Educating the consumer about the social and ecological aims of the group is also helpful in giving greater value to the textiles and in building a connection between the makers and the buyers. In my work with co-op women, I have tried to promote such initiatives as Grimes (this volume) practices in her shop. For example, ACPN makers' profiles or printed information outlining the benefits brought to the Tibetan refugee community through the sale of carpets give consumers an idea of the individuals and communities involved in making their craft products. It is also interesting to note that in Europe, the fair trade movement has been instrumental in successfully marketing a range of food products in supermarkets—including coffee, tea, and chocolate—through the use of various fair trademarks (see Grimes, this volume). These symbols clearly identify fairly traded products and often are paired with producer profiles and other support material. In North America, where fairly traded goods are more often craft products than foods, the use of such identifying seals could help to alleviate some of the confusion about what constitutes a fairly made product and thus aid in consumer education. Although there is still much that can be done to build on the successes of fair trade in terms of marketing and distribution, the fair trade movement has been instrumental for Nepalese producers in connecting the artisans with supportive buyers who are interested in the groups' goals and who are willing to educate their customers.

Many well-intended projects geared toward income generation through craft production are not based closely enough on local resources or on local textile forms, however. The participating women may be taught to make a specific product that may not have a specific target market. No effort may be made to turn the textile production process over to the producers themselves or to involve them in determining the goals of the project. In such cases, neither the long-term needs of the women nor the demands of the consumer are considered. The project serves no one and often flounders, leaving the women without work and justly suspicious of future craft-based projects (see Milgram, this volume). The relationship between facilitator and craftspeople must be long term. Changes must evolve slowly with the full participation of and input from the craftspeople. Inevitably, an outsider is seen as an "expert" rather than as a collaborator. Only through working together over time can these expectations and barriers be broken down and a more collaborative and mutually rewarding relationship develop.

The results of my own collaboration with Nepalese craftspeople were shown as part of my graduate project at Central Saint Martins College of Art and Design in London, England, in 1998. Carpets made by the weavers at the Dupgyal Cooperative were exhibited alongside yardages showing experiments in resist dyeing on hemp, nettle, silk, and pashmina fibers woven by women artisans involved with ACPN and Eco-Himal. Cushions, bags, scarves, and other sample products were also displayed. There was commercial interest in the textiles from high-end retailers, and many visitors commented not only on the high quality of the products, but on the unusual fibers and techniques. It is too soon to tell what the outcome will be for the producers, but on my next trip to Nepal, I anticipate developing further my collaboration with the co-ops in order to bring some of these products to market.

CONCLUSION

In Nepal, artisan groups may be organized as projects by social activists according to community or ethnic affiliations or as family-run enterprises, but all grow out of local conditions in response to local needs. However, the cooperatives I have discussed not only provide cash income for low-caste women, but are also a part of an ongoing movement for social justice. As such, they function as sites where disadvantaged Nepalese women can participate in furthering social change for themselves and for their families. These women are involved both in substantially altering their own economic conditions and in actively shaping new social attitudes and spaces for themselves and their daughters. As an alternative to capitalist structures, artisan collectives often provide access to services not otherwise available to low-caste women and provide access for craftspeople to reach international markets. The fair trade network is important to these producers because it enables them to maintain a greater degree of control over production while directing their textiles to interested consumers. It also provides women with a sense of outside support and a connection with those who are sympathetic to their goals. In my work with female artisans, I have been in a position where I move back and forth between two cultures to mediate a slow, collaborative process of change. I feel I have been fortunate to work with these women as they meet complex challenges and strive to create a better life for themselves and their communities.

NOTES

[1] My research in Nepal was in part funded through the Canada Council for the Arts. I would like to thank Meera Bhattarai and the women of the ACPN; Dundup and Khandro Tsering and the Tibetan Community of Pokhara; Mr. Shankar Pradhan and his family; and Professors Prem Khatry and Punya Khatry of the Centre for South Asian and Nepal Studies for their assistance.

[2] See Grimes (this volume) for a discussion of fair trade.

[3] The British Gurkha Regiment is made up of Gurang men from Nepal.

[4] Elsewhere (MacHenry 1998), I have discussed at greater length the historical and political context of Nepalese cooperative craft production.

[5] These may be aid-based organizations, such as Oxfam in Britain, or fair trade importer-wholesalers, such as Tara Handknits in the United States.

[6] See Page-Reeves (1998) for a description of the Bolivian handknit sweater industry.

[7] In the Pokhara Valley, agricultural day labor is the most usual paid work for women outside the home. They receive five rupees a day in comparison with the ten to fifteen rupees paid to men. For weaving, they are paid by the centimeter and may earn up to twenty-five rupees a day.

[8] See Thakar (1995, 231–48) for a study of exploitative carpet workshops in Nepal.

[9] There are approximately thirty different ethnic groups in Nepal, each with its own language and cultural practices; however, all share the same rigid caste structure.

[10] See Eber (this volume) and Burkert (1994) for similar situations faced by women craft producers in other regions in the world.

[11] The foothills of the Himalayas used to be covered in teak forests. However, these trees were ruthlessly harvested to supply the West's demand for teak, leaving the hillsides bare and subject to erosion. Recently, the government has returned control of the forests to local communities, who have had considerable success in replanting and managing this important resource.

[12] See Mies and Shiva (1993) for further discussion of the ecological effects of pesticides and other imported agricultural methods.

[13] Another European ecological protection law that has affected textile production in South Asia forbids the import of textiles dyed with AZO dyes. This has caused all producers, both commercial and cooperative, to switch to non-AZO dyes, which are supposedly less harmful.

[14] The legal age for work varies between twelve and fourteen years through South Asia. India, Pakistan, Bangladesh, Sri Lanka, Nepal, and Bhutan all have laws prohibiting child labor.

[15] Although primary education in Nepal is free, the low status of girl children in the family often means that they are not seen as worthy of an education. Many families feel that they cannot afford to do without their daughters' household and farm labor, and are unable to afford books and school uniforms for them. In poor families, boys are more likely to attend primary school than are girls. The illiteracy rate for young women ages fifteen to twenty-four is 85 percent, whereas the rate for men in the same age bracket is 55 percent. Current school attendance continues to reflect this imbalance with a 2.7 to 1 boy-to-girl ratio at the primary level (UNICEF 1996, 15).

[16] Further discussion of the role of the designer in developing crafts for the marketplace can be found in Tyabji (1998).

[17] Some fair trade companies, such as DZI, are successful in marketing clothing and paying the producers fair wages. Located in Washington, D.C., DZI works with Tibetan refugee producers in Dharamsala, India. Working with women producers in India, Marketplace of India has also built a successful clothing business (see Grimes, this volume).

CHRISTINE E. EBER

4. "THAT THEY BE IN THE MIDDLE, LORD"

WOMEN, WEAVING, AND CULTURAL SURVIVAL IN HIGHLAND CHIAPAS, MEXICO

Take care of us, Lord, on this day.
Not only today when the women are here,
but on other days that they come here.
On each trip, Lord, care for the women,
the representatives,
and the women who keep coming here
to leave their work,
to leave their weavings.

Care for us, Lord,
and also the Holy Virgin Mary of Guadalupe,
help us all your Saints.

We ask, Lord, for your great help and blessing,
for the women to whom you gave your grace,
for them to learn the work of weaving,
that the work they brought here today
be beautiful,
be marvelous.

When the women work
and make weavings,
in this way they find money to feed their
husbands and their children.

They work day and night,
sometimes suffering,
with pain,
and with sadness.
But we ask you, Lord,
give them more grace and help.

Lord, all the people gathered here,
help us this day,
that no illness falls on us,
no stomach pain,
no diarrhea,
no fever,
nothing.

But we ask you, Lord,
When they travel on the road,
take care of us,
the women,
that nothing happens on the road,
in the van.

The drivers in the vans,
open the road ahead of them,
and open the eyes of each driver.

I am crossing my hands,
and kneeling,
to ask your blessing on everyone
who is present,
and most importantly on the women.

The story of the women artisans, Lord,
we ask you to put it in the middle of your hand,
of your document,
of your book,
that they be in the middle, Lord.[1]

The respected elder knelt on a bed of pine needles before twenty-four candles and asked God to protect the twenty-four people gathered around him. The elder's prayer opened a weaving competition and celebration in San Cristóbal de Las Casas, Chiapas, Mexico, on June 27, 1998. Although the structure and function of his prayer derive from a Maya tradition with deep historical roots, many of the images in the prayer speak of a world that the ancestors could have seen only in dreams. For example, the elder's focus on women in his prayer reflects the dependence of his people on the cash women earn through selling their weavings. Never in the history of Maya peoples has money played such a central role in daily survival. His request of God to put the weavers' story in the middle of his hand, of his account of the world, indicates his people's respect for the central role women artisans play in their people's material and spiritual survival at the end of the twentieth century.

In this chapter, I tell a part of the weavers' story that the shaman entrusted to God. My understanding of this story comes from my applied work with Tsobol Antzetik (Women United), the weaving cooperative that the shaman asked God to protect.[2] I began to work with Tsobol Antzetik in 1988 in San Pedro Chenalhó, the highland Chiapas township where members of Tsobol Antzetik live. In my research on women's relation to their own and others' drinking, I observed how women used their astute analyses of problem drinking as a springboard on which to deal with other related problems, such as poverty, male dominance, and political corruption (Eber 1995). They also used their analyses of problem drinking as a way to legitimate their right to offer their points of view in public forums, a freedom they had not enjoyed before this time. In the groups women created in Chenalhó in the 1980s, such as weaving cooperatives, they developed leadership skills and began to gain more control over their work and lives. In 1988, I asked the women what I could do to support their women's groups, to reciprocate in some way for the abundant help I had received from them and their families. The women asked me to help them earn cash by expanding markets for selling their weavings.

The twenty-four women and their children who belong to Tsobol Antzetik live in several hamlets in Chenalhó, a township with a strong base of support for the Ejército Zapatista de Liberación Nacional (EZLN, Zapatista Army of National Liberation) and for the growing democracy movement. The shaman's prayer opened a weaving competition and celebration that members of Tsobol Antzetik asked me to help organize with donations from individuals and groups in the United States. Weaving competitions originated with cooperatives started by the Instituto Nacional Indigenista (INI, National Indigenous Institute), a government organization.

Drawing attention to individual women for their talents by giving them cash prizes first struck me as contradictory to the communal ethos of life in Chenalhó, but soon it became clear that the women responded to the weaving competition as they have to other outside traditions, by accommodating it to their people's central values of respect, hard work, and service. For example, spreading sacred pine needles on the ground where the competition took place and choosing an elder to open the event with a prayer, the women acknowledged the debt that humans owe the powerful spiritual beings who guide and protect them. By making sure that all weavers received some prize, the women further demonstrated their respect for the labor intensiveness of weaving and the importance of everyone working together to surmount the hardships they face (Eber 1995, 249).

The weaving competition in 1998 was unusual in that it came at a time when the weavers were recovering from the massacre of forty-five women, men, and children in Acteal, Chenalhó, on December 22, 1997. Despite the complicity of the Mexican army in the massacre (Marín 1998), Mexican troops and paramilitary groups continued to operate in Chenalhó, making for a virtual state of siege in the township (*Global Exchange* 1998). Those of us from outside of Chenalhó who gave out the prizes and filmed the event wanted to assure the women that their work and lives have inspired many people throughout the world and that we would not abandon them in their quest for economic and social justice.[3]

One of the specific aims of this chapter is to describe how women in Tsobol Antzetik are using their cooperative to obtain cash to survive, renegotiate their identities and relationships, and reinvigorate valued traditions—all in the context of a radical restructuring of their society. I also discuss women's efforts to accommodate their craft traditions to market demands and the help I have given to the women making these accommodations.

WEAVING FOR CASH

Weaving cooperatives are a relatively recent development in a long legacy of resistance to economic and social injustice that Pedranos (the name for the indigenous residents of Chenalhó) have been waging throughout the twentieth century (Eber n.d.). Women artisans began to intensify their household craft production and seek markets for their products in the early 1980s when they began to feel the effects of the debt crisis. At this time, Mexican policymakers were restructuring their nation's economy in response to the debt crisis, International Monetary Fund (IMF) guidelines, and internal limits of import-substitution industrialization. These policymakers instituted an austerity program that involved trade liberalization, promotion of foreign investment and exports, and massive cutbacks in government social spending. Although the international financial community has hailed Mexico's lowered inflation, growing exports, and timely payments of the interest on its foreign debt, these so-called advances have been made at the expense of the majority of Mexicans. Poverty and unemployment are increasing; real wages are falling; and wealth continues to be concentrated in the hands of a few powerful men. These conditions are exacerbated in Chiapas by the effects of a low-intensity war, making it increasingly difficult for people to plant and harvest crops, which the majority of indigenous people depend on for subsistence.

The lack of wage labor opportunities, combined with the decreasing capacity of milpa production to provide a viable means of subsistence, makes selling crafts, agricultural products, or firewood one of the only means indigenous people in Chiapas have to earn cash to buy the food and other necessities they cannot produce (Rus 1995). Since the early 1980s, households have become increasingly dependent on the cash women provide through selling products they produce or gather (Rus 1990, O'Brian 1997). In a census conducted in 1987 and 1988, as many as 60 percent of women in some hamlets of Chamula, a neighboring township to Chenalhó, were involved in producing artisan goods for the tourist market (Rus 1995). However, at the same time as women have been making more products for the market, demand has not increased. In fact, political instability and violence in Chiapas have caused market demand to shrink.

Nonetheless, with normal economic activity interrupted in Chenalhó, weaving in the relative safety of one's home remains one of the few ways to earn cash. For the more than ten thousand Pedranos driven from their homes by paramilitaries and living in refugee camps in Chenalhó, weaving has emerged as the most viable way to earn cash.

The elder's prayer at the weaving competition petitioned God to protect the weavers from dangers on the road from Chenalhó to San Cristóbal and on the streets of this big city. His words speak to the increased mobility of women outside their townships and the challenges this mobility poses to them and their families. Even though Pedranos have always been tied to the economy in San Cristóbal, it has been a hostile place to them. The city is especially intimidating to indigenous women, most of whom are monolingual in Tzotzil. For these women and even for women who speak Spanish, San Cristóbal is the land of *ladinos* (nonindigenous people) with their stores and government offices. In contrast, Chenalhó is the land of the ancestors, with milpa plots scattered throughout a sacred geography.

When tourism began to increase in highland Chiapas in the 1970s, the only outlets open to women to sell their weavings were stores run by nonindigenous people in San Cristóbal. Until the road between Chenalhó and San Cristóbal was paved in the early 1990s, the trip was long and arduous and usually necessitated staying overnight. If women were lucky, they sold their weavings to one of the tourist shops lining the colonial streets. Shopkeepers rarely paid women what their weavings were worth and later sold the weavings for a hefty profit. Sometimes women were so fearful of their encounters with shopkeepers that they sold weavings that took several weeks to make for the price of a handful of fruit (Nash 1993a, 15).

Government representatives started the first craft cooperatives in the 1950s and 1960s in response to a government initiative to support indigenous crafts as an entry point for tourist dollars. The cooperative movement was encouraged by INI as part of its national indigenous peoples policy. The institute held the first weaving fair in 1972 (Morris 1991, Nash 1993a).

Women began to join government-sponsored cooperatives in the 1970s as a way to survive that did not involve them in the exploitative markets that dominated craft sales up until that time. The first member of Tsobol Antzetik to join a weaving cooperative was María,[4] the eldest member of the group and the mother and grandmother of ten other group members. In 1981, María heard about a group sponsored by INI that had formed in the head town of Chenalhó. She and her teenage daughters joined the group, but eventually they left this co-op because they began to doubt whether the representative was giving them all the money she received at the INI store for their weavings. Although the representative was a Pedrana like themselves, the women viewed her as identifying more with the ladino world, as evidenced by her facility with Spanish, a son who had become mestizoized through his teacher training, and her many contacts outside of the township.

Around the time María and her daughters were considering leaving the INI co-op, she heard about a weaving cooperative that had opened a store in San Cristóbal and was inviting indigenous women to join. Through María's initiative, her four daughters, several of their relatives, and people from neighboring hamlets joined Sna Jolobil (House of the Weaver). In accordance with INI's and Sna Jolobil's structure, the women chose one of their members to represent their local group. The representative's duties included delivering weavings to the co-op store, collecting payments, and delivering them to co-op members. Members in turn contributed a small percentage of the sale price of each of their weavings to cover the representative's bus fare to San Cristóbal and some refreshments while there. From the early 1980s until 1996, María's second eldest daughter, Antonia, served as the representative of the cooperative. Although María was a veteran weaver and a respected elder, she could not serve as representative because she was monolingual in Tzotzil. In contrast, Antonia had attended six years of school, where she had learned to speak, read, and write Spanish.

In the early years of their affiliation with Sna Jolobil, the women said it was truly "their house." The women explained that they felt this way because they contributed a small amount of cash each year to the larger group and attended annual meetings, where they felt they had a voice in the governance of the organization. Sna Jolobil also started study grants to enable women to study older designs that all but one or two veteran weavers in their communities had forgotten how to make. After learning how to reproduce the older weaving designs, the women in the study groups then taught other women how to make them. Local groups also held annual or biannual competitions in their hamlets, which encouraged high quality and creativity.

The weaving cooperative structure continues to meet women's needs because it enables them to work at home, where their major responsibilities lie, while still feeling connected to other women through the group. Women in Tsobol Antzetik choose not to have many meetings. They live dispersed on the mountainsides and have much work to do, so frequent meetings create hardships. When they do meet, about every four or five weeks, the weavers often spend half a day at the representative's house, discussing current co-op issues while finishing up a weaving, gossiping, joking, and drinking cups of coffee or soda.

Despite benefits from collective work, several significant drawbacks keep women from joining cooperatives and influence them to leave after they have joined (Eber and Rosenbaum 1993, 168–69). A critical drawback is the persistent cash flow problem. In the past, the women of Sna Jolobil sometimes had to wait eight months to be paid for weavings that Antonia had delivered to the co-op store in San Cristóbal. This situation was never acceptable but became intolerable as the economic crisis deepened, and the women began to doubt that Sna Jolobil was really "their house." Many times when Antonia went to San Cristóbal to pick up payments for weavings she had delivered several months earlier, the co-op store representatives told her that there was no money. Antonia said that the women had trouble believing that there was no money at all. They suspected that if the store representatives' children needed food or medicine, they would find money somewhere. Meanwhile, Antonia and the other women in her co-op had no other source of cash for these necessities. Throughout the time the women were involved in the cooperative, the director of Sna Jolobil was Pedro Mesa Mesa, an indigenous man from Tenejapa whose grandmother had taught him to weave. Although the women respected Pedro, they were critical of the large amounts of money he spent on operating costs, including entertaining prospective buyers.

The women's experiences with governmental and nongovernmental organizations have led them to view both types of organizations with suspicion. They tend to see any outside group as having the potential to control them for its own aims. Around 1990, the women who eventually belonged to Tsobol Antzetik separated from Sna Jolobil and began to reform themselves as an independent group. With this decision, they opted for a more decentralized model that gave them greater autonomy.[5]

While the weavers were experimenting with collective models, I was seeking markets for them in the United States among members of community and church groups concerned about social justice. Unable to devote myself full-time to this work and having little capital to invest in it, I obtained markets for the women by presenting talks and slide shows to community groups. By asking U.S. consumers to prepay, I was able to send the money in advance to the women. Some women used the money to buy thread, others to buy food or household needs. Still others preferred to wait to be paid until they had finished their weavings. What mattered was that the women did not have to wait to be paid if they chose not to.

This method of working has limitations, the most pressing being the women's dependence on me or on students at the three U.S. universities where I have taught. Since I began teaching in 1992, many of my students have taken an interest in Tsobol Antzetik. For example, during the 1997–98 academic year, members of the Student Association for Latin American Studies (SALAS) at New Mexico State University supported the cooperative by creating notebooks with background on the weavers and samples, which they then circulated in the university and Las Cruces community to solicit orders or donations. Students also sent moral support in the form of letters, which the women of Tsobol Antzetik shared with their families and read out loud at hamlet meetings.

The work of university students and others concerned about social justice has opened up a new market niche among people whose primary motivation for purchasing products from marginalized producers is to support these people in their struggle for social justice (see Rosenbaum, this volume). When people purchase from this perspective, they are usually willing to buy whatever the group they support produces. This kind of buyers trust that they will find a use for the products and that what the products may lack in refinement, they make up for in heart. Consumers working from these premises assume that the creators of the products are doing the best they can with the scarce resources at hand under highly difficult conditions.

In addition to trying to connect members of Tsobol Antzetik to concerned groups and individuals, I have also tried to connect them to alternative trading organizations (ATOs; see Grimes, this volume). My only attempt to date to establish this sort of connection was unsuccessful. However, it educated the women and me, and underscored the unfair risks marginalized producers take in engaging even in fair trade relations.

After a couple of years of discussions with Pueblo to People about carrying a product from Tsobol Antzetik, in 1996 the well-respected ATO agreed to carry a table runner. That fall it ordered twenty-five brocaded table runners from Tsobol Antzetik. A brief editorial about the co-op accompanied the photo of the weaving in the catalog. Pueblo to People sold all the table runners even before they arrived and immediately placed another order for five times as many table runners. Unfortunately, Pueblo to People was unable to pay its producer groups for three months, and the women had not yet received payment for the first order when they received the second. When we considered whether the weavers should work with Pueblo to People, the women didn't want to wait the three months to be paid, but faced with having to produce a large order for which they did not have the cash to buy the threads to weave, they accepted the terms set by the ATO. In the summer prior to completing the first order, high winds had destroyed many of the corn crops in Chenalhó, and many of the women needed to use whatever cash they could find to buy corn. Consequently, they never filled the order for Pueblo to People and lost this connection.

Pueblo to People went out of business soon after my effort to connect Tsobol Antzetik to it. This ATO had a long history of serving marginalized and third world craftspeople, but it was not able to resolve many of the problems that plague ATOs— cash flow being one of the most pressing. Pueblo to People representatives informed me from the start that they were urging marginalized groups such as Tsobol Antzetik to link up with other similar groups in regional confederations with which Pueblo to People could then work more effectively. Researchers's assessments of changes in social movements in Latin America reveal that successful movements in the 1990s tend to be those started by small grassroots organizations with relatively concrete goals that connect themselves with similar groups in wider organizations (Hellman 1997, 18). Such connections are nearly impossible for the women of Tsobol Antzetik to make in these unstable times.

The following summer when I returned to Chenalhó, we set up a loan fund with donations from U.S. supporters roughly along the lines of the Grameen Bank model. Our aim was to create a fund that would tide the women over in situations like the one with Pueblo to People and help them create new income-generating projects. The loan fund softened some of the worst effects of the inequitable marketing relationships in Chiapas. Still, it is in its infancy, and the women have not yet developed the educational component of the project—how to plan longer-term development projects that arise from analyses of their households' and the community's needs.

Even with all that is against them, the weavers cleverly adapt traditional ideas about economic equality to new market relations to maintain a sense that they are all progressing together. For example, in the early 1990s, Tsobol Antzetik started a project to invest monetary donations in buying and selling bulls. Calves were tethered at members' homes on a rotating basis, enabling women who could not weave for various reasons—they were ill or pregnant or caring for an infant or sick family member—to feel that they were still progressing along with the other members. Eventually, the co-op sold the bulls for a profit and reinvested the money in more calves or used it for co-op expenses or emergencies.

Despite the loan project and other creative ideas the women of Tsobol Antzetik have devised, cooperatives are a poignant reminder of alternatives to a cash economy that indigenous people used successfully before capitalism squashed these alternatives. In the late 1990s, cooperatives survived only through external support from ATOs, government and nongovernmental agencies, and church and solidarity groups in the United States and other countries (Morris 1991; Nash 1993a; Eber and Rosenbaum 1993; Rovira 1997, 199–236).

WEAVING AND SOCIAL RESTRUCTURING

The growing importance of women as providers of cash and their increased mobility have caused relations in households to shift. Pedranos still identify themselves as farmers and weavers, even though semisubsistence farming has become increasingly difficult to continue over the past decades throughout highland Chiapas. Whereas women uphold many of their understandings of themselves as women through weaving, men often cannot rely on milpa farming as a central aspect of their identities (Rus 1995). Faced with this imbalance in traditional ideas about gender complementary, women sometimes bring their husbands into cooperative work as advisors or mediators with outlets (Rus 1990). In general, the husbands have been supportive of their weaver wives, but at one time or another most have shown resentment to their wives over their greater potential to earn cash.

The social risks women face when they join cooperatives extend beyond their households. Cooperatives in Chiapas are symbols of change, and relatives and neighbors who fear change are often suspicious of these ventures. The sector of Pedrano society opposing the Zapatista movement is especially critical of cooperatives. Many of these people have gone as far as to support the escalation of the low-intensity war against democracy advocates in Chenalhó. This war has caused many women in cooperatives to fear for their physical safety, not to mention their emotional well-being. For example, women of J'pas Joloviletik (Those Who Weave), a cooperative in San Cristóbal, have been harassed on numerous occasions by men with military haircuts and demeanor. One member received a death threat, and the director was chased several blocks by two men brandishing a loaded gun in a truck (May and Craig 1994). In the context of the backlash against the democracy movement, hundreds of women have been raped by men in paramilitary groups or by Mexican soldiers. Rosa Gómez, an indigenous woman from Jitotol, was killed with a machete by her husband, who resented her frequent trips to meetings to discuss women's issues, even though she also participated with her husband in a peasant organization (Hernández Castillo 1998, 13). Just as women are beginning to enjoy greater freedoms resulting from their collective work in Chiapas, many are having to contend with family members either confining them to their homes in order to protect them or retaliating against them out of fear or resentment.[6]

At the same time as women have joined weaving cooperatives, they have joined other collectives, such as agricultural co-ops and Catholic community groups that meet to apply Jesus's biblical teachings to their daily lives. The latter groups formed through the Word of God, the name indigenous people give to the Preferential Option for the Poor, which characterizes the thrust of the Catholic diocese work throughout Chiapas. Like weaving cooperatives, these groups provide spaces within which women can confront economic injustice, social discrimination, and the domination of the Partido Revolucionario Institucional (PRI, Revolutionary Institutional Party), the political party in Mexico that has been in power for most of the twentieth century. Protestant churches also provide women with social and spiritual support, which they use to improve their lives. However, these groups do not focus on social action to as great an extent as do Catholic groups in the Preferential Option for the Poor.

Since its beginnings, Tsobol Antzetik has kept the cooperative open to women of all religious and political affiliations. Even so, it has always had a majority of traditionalists, women who still follow the folk Catholicism that has evolved out of almost five centuries of contact with the Catholic Church. As the democracy movement has spread throughout Chenalhó since the Zapatista uprising in 1994, about half of the women in Tsobol Antzetik have either joined groups that support the Zapatistas or the Sociedad Civil las Abejas (Bees Civil Society), a Catholic group that supports democracy and the Zapatistas' ideals but does not support their use of arms or their more radical socialist agenda. In the spring of 1998, the women in Tsobol Antzetik had to ask one member to leave the cooperative, the only member they have expelled. The women said they were forced to expel her because she had begun to believe the rhetoric of the PRI township authorities, who maintain that foreigners are the cause of the problems in Chenalhó and who have supported paramilitary activities in the township, the most tragic of which was the Acteal massacre. Since the massacre, the women have heard that paramilitary groups are talking about "finishing off" democracy supporters such as themselves.

In light of increasing fear of and repression by PRI officials, paramilitary groups, and the Mexican army, the women of Tsobol Antzetik are working to reduce the differences that have divided the two democracy factions represented in the township and in their group—the Zapatistas and the Bees. Until recently, Tsobol Antzetik members experienced tension between the two democracy factions. For example, María's family is divided into members who support the Zapatistas and others who support Las Abejas. During the height of tension, Antonia, a dedicated Zapatista base member, said she felt that her younger sister Anita and her other relatives in Las Abejas bases were holding back the democracy movement by not putting themselves behind the Zapatistas. Anita and her husband, Andres, on the other hand, expressed concern that some of the Zapatista practices and beliefs were too radical and costly. They preferred to work with Las Abejas also because this group rejects armed struggle. However, it was Las Abejas members who lost their lives in the Acteal massacre because they refused to support paramilitary groups bent on crushing the Zapatista movement. In the months following this tragic event, Pedranos in both Las Abejas and the Zapatista movement created a reconciliation committee, the aim of which was to create a shared strategy to bring justice and peace. On a smaller scale, Tsobol Antzetik's recent experiences reflect this reconciliation effort. For example, Antonia and Anita, the current representatives of Tsobol Antzetik, say that the Zapatistas and Las Abejas are on parallel paths.

WEAVING AND WOMEN'S CHANGING ROLES

Antonia is a model to the other women in the co-op of how to balance the many roles and allegiances women have. Women in Zapatista bases are creating quite new lives for themselves, but all within the context of respect for their unique identities as Pedranos (Eber 1999, Eber n.d.). For example, women who become *responsables* (representatives) or officers in women's groups in Zapatista bases of support must attend weekly meetings, often in distant hamlets. Most women have many children and face formidable obstacles to attending meetings that range from the need for child care, the cost of transportation to meetings, and exhaustion from adding organizing work to housework, child care, fieldwork, and weaving. They must also work at home to assert their rights as women—for example, in dividing household tasks in a more equitable manner between themselves and their kinsmen. Being subject to both age and gender subordination, young women face the challenge of trying to assert their needs while retaining the rewards they receive from their embeddedness in a society with clear rights and responsibilities. Even in the years leading up to the Zapatista rebellion, both women and children were starting to confront men's and elders' greater privileges in their society (Eber 1999).

Antonia has served in two offices in her Zapatista base—as president of a bakery cooperative and representative for fifteen hundred women refugees of political violence who have recently begun to organize themselves to find markets for their weavings. The year following the rebellion, she retired from her position as representative of Tsobol Antzetik in order to devote herself to the Zapatista movement. Although she declined the nomination to be one of the four women representatives of the base in her hamlet, she eventually became president of the bakery cooperative. Antonia continues to be involved in Tsobol Antzetik but devotes the majority of her time to the Zapatista bakers and refugee women weavers. Since spring 1998, Antonia has been making the sacrifice to travel twice a month to Polhó, in the north of the township, to meet with the women refugees there. Because she has six children and many responsibilities, this work is an additional burden for her, yet her commitment to these refugee women illustrates the indomitable spirit of women representatives in Zapatista bases as well as the tremendous obstacles they face. In 1999, Antonia joined another weaving co-op called Mujeres por la Dignídad composed of women Zapatista supporters from four highland townships.

Antonia's commitment also illustrates a belief many Pedranos retain that growing up is a process of "making one's soul arrive" through serving one's community in civil or religious duties called *cargos* (Eber and Rosenbaum n.d.). The belief that souls require ongoing care and protection also undergirds the conviction many Pedranos hold that their souls are connected to the souls of their ancestors and of their land. They take their connections to the land and the ancestors seriously. In addition to individual souls, they conceive of a collective soul that all are responsible to nourish. Even when they join Protestant groups, they may continue to serve their communities, for example as *mayoletik* (policemen) or by means of other civil cargos. Carrying out civil or religious cargos—for example, as midwives, shamans, or fiesta leaders—is work that the women say empowers them (Eber 1995, 107).

Anita's cargo as representative for the cooperative and her membership in Las Abejas also reflect her desire to fulfill her duty to her people. This work has increased her commitment to social change, although she remains skeptical of the Zapatista movement that Antonia embraces with her whole being. In contrast to her sister, who is willing to work with fifteen hundred refugee women, Anita says she would prefer to keep Tsobol Antzetik's membership small so that she has a better chance of selling what the women produce. Although Antonia says she, too, fears not fulfilling her commitment to the women by not being able to sell their weavings, she manages to submerge these fears beneath her passion for what she calls "la santa lucha," or "the holy struggle."

WEAVING AND IDENTITY

A report that was transmitted via electronic mail soon after the Acteal massacre told the story of a woman who had survived the massacre but was walking around in dirty, torn, and bloodstained clothes. When a group of people came to help the survivors, they offered the woman the used clothes of a ladina. The woman refused to take the clothes, replying in effect, "No thank you. I am not a *mestiza* [ladina]. I am from Chenalhó. These are not my clothes. It's better for me to walk around in the clothing of my people even though it's torn and dirty."

At a meeting of Tsobol Antzetik in July 1996, women expressed similar convictions that it would be incongruent with their identities to wear anything but their traditional clothing. I was struck by the strong agreement among them that it was important to continue to weave their own and other family members' clothes. One woman addressed the important role dress plays as a boundary marker when she described the unfortunate situation that might happen if she were to wear a ladina's clothes and someone were to speak to her in Spanish. She speaks only Tzotzil, so she wouldn't be able to answer. This situation would be unfair to the person and herself because they would not know how to act. She would be pretending to be something that she was not, in essence deceiving the person. The experience would not make sense to either party.

The responses from the refugee woman and the women of Tsobol Antzetik illustrate how the women of Chenalhó intertwine language, dress, and ethnicity in thought and behavior. Women in Zapatista bases take this amalgamation to a more self-conscious level in the cultural revitalization movement that they have been creating (Eber n.d.). For Antonia and others in Zapatista bases, wearing traditional clothing is also part of a larger project to cleanse themselves of the contamination of ladino and other nonindigenous influences. Pedranos in the democracy movement are recommitting themselves to traditions that they perceive to be empowering, including weaving and wearing traditional clothing. Many men wear Western-style pants while working in the milpa, but this is mostly to protect their legs because traditional tunics leave them exposed to midthigh. Children often wear Western-style clothes because their mothers cannot weave enough to clothe them every day in traditional clothing. Women never wear Western-style clothing, except for sweaters when it is cold and shoes to protect their feet—also because they find them attractive—when they can afford to buy them. But all Pedranas living in Chenalhó wear their traditional indigo skirts and brightly brocaded blouses, only occasionally wearing a blouse made by an indigenous woman from a neighboring township, a quite recent choice that seems to reflect women's delight in the work of other women as well as a wider sense of themselves as indigenous people in a shared struggle for autonomy and cultural survival.

Although Pedranos are reinvigorating time-honored identities, they also show their flexibility and adaptability. For example, although weaving has traditionally been women's work, more and more sons of women in the cooperative are weaving or embroidering for cash. Boys still tend to follow their fathers as milpa farmers, but the decreasing capacity of farming to support households and the need for cash to buy corn have pushed young men and boys to seek additional means to earn cash. For some time, men and boys have been intensifying their production of the cotton bags that all Pedranos use to carry food, produce, or other possessions when traveling from place to place. Men traditionally make these bags using a macramé technique, but until recently few boys have shown interest in backstrap weaving. My first hint of boys beginning to weave came in early December 1997, when a box from the cooperative arrived at my home in New Mexico. Halfway through the box of weavings, my fingers unraveled a scarf caught in the folds of a blouse. Its border was a parade of colors that came together in a whimsical way. The name on the tag was Sebastian, Antonia's fifteen-year-old son. Since his parents became committed to the democracy movement, Sebastian has been taking over much of his father's work in the fields. I knew Sebastian to be a passionate farmer and diligent worker, and was not aware that he had any interest in weaving. When I saw him in July 1998, I complimented him on his fine weaving and asked him how and why he got started. He told me that he saw that his mother was earning cash, and he, too, wanted to earn it. He learned to weave scarves, tortilla cloths, and baby boys' tunics over a period of about three to four months in 1997 and 1998, sitting by his mother's side and copying her. I commented to Antonia on how rapidly Sebastian had learned and on his fine work, which she attributed to his strong heart and determination to earn money.[7]

SUPPORTING A SACRED STRUGGLE

My work with Tsobol Antzetik is based on several assumptions of feminist scholarship. The most relevant to this chapter is that research unfolds within ongoing dialogues aimed at decentering researchers from positions of privilege in order to ameliorate the worst effects of inequality between ourselves and the people we study, as well as within the communities we study (Nash 1997, Wolf 1996). Observing the women in Chenalhó struggling to represent themselves and to control their lives in the wake of the Zapatista uprising has impressed on me the importance of not neglecting or disrespecting their ideas and analyses. I have tried to work with the women in ways that respect them as negotiators of change, picking and choosing among those ideas that come from outside and then reworking them in ways that make sense from their points of view. The women's personal histories make clear their deep consciousness of place and change, as well as the complex and layered roles they play as producers of knowledge and as people of action in their communities and beyond. Much can be lost in theorizing about economic change and poor artisans when researchers and fair trade advocates do not try to dislodge themselves from positions of power and to approach their work as an ongoing dialogue.

Working from the premise of collaborative empowerment in unstable times across international boundaries means that I move slowly with the women of Tsobol Antzetik, checking with them as much as possible about how they feel about the nature and pace of our work and the demands these place on them. Above all, I have tried to convey to the women—for example, in a speech at the weaving competition—that I understand and am trying to help others understand that the women's ways of knowing and being in the world are as valid as those ways being forced on them by neoliberal economic promoters with narrow understandings of development. In keeping with their people's concern for reciprocity, Antonia and Anita replied to my speech by sharing some details of the suffering the women had experienced during the past year and their resolve to keep struggling for peace and justice.

Mainly because of time constraints, I have moved slowly with the weavers in terms of asking them to make new products that respond to the tastes of Americans and other foreigners. Another important reason for moving slowly, however, is the type of markets I tap. As mentioned above, I have solicited orders from a sector of the U.S. public that appreciates products that embody cultural values and alternative economic visions. People in this sector try to understand the obstacles facing poor producers.

Relying on sales from this sector has meant that I have not had to impose on the women too many demands that add to their already taxing lives or that would be difficult for them to accept. It has also meant that I have been able to sell the types of weavings that the women make for themselves and their families, and what they had already been making in the cooperative movement before I met them. All of these items are labor intensive and require finely honed skills to make. Socially conscious buyers have the patience to wait for these products and are willing to pay what they are worth.

These labor-intensive products embody cultural beliefs about continuity and connections with the ancestors that socially conscious buyers respect. Apart from the symbols that have their roots in Classic-era Maya civilizations (A.D. 600–900), the weavings from Chenalhó embody a central understanding about cloth that continuous weaving transmits spiritual force. In several contemporary societies, this belief about cloth is supported by taboos about cutting (Hughes cited in Weiner and Schneider 1989, 15). Although I am unaware of any taboos on cutting in Chenalhó, weavers there never cut their cloth. Their reticence to cut is most likely connected to a central belief in Pedrano culture that people are responsible to nurture a collective soul that has always existed and will continue to exist in the future, so I have not suggested to the weavers that they cut their weavings to fashion them according to current styles and tastes in the United States.

Items that we have been able to market successfully and that embody cultural values include many types of cloths in which to wrap tortillas or to place over food on tables, as well as men's and boys tunics and women's and girls' blouses, shawls, and purses. We have also come up with about a half-dozen new products that are mostly for foreign consumers—including bookmarks, a tray, a table runner, place mats and napkins, and a shoulder bag replicating the design on a ceremonial blouse. These products have been quite successful due in part to their usefulness. They represent compromises through which the women depart somewhat from traditional designs but receive benefits for doing so in increased orders. Although these new items came through my own and friends' efforts to develop marketable products, our objective has been for the women to maintain control over adapting the new forms to their traditional ways of working. As we work out the new designs, sometimes the women request that I be more specific about exactly what U.S. buyers want so that they can meet their size, style, and color preferences.[8]

I have also tried to introduce ideas for products that make sense to the women weavers. A case in point is the bookmark that they started to make in 1998. No woman in the co-op has books in her home, except perhaps a Bible or a child's school work-book, but the women have begun to understand that others learn about their situation and become inspired to support them through written materials, such as books. The Zapatistas have also made education a focal point of their development projects. In June 1998, I gave Antonia a copy of a book published earlier in the year about violence toward women in Chiapas, *La otra palabra: Mujeres y violencia en Chiapas, antes y despues Acteal* (The Other Word: Women and Violence in Chiapas, before and after Acteal; Hernández Castillo 1998). What interested Antonia most in the book was the section in the back with photos of the aftermath of the massacre at Acteal. She seemed moved that there were people who would care enough about them to write a book about their struggles against injustice, with photos showing the reality of their lives. She said that the book was an important gift that she will share with women in all the groups to which she belongs. A piece of fabric to mark one's place in a book may now have significance for women like Antonia, beyond just being an item foreigners use that is part of our strange life, a life that provides free time to read.

CONCLUSION

When I began to work with Tsobol Antzetik in the late 1980s, it was clear that weaving was becoming an important source for obtaining cash and that weaving cooperatives were creating new social spaces for women in which they could develop leadership skills. But I did not anticipate the extent to which families with weavers would come to depend on selling the weavings for their survival, nor did I foresee the key role that women's groups would play a decade later in restructuring indigenous communities. Like poor women throughout Latin America, women in Chenalhó demonstrate that they are fully capable of articulating their ideal society and acting in order to survive the best way they can at any moment in time (Eber 1999; see also Milgram, this vol-ume, for comparable evidence among Filipino women traders).

The women's work in Tsobol Antzetik holds out an alternative to incorpora-tion into capitalist structures that pit producers against each other. Worldwide atten-tion to and support for the democracy movement in Chiapas have increased the women's awareness of their embeddedness in a world system that includes greedy capitalists as well as many sympathetic people. Some people in the latter category have become con-nected to Tsobol Antzetik through fair trade delegations that bring representatives into the women's homes, as well as through donations and orders for weavings.[9] The fair trade market is an important one for the weavers, as is the expanding market made up of members of solidarity and other social justice groups in the United States and throughout the world.

The constraints on the women of Tsobol Antzetik to work with outsiders are many and now include intensifying assaults against their lives. Still, the women keep weaving. Their weaving is an act of faith in the future, and their faith strengthens both themselves and those of us who are privileged to work with them.

NOTES

[1] Cristóbal Ruíz Arias provided the Spanish translation of this prayer in Tzotzil for inclusion in the film *Chiapas: Prayer for the Weavers* (Gleason 1999). The English translation is mine.

[2] Support for my research in San Pedro Chenalhó in the summers of 1997 and 1998 came from a New Mexico State University Mini Grant (1997), an NMSU-Mexico Small Grants Program grant (1997), and an NMSU Summer Research Award (1998). The current climate of militarization and repression of research and human rights work in Chiapas prevented me from entering Chenalhó in the summers of 1998 and 1999. I obtained my information about current conditions in weaving cooperatives in Chenalhó from women and their families who were able to travel from their rural hamlets in Chenalhó to the weaving competition and celebration in June 1998 in San Cristóbal de Las Casas, the urban center of highland Chiapas. During this event, the women of Tsobol Antzetik asked me to convey their gratitude to the North Americans who have supported the co-op and the democracy movement by purchasing weavings, sending donations, or educating people about their lives. I, too, would like to thank these people as well as the editors of and contributors to this volume.

[3] *Chiapas: Prayer for the Weavers* by Judith Gleason is distributed by Filmmakers Library.

[4] Throughout the chapter, I use pseudonyms to refer to the women in Tsobol Antzetik.

[5] Inuit artists express similar concerns for trade practices that honor cultural values, particularly those surrounding reciprocity and autonomy (Driscoll-Engelstad 1998).

[6] For discussions about violence toward women in Chiapas, see Hernández Castillo (1998).

[7] Girls in Chenalhó who want to weave usually begin to learn at around seven or eight years of age. They begin by embroidering designs on purchased or woven cloth and later learn to brocade on backstrap looms. By the time they are teenagers, many can weave well enough to sell their work (Chen n.d., Eber and Rosenbaum 1993).

[8] See Lynd (this volume) and Rosenbaum and Goldin (1997) for a discussion of changes in marketing traditional designs produced on backstrap looms in Guatemala and Chiapas, particularly the consequences of internationalizing production.

[9] Global Exchange and Cloudforest Initiatives have offices in San Cristóbal de Las Casas, where they organize delegations to indigenous communities focusing on a range of topics, including fair trade and sustainable development. For Global Exchange's address, see Grimes (this volume, note 10). Cloudforest Initiatives' address is P.O. Box 13149, Minneapolis, MN 55414; (651) 592-4143; cloudforest@hwpics.com.

MARTHA LYND

5. THE INTERNATIONAL CRAFT MARKET

A DOUBLE-EDGED SWORD FOR
GUATEMALAN MAYA WOMEN

Throughout human history, people have expended time, energy and resources to both produce and adjust to change while preserving their culture from being assimilated wholesale into another one. For the most part, they prefer to integrate themselves into the larger society on their own terms. They accept and affirm their ethnic identity but not the material and social conditions to which they are subjected.
—*Charles Kleymeyer*, Cultural Expression and Grassroots Development

Women's weaving groups in the rural western highlands of Guatemala are poignantly experiencing the process of adaptation to change. Women weavers who have joined craft groups in the states of Sololá and El Quiche are handling a double-edged sword as they engage in the international crafts market. Of their own volition, indigenous weavers have struggled to gain the contacts to enable them to export their goods. Though weaving is something the women do with great skill, they are unable to get ahead in the local markets because of intense competition, so selling in the international craft market becomes an attractive option. At the same time that they want to succeed in this international arena, they want to maintain their cultures. Their textiles and perceptions change as they make the necessary adjustments to sell their work.

In this chapter, I explore how anthropologists and people involved in the fair trade movement can be proactive agents for change.[1] These cultural facilitators can perhaps help to lesson the negative effects of change, while using their skills in traveling between cultural contexts to assist indigenous craftspeople to wield this double-edged sword. I also suggest an approach that can meet the dual needs of succeeding in the international crafts market while at the same time participating in projects that help foster the economic and cultural well-being of indigenous crafts groups.

I first discuss my long-term working relationship with women's weaving associations in Guatemala. As a weaver myself, I used art as a vehicle through which to begin a dialogue with the women and to learn of their priorities. Second, the chapter explores how anthropology and a fair trade commitment can be combined with business. I explore how developing trust through long-term business connections can create the basis on which to branch out into supporting or creating projects that benefit the weaving groups. I also describe some of the lessons we have learned at Maya Traditions in terms of the nuts and bolts of building a business that can incorporate quality control so that weavers' products can be successful in the international market. Maya Traditions is a fair trade wholesale business that works with Maya weaving groups, promotes and provides orders for high-quality weaving, and supports weavers and their families through education and health programs.

After examining the marriage of weaving as an income-generating activity with community-based social programs, I explore how this combination is a form of resistance to "wholesale" cultural assimilation, as Kleymeyer (1994) suggests in the epigraph to this chapter. Finally, I share a case study of a participatory evaluation of a craft group's long-term involvement with such projects; I examine how implementing this type of evaluation can be important in truly creating a team atmosphere. This sense of teamwork between craft groups and fair trade businesses with a broad social trajectory can then serve to improve both the crafts being produced and the commitment to proceed with further projects that meet the needs of producer groups.

HECHOS NO DICHOS—ACTION NOT TALK

While in academia, I became frustrated by the high proportion of social and anthropological work that failed to address the needs of Native American communities in the United States.[2] At the time, I was too inexperienced to handle the direct and justified historically based outrage of many Native Americans, but I still wanted to work with indigenous people to build on commonalities and interests rather than differences. Intrigued by the highly skilled colorful textiles in Guatemala, woven by a population that is roughly 60 percent indigenous, I made a commitment to work with weavers in Guatemala and help them develop broader markets for their products.

My interest in weaving began when I learned to do floor-loom weaving while still in high school. Subsequently, I worked as a production weaver for Vovaka Textiles in Boulder, Colorado, producing bolts of upholstery, blankets, rugs, and specialty fabrics. In 1992, I was part of a Witness for Peace delegation that visited Guatemalan refugee camps in Chiapas, Mexico, and marginalized areas in Guatemala. The experience gave me a sense of the political, historical, and economic background of the country and its people; weaving served as an excellent medium through which to understand and gain trust with the indigenous women I met.

I later attended a language institute in Quetzaltenango, where I met representatives of women's weaving associations. I purchased weavings directly from the artists, who live in isolated highland villages and who typically receive very little money for their work. Members in one of the weaving groups invited me to live in their village for a month and learn how to do backstrap weaving. In exchange, I assisted in starting a project to get a market outlet for their work. Though one month is a short fieldwork stay, I experienced life in a Kiche farming village where few women speak Spanish and where Maya traditions and culture persist despite colonization and the recent civil war. I decided that I would learn whatever it was that people felt like sharing with me about their lives without imposing predetermined research questions on them. My goal was to understand their needs and priorities by living with them and listening to their stories. I discovered that income-producing activities were of primary importance to both the women and their husbands.

Gaining people's trust is the most fundamental task that enables truly valuable and relevant work to take place. When I first met these women, they explained that their group was composed of widows of the war—an identity designed to win the sympathies of young politically interested language students. When I actually went to live with this group, however, they admitted that they had not told the truth, explaining that outsiders are not as sympathetic to their needs if they simply say that they are impoverished and need money. From this experience, I realized that poverty is a form of political violence that many middle-class people like myself often do not understand, and that people in dire circumstances will at times say anything to survive. Only after an outsider builds trust with the producers with whom he or she works can such producers begin to share more openly the dynamics of their experiences.

The weavers I met in highland Guatemala asked me to find an international market for their work. Because weaving is the primary way women make money in the rural sector of Guatemala, I accepted their challenge as a form of applied anthropological work. I saw it as a way to contribute to the communities in which I lived and with which I have had contact. I share this story as the background that contextualizes how I started to develop a working relationship with weaving associations. As a father of one of the families in the village where I lived said, "Lo que queremos ver son hechos, no dichos" (what we really want to see are actions, not talk).

WEAVING IN HIGHLAND GUATEMALA

A web of related factors has made it extremely difficult to live a subsistence lifestyle in the highlands without the need of cash or services from the outside world. Loss of land, war, overpopulation, exploitative labor practices, migration, tourism, and an export-oriented economy influence the lifeways of indigenous upland communities. Guatemala supports a population of approximately 10.6 million people. Eighty percent live in poverty, 60 to 70 percent of which live in extreme destitution (Villatoro 1996, 110).[3] To compound this situation, Guatemala is coming out of a thirty-six year civil war, which "officially" ended in December 1996. As Villatoro explained, "For five hundred years the dominant culture has tried to rob the identity, social consciousness, spirituality and material world of the Maya. But Guatemalans have resisted and persisted even with war, racism, discrimination and poverty."[4] The recent civil war is part of a long historical process. Although all Guatemalans are affected by the conflict, it is principally the Maya of the central western highlands who have suffered the most serious consequences (Villatoro 1996, 109).

Land ownership is of central importance in the conflict. Whereas in the past children inherited enough land from which they could meet basic needs, today this is no longer possible in most villages. Partitioning of family plots over the years has left parents with insufficient lands to sustain themselves and their many children. Family members have responded by uniting with other community members in various economic ventures to earn needed cash and desired services.

Weaving groups are one popular strategy chosen by women to fight desperation and increase family income. Weaving is a traditional activity that allows women to maintain their role as primary homemakers. They typically weave four to five hours per day—work interspersed with the daily activities of cooking, caring for children, feeding animals, and washing clothes. Participating in weaving groups gives them a break from the isolation in their homes and provides income, while at the same time keeping their weaving traditions alive. Women also gain secondary benefits in learning to express themselves through the group decision-making processes. The leader of the San Juan weaving group, Teresa Ujpan Pérez, discussed what being in a group means to her: "With the money from weaving, we can maintain our children, pay for clothing and education. We combat the violence. We don't want our children to be out there on the street. We are succeeding little by little. Now our weavings are valued."[5] When I asked Teresa what she meant by combating the violence, she said that women have a lot of fear from the time of the war. People were killed or disappeared in nearby villages. The women were afraid to leave their houses or travel because they might not return. Now they are fighting against this fear when they make the decision to participate in groups, to organize, and to speak.

By participating in organized groups, they also gain access to different types of training, an important benefit for women who typically have not studied past third grade (see also Eber, this volume). Although weaving does not generate a great deal of income, it can help women to buy corn when the yearly stock is depleted, medicine, or shoes and schoolbooks for children. It also enables women to have more equality in their relationships because they are generating revenue for the household. Admittedly, there are sometimes martial problems as husbands adjust to their wives not always being in the home as they participate in meetings and sometimes travel to training sessions.

HELPING WEAVING GROUPS SUCCEED IN THE INTERNATIONAL CRAFTS MARKET

Understanding the needs of these women who are materially poor led me to become involved with the alternative trade organization Maya Traditions.[6] People need to eat today, yet at the same time they look for long-term economic and cultural survival strategies that meet their needs and interests in culturally appropriate ways. Maya Traditions is concerned with helping weavers achieve these goals. Founded by Jane Mintz, a former social worker and textile weaver, Maya Traditions is a member of the Fair Trade Federation (FTF).[7] It strives to preserve backstrap weaving and to provide consistent work for weaving cooperatives or associations in the Guatemalan highlands. With two offices—one in Panajachel, Guatemala, the other in San Francisco—Maya Traditions buys directly from weavers from Nahuala, El Quiche, and Sololá, and exports their products to stores in the United States. We work together with weavers to develop woven products that incorporate new color combinations and traditional designs, and to highlight the different weaving techniques that are distinctive to each village. In addition, in accordance with fair trade's philosophy of working to enhance the quality of life of artisan groups, I conducted a needs assessment survey with the Nahaula and Sololá groups in 1996 in order to identify their concerns and priorities. The groups stated six main priorities: steady orders for their weavings, education for their children, access to health care, capital for thread or loans, more land, and a place to meet outside of their homes.[8]

My work with Maya Traditions includes design work, quality control, managing orders, continuous contact with the weaving groups, and participation in social and health projects with members. The experience of living in Guatemala and engaging in weekly contact with the weavers has taught me many things that I would not have learned otherwise. The following section outlines five fundamental lessons that have served to improve the quality of our work and consequently our overall sales.

First, to provide the groups with steady orders and income, it was important to create a few low-cost items. We combine small pieces of distinctive traditional weavings with less expensive cloth in order to keep the costs lower and increase affordability for the average North American buyer. Although many people cannot afford an expensive woven wall hanging, most can purchase a colorful, small change purse.

Second, it is beneficial to recognize the potential skills of individual weavers in each group and to be particularly knowledgeable about the best weavers' capabilities. This lesson can be applied to other kinds of crafts and producer groups as well. Previously, our usual method of communicating orders was to transmit orally to the weavers the written or drawn text on the order forms, but even when bilingual literate weavers explained the orders, we still had problems with the artisans producing precise work. We discovered that not all women have the same capacity to capture design changes, combine colors, or learn orally. We remedied the problem by identifying the best weavers who have the skills or creativity to handle new color combinations and measurements. These highly skilled weavers create new samples that the other weavers can copy and use as tangible references. Correct samples are passed around to each member of the group, who in turn counts threads and measures using finger widths, or who devises her own method to remember the design or color combinations.

The third lesson involves discounting the price paid for finished work when it does not meet quality standards. At first, when weavings did not meet the specifications, I had to learn to control my instinct for leniency and to avoid accepting all pieces in response to the women's poverty. Our current strategy is to explain to producers that if they want to increase sales, they need to take individual responsibility for making their work the best quality possible and to correct mistakes independently. To introduce this system, we do not discount the price paid if producers make mistakes on new pieces the first time we ask for sample weavings. However, after the second or third delivery, we deduct a percentage from the total due if the work does not reflect what has been ordered. This new tactic has proven an effective form of quality control. For example, the small weaving group located in a village near the market town of Chichicastenango typically weaves extremely bright *huipiles* or handwoven blouses. When we asked them to use less of the hot pinks, lime greens, and oranges, they replied that the weavings would then be *triste* or sad. We had to explain that every culture has different ideas of aesthetics and that North Americans prefer only a bit of these colors.

They nodded in agreement, but later the hot pinks and lemon yellows again appeared. We then had to sit down with weavers and painstakingly review with them the colors in each design. We continue to discount when weavers do not follow the design. Currently this group produces dynamic work that is popular and thus provides weavers a steady source of income for four families. The women are pleased to receive repeat orders, and the youngest weaver has become a sample expert who can readily create new designs and color combinations for us.[9]

We acknowledge that introducing new designs and color combinations is a delicate issue. On the one hand, we want to help the women succeed in the international market. On the other hand, as a fair trade business committed to preserve producer groups' traditions, we do not want producers to lose the integrity of their weavings. In such a situation, the fair trade advocate must try to wield a double-edged sword. As a cultural facilitator, we try to educate North American consumers about the cultural meanings and context of particular weavings, while helping the artisans understand the range of North American tastes.

We have also learned that the practice of discounting can be useful only up to a point. It does motivate weavers to do their very best work. Once there is internal quality control on the part of the groups, however, we must consider what is culturally acceptable and possible given particular weaving techniques. Constant dialogue between the producers and marketers becomes essential. With backstrap weaving, it is unrealistic to make items with small margins for error, so we have changed the product design for items that were causing repeated trouble for the weavers. This way of working with weavers has reduced problems in production and has yielded high-quality textiles that appeal to our customers.

Our fourth lesson is that product development is a slow process. To reduce risk, we produce a series of samples before placing a large order. Similarly, the fifth lesson entails providing weavers with ample time to fill the orders. As semisubsistence farmers, the weavers must often accomplish other daily activities before they can weave. They must contend with unexpected events, such as deaths or natural disasters, and devote time to cyclical events, such as corn and coffee harvests or community festivals. Respecting their cultures means planning for slower production during these times. Likewise, during certain months—such as October, when a family's corn supplies are exhausted—sales from weavings are more important (see also MacHenry, this volume).

The weaving groups were originally organized to try to earn a better price for their work. However, one of the most difficult tasks weavers face is determining the value of each weaving, given that production is interspersed with other daily house-hold chores. With intense local competition and destitute weavers undercutting each other's prices to make sales, this situation is further compounded by shop owners and tourists who haggle to get the best possible bargain (see both Eber and Milgram, this volume).

We at Maya Traditions together with the weaving groups' representatives cal-culate the production costs—the cost of thread and the time involved in producing a weaving. We factor in the additional costs for other materials and the sewing time re-quired to manufacture the weaving into a finished product. By comparing these costs with an estimation of the amount we can charge for the item in the U.S. market, we can determine whether an item will be competitively priced or whether it will be too ex-pensive. We pay the weavers the highest price the business can afford. Part of our fair trade commitment means that we maintain a low markup.

Some fair trade organizations—such as Peoplink, in which artisans market directly to first world consumers on the Internet—obviously provide an even better return to the artisans.[10] The artisans with whom we work, however, do not have the marketing skills, English- and Spanish-language skills, knowledge of foreign tastes, or sufficient capital to create a feasible consumer base on their own. Moreover, many do not have the time to gain the necessary skills to assume the marketing role; they want to weave and have someone else sell. Many obstacles need to be analyzed to understand how to empower groups further if they have the desire at some future time to export and market.

PROFILES OF THE WEAVING GROUPS

Each weaving group differs in size and character; they range from six to twenty-eight members. They are organized as associations in which decisions are made collectively, and the boards of directors are responsible to their memberships.[11] Orders are spread among members so that everyone benefits. By learning the history of the groups and how each functions, we have gained an understanding of their strengths and weak-nesses, and have identified differing needs and goals. We visit the groups periodically in their communities and have been able to talk at more length, albeit through inter-preters.[12]

The Sololá group, organized by widows, was established after violence hit their community in 1982. A Maya organization called Mayalan[13] provided the group with information on how to form a board of directors and administer monies. Significantly, Mayalan advised the women to take 10 percent of the profit from each woman's weaving and donate it to a group fund. The group is now in the process of successfully paying off a loan for a piece of land held in common that will be used to grow corn and other vegetables. Because the group is well organized, it has taken advantage of opportunities to participate in other productive activities as well as consciousness-raising and educational workshops.

The other groups have had more problems. The Nahuala group has so few people who read, write, and speak Spanish or who can balance accounts that the same leaders are begrudgingly reelected year after year. This educated elite is resented, yet the bulk of the group lacks the skill or self-confidence to take on leadership positions (see Milgram, this volume). To protest this situation, the group elected a treasurer from outside the educated elite, but this person could not subtract. The new treasurer administered individual loans and failed to record the amount each member received. Consequently, there was not enough money for the group to buy threads. The need for education in particular areas is painfully apparent. Groups persevere because of the financial needs of their members, but they could potentially function better. For example, another group from San Juan la Laguna experienced a scandal when it received money from the United States Agency for International Development (USAID) and the male administrator stole the funds to build his own private house, leaving members stranded.

We also work with a splinter weaving group that lives outside the colorful market town of Chichicastenango. This group separated from the larger group because of problems over a loan that the original group received in order to learn how to use the upright, European-style loom (used for weaving *cortes,* the traditional-style skirt worn by women). Lacking the foresight or training to understand how the payback schedule would affect their lives, many women resented the loan to which they had agreed. In the splinter group, extended family and close friends work together, so in this case, group cohesion and trust became more important than financial concerns.

All of these situations exemplify the need for orientation and training in the formation and functioning of craft associations. The craft groups, once formed, do more than produce beautiful art work. They become social units that serve as the basis for self-help projects and for gaining access to credit or nongovernmental organization (NGO) training programs. The women's groups have been involved in various projects, including livestock fattening, analysis of wage and human rights issues, and Maya cosmovision workshops. Each group has a distinct set of experiences and history, which in turn greatly affects its character.

Close contact with weaving groups allows the facilitator to help groups find alternative ways to meet their needs in a multidimensional way. As we come to know the women better, we have become involved in other projects that are not directly related to craft production. We have learned the importance of group organization and of the provision of adequate training and orientation to prepare members for the responsibilities of new projects.

BEYOND CRAFTS: ADDRESSING COMMUNITY NEEDS

Just as supporting the preservation of traditional weaving techniques reinforces cultural expression, it is important to think about what types of projects accomplish the dual goals of satisfying material needs while building on a cultural foundation. Group members and local indigenous leaders repeatedly stressed this idea in interviews. As Julia Par Yaxon (1998), a grassroots organizer for Mayalan, states:

> The kinds of projects that work in the countryside besides *artesania* (craft production) are ones that have to do with what people know. What works is planting and selling onions, potatoes, or raising chickens and selling the eggs. Also raising bulls to slaughter or growing tomatoes, fruit or something from here. One woman planted Chinese cabbage to export, but this is not something we know about. It doesn't have anything to do with our culture. . . . This is also how we have failure in work . . . when we learn how to grow something we don't eat or know how to use. And then people don't even want to wear their *traje* (traditional clothing). In this way the young people lose their culture.

Securing a market or demand for whatever product or service offered is an important issue for Maya communities. The people in these communities do not have the luxury of changing their minds several times about the kinds of skills they seek and opportunities to learn. Women are most concerned about feeding, caring for, and educating their families; practicality is an essential element with people who have limited economic resources and time. Therefore, in terms of anticipating long-term success, it is important to support projects that meet the needs of people locally and build on their knowledge and culture.

With globalization, there is increasing pressure on people to abandon their subsistence-farming lifestyles and to work as wage laborers on monocrop plantations that provide food for urban populations. As local subsistence economies are destroyed, people's cultures are ravaged. Consequently, cultural diversity decreases and environmental problems often accompany social problems. As Wali (1994) has suggested, "In recent years, the battle over resources has been framed as a debate about development. Many of Latin America's efforts to modernize since World War II have focused on homogenizing populations on the theory that this would grease the wheels of economic growth. This scenario visualized local culture and social differences as obstacles to be overcome, not opportunities to be seized" (167). An integrated approach called *desarollo integral,* however, strengthens rural communities in Guatemala by supporting indigenous cultures and their local economies and respecting their communities' sovereignties. This type of approach prioritizes the participation and leadership of community or group members in any type of project. In small-scale practical terms, this means supporting projects that strengthen community ties and foster well-being in a deeper sense than can be measured simply by indexes of economic profit. I now turn to two such projects we support that illustrate this point.

THE EDUCATION PROJECT

As Teresa Ujpan Pérez, the San Juan group leader, has stated so well, "With education you can combat discrimination. When you graduate from the university, you're seen as an equal. Otherwise they discriminate against you when they see your *corte.* If you're well educated, even if you wear your corte, the high-class people have to take what you say in account. And I've seen some people come back from the university and support the community. I've seen some people do this. I knew a nurse who would talk to the people and explain things to them."

In addition to helping groups increase income in the short term, we are working together to better prepare for the future. We began a scholarship program after Sophia, daughter of a weaver, asked for help in attending secondary school. Her father was killed during the war, and her mother struggled to put her through school by selling weavings. Because schools beyond sixth grade seldom exist in rural areas, room, board, and transportation become prohibitive barriers to education for poor families. The Sololá women's group desired to find a way to educate their children. We agreed to help because education would provide an enduring benefit. Although Maya Traditions donates money for school supplies for elementary children, its primary focus is on helping older youths stay in school so they can have a voice in society and assist their communities.

The scholarship project also expresses our fair trade commitment. It provides weaver families with the opportunity for formal schooling, which they could not afford otherwise. Private donations are used to fund the scholarships, and we donate our time to facilitate the program. In 1998, we funded eighty-three elementary school children and thirty-one junior high school students. In 1998, we also gave support to seventeen high school students.

Concerned about the older youth who are leaving their communities and facing the pressures to assimilate into the dominant culture, we discussed the issue at length with group members and with community organizer, Julia Par Yaxon. She explained, "It all depends on the formation of the young person in the home. . . . If the person was told from the time he was little to value his culture, have respect for your family, do what is right, and not do bad things, well, the person carries this around inside of them wherever they go." When asked about students' relationships to native communities after completing school, she remarked, "The people who work for the good of the community, even if they don't volunteer their time, if they identify with the community, then we say their education is worth something, if they support the community. For example, if a person becomes mayor and helps those in need for the benefit of the community, then their study is valid. . . . There are young people who help and those who don't. But it's more common that they'll help because of the times we're in" (Par Yaxon 1998).[14]

In return for economic support, each student is required to perform community service that in some way benefits the women in the groups. The women and students together decide what classes will be taught each year. Students teach classes during school vacations. Literacy and oral Spanish classes were taught in two communities in 1997. In another, students taught how to maintain personal hygiene and how to plant family garden plots to supplement the traditional bean and tortilla diet. This program helps provide students a way to reintegrate with their community.

The Spanish classes have taught many of the weavers to speak, read, and write some Spanish, which has in turn improved group decision making and consensus. As a board member from the Nahuala group stated, "We had problems with group elections. Nobody wanted to be the president or secretary or treasurer. Why? Because they can't speak Spanish. They have to travel a lot and speak with people who only speak Spanish." Maya Traditions plans to continue supporting this project in which the students give back to their mothers, gain teaching experience, and honor women who are marginalized by Guatemalan society as a whole.

Through access to education, these young high school students are becoming more highly skilled. They have a choice either to leave their villages to pursue other occupations or to stay in their communities to become future craft group presidents or teachers. Whatever they choose, it is certain that by being educated, they are better prepared to handle a changing world and to defend their rights as indigenous people.

WEAVERS, MAYA TRADITIONS, AND NGOS COLLABORATE: AN INTEGRATED HEALTH PROJECT

Vivamos Mejor (Let's Live Better)—a Swiss-funded, Guatemalan-run NGO—organizes sustainable grassroots community projects, such as a project to revive natural Maya medicine practices in the state of Sololá. After learning of this project, I connected the Sololá weaving group with a local health promoter, Andres Matzar, from this NGO.[15] Because improving health care was one of the long-term needs expressed by the group, I thought that they would be receptive when asked if they wanted to participate. In February 1998, the group began attending workshops on how to cure common sicknesses with herbs found locally. Although the women are familiar with many of the herbs, they do not always know all their uses or the appropriate doses. Matzar teaches in Kakchiquel, the language of the women, and utilizes a teaching style that combines aural learning, simple charts, hands-on activities, and oral quizzing of the women. He also does all the necessary translation for the group.

By responding to the most common health needs in this region, this program undertakes an integrated approach to health care. Many of the women suffer from nervous tension and gastrointestinal problems that, as they themselves affirm, are in part side effects from living through massacres in their villages. The Sololá weaving group has many women who suffer from these health problems as well as from psychological effects from the war. Maya pathology recognizes health and sickness as a continuum that plays itself out in the body, mind, and spirit.

Because of their recognition and receptiveness, the women have been treating these illnesses with the help of two community psychology students. The psychologists use participatory dynamics translated in Kakchiquel, which are based on elements of life in the countryside and on Maya values, to help the women unload their pain from the war. The health promoter teaches them about herbs that help heal their gastritis, and the psychologists help them build group unity. The group thus not only helps meet economic needs through its focus on weaving and other productive projects, but also serves as a source of spiritual renewal.

Becoming part of the mental health team at Vivamos Mejor, I have accompanied the health promoter and psychologists, and have learned about their work with indigenous groups and their use of participatory techniques. Vivamos Mejor values my input as a facilitator because I have been in contact with the Sololá weaving group since 1992, which has proven an important factor in the group's acceptance of the project.

PARTICIPATORY EVALUATION OF PROJECTS

"What we want is a solar plant dryer. . . . We need all the herbal remedies to be written down, and we want to learn better the uses of each plant. . . . We forget a lot. . . . We feel good that we are learning how to get our sadness out": these comments were made during a team-run participatory evaluation conducted with seventeen Kakchiquel women in the Sololá weaving group. When previously asked direct questions about how the group valued the herbal medicine and mental health project, they had responded in a superficially positive manner; in other words, they had no criticisms or suggestions. What would seem like a straightforward matter in the West of examining strengths and weaknesses of a program in an unabashed way is complicated in Guatemala by power and cultural differences. Many groups in the countryside feel that if they say what they think a potential funder wants to hear, they will continue to receive funding for a project they desire to continue.[16] As facilitators or service providers who have direct contact with NGOs, we are seen as having the power to determine the fate of future projects. Culturally, as well, rural Guatemalans tend to avoid offering direct criticism, and indigenous women especially have been trained to repress dissatisfaction or not to reveal their true feelings.

Through the forces of machismo, women are taught to defer to their husbands or fathers, and in dealing with nonindigenous people, they have learned to yield because of the historic effects of colonialism, discrimination, and the recent war. As one group leader stated, "There are some groups who won't talk for anything, and I ask myself why? I think it is because of the violence when family members were dragged out of their houses and killed. I think it has left a big effect in the people. They especially feel aversion to talk to an outsider." Silence has been a survival tactic in the village of this particular weaving group, where people were killed for reasons often unclear to them.[17]

We recognized that any type of project evaluation must be grounded in trust. To do so, we first made clear to the weavers that this activity was optional and that we respected their authority in deciding whether or not to participate. We explained that the evaluation was to help their group and us understand what elements helped past projects to succeed or fail. Our hopes were to engage in a mutual learning process that could be applied to our current projects as well as future ones. We listened to their past experiences with different projects to glean factors that contributed to the results of each project, including internal group dynamics and outside forces. Their responses informed us and sparked group insights as the women reviewed the history of both the smooth and difficult moments.

The participatory evaluation methods that we have used are based on popular education models in which the emphasis is on starting at the education level or life experience of the participants. Information and the structure of activities are arranged in such a way as to make the evaluation completely accessible and relevant to the participants, while simultaneously building participants' communication skills. Although many books on popular education techniques are available, I had a difficult time finding evaluation methods appropriate for groups that are predominantly illiterate.[18] We decided to learn from the women's personal experiences by using pictures that the women drew. The women symbolically represented their assessments of each project, an activity that then could be applied in multiple ways to group work in which the majority of the members are illiterate.

I was encouraged by the honest feedback from members about why they chose the symbols they did to evaluate the projects. Several themes emerged. Members agreed that the most common problems in dealing with outsiders who offer assistance are the lack of follow-up and insufficient training. For example, in examining a thread-dyeing project, members revealed that the project failed because the women received only one day of training and forgot most of the steps afterward. In the evaluation of a sewing and tailoring workshop, it emerged that the British funder who supplied the sewing machines assumed that all the women in the group knew how to sew and how to use the machines. Rather than understanding that the group wanted to learn how to sew, the funder neglected to assess the women's skills, and because they wanted to secure the sewing machines, the women omitted stating their actual need for intense training.

Other types of issues arose. Some of the literacy classes failed to achieve their desired results because the teachers did not schedule enough time for students to practice their lessons orally. The women discussed the importance of practice and theory going hand in hand.[19] A loan project to raise bulls for slaughter and to use a portion of the profits to pay back the loan was a success. However, the second time the group took out a loan for more bulls, they discovered that other groups in the communities had also. Unfortunately, there was not enough grass to feed all the bulls. The women gained a more thorough understanding of the problem of competition for natural resources. Later, only those who had enough grass on their lands continued to participate in the project.

In another project, the weavers were advised to purchase threads from small producers rather than from the large factories. However, the group failed to check the quality of the thread to ensure its colorfast quality. As a result, they lost their client, whose European customers demanded refunds when the colors in the inferior textiles bled. The group learned to examine their options more carefully before making decisions. A workshop on women's rights, especially indigenous women's rights, was successful in empowering the weavers. In the past, everyone was sad when a female child was born. Currently, however, they have learned to value themselves and other females, and they work harder to educate girls as well as boys. Other consciousness-raising workshops discussed preserving Maya ceremonies and wearing traditional clothing— actions that improve Maya women's self-esteem.

The projects supported by Maya Traditions have, for the most part, achieved our goal of helping to enhance the quality of life for the weavers and their families. We are beginning to apply participatory evaluation methods to our projects to ensure that every women's voice is heard, in contrast to meetings or reviews in which only the leaders speak and in which shy women unobtrusively listen and balk direct questions. At the end of one evaluation, Pascuala, the founder of one of the groups, exclaimed that she could appreciate the road their group had traveled together: "We are like a family who has happy and difficult times. Now I see that when we have hard times, we just need to get through them and try to understand why."

CONCLUSION

Having the capacity to adjust to change while still preserving those elements of culture that are highly valued is the essence of indigenous resistance. People maintaining power over their lives and their futures is most important in a world where dominant cultures want to destroy indigenous cultures, lifestyles, traditions, and languages. Cultural facilitators can serve a useful role by understanding the multifaceted nature of resistance to wholesale assimilation and by helping strengthen producer groups' diversified subsistence base.[20] People whose basic needs are met have the physical and mental energy to work for and encourage cultural preservation.

Focusing on selling weavings is a practical attempt at providing a small income base in a culturally appropriate manner. Projects or businesses that help people to meet their basic needs, in addition to subsistence agriculture, can be viewed as the first step in a strategy of economic diversification. Other projects that affirm cultural identity and individual well-being, such as the mental health and herbal medicine workshops set up by Maya Traditions, are a second step to cultural survival. I believe that these strategies are key to indigenous rural communities' ability to meet their material needs and to stay on their lands; at the same time, these programs help members preserve and gain more power to participate in the decisions that affect their lives. The international market can be brutal, but perhaps indigenous peoples can use the tools of the new conquistador to take advantage of this opening market, while defending their communities and their rights.

The "modern" world is encroaching on rural Guatemala. Some tools of Western societies, such as computers, can be quite helpful, but other nonessential goods, such as factory-made candies in plastic wrap or cigarettes, are not only polluting the Guatemalan countryside but binding indigenous people more closely to national and international markets. The fundamental challenge I see in the future involves helping rural indigenous women to gain the skills they need to reflect on and to analyze their social, economic, political, and cultural circumstances. Although some women are confident in this area, particularly those who have been active for a long time in social organizations, there are still many women who are plagued by fear and have yet to learn how to critically examine their lives and the macrolevel structures in which they are situated.

Women must develop more critical thinking skills so that they can chart their own course with their families and communities. Technical training in one income-producing area is not enough. Neither are consciousness-raising workshops that do not devise ways to ensure the participation of all group members. Cultural facilitators who aid indigenous women in their pursuits are in fact helping them to articulate and carry out their visions for their own lives and for reweaving the social fabric of Guatemala.

NOTES

[1] See Grimes, this volume, for information on fair trade. See also Rosenbaum, this volume, for more information on Guatemala.

[2] At this time, I had yet to hear of applied or action anthropology.

[3] "Poverty is officially separated into two categories: 1)those without the ability to meet basic material (housing, transportation, medicine, etc.) and food requirements are defined as living below the poverty line, and 2)those who cannot even meet their basic food needs, let alone other basic needs, are classified as experiencing extreme poverty" (Barry 1992, 95). Other nonmaterial needs could also be considered—such as human rights, self-realization, and the quality of one's environment. Although the weavers with whom we work are materially poor, it must be remembered that they possess a huge cultural richness. Often, development or antipoverty schemes enacted in Guatemala fail to recognize this distinction.

[4] From an interview with Guatemalan anthropologist, Elba Villatoro, Guatemala City, March 1998.

[5] From an interview with Teresa Ujpan Pérez, Panajachel, Guatemala, October 1998.

[6] To receive a copy of Maya Traditions' catalog, write to 3922 Mission Street, San Francisco, CA 94112; phone: 415-550-1449; fax: 415-821-3202; or e-mail, mayatrad@earthlink.net.

[7] By focusing on the fair trade niche, we have gained some loyal customers who share our goals. Though a small market, it is growing quickly.

[8] Many of rural Guatemalan women's needs are similar to those of other women in the third world. For example, Bhanti's research (1998) shows that women in three rural villages in India identified education, health, income-generating projects, political awareness, and social justice to be their top concerns.

[9] Maya textiles have evolved over time. So-called traditional colors may be relatively recent innovations, although usually they are combined with some elements of the past. An example of this is the explosion of color from synthetic dyes introduced in Europe in the 1850s, which quickly found their way to Guatemala and dramatically changed Guatemalan textiles (Schevill and Foxx 1997, 136–37). Maya weavers, however, still typically weave and wear what they view as "traditional" for their own and their families' uses.

[10] See Grimes, this volume, for information on Peoplink.

[11] The process to become a legal cooperative in Guatemala is prohibitively expensive for these groups. They are classified in Guatemala as associations, although they function like what in the United States is called a cooperative.

[12] The groups with whom we work speak three native languages: Kiche, Kakchiquel, and Tz'utujil.

[13] Mayalan is dedicated to assisting income-generating projects for Maya women and to promoting women's rights and Maya spirituality and identity.

[14] Acknowledging that Maya youth are heavily influenced by outside pressures, which often compel

them to lose part of their identities and cultures, we invited Mayalan to give a workshop to ten youths in 1998. The workshop, entitled "Maya Cosmovision and the Current Social Context," explored Maya spiritual and philosophical views of the world while also considering the influences of the Western world. Students broke up into small groups to write and draw responses to questions, reflecting their views and feelings about their relationships with family members, friends, community, and land. They also analyzed problems in society today that affect Maya youth. The result of the workshop was that it allowed the youths to express their desires for opportunities while acknowledging the realities of discrimination, the war, and pressures to assimilate into the ladino society. They affirmed their own identities as indigenous peoples with the privilege and responsibility of receiving formal education.

[15] Matzar is Maya and has training in traditional Maya, herbal, and allopathic medicine.

[16] Juan Skinner, executive director of the Lake Atitlán Watershed Environmental Authority, warned me about the frequency of community groups trying to please NGOs to get funding for projects.

[17] Though accurate statistics do not exist, it is generally accepted that the majority of the 140,000 casualties in the war were poor Maya peasants who were not allied with either side (Hedstrom 1997).

[18] I found that most of the recommended methods—such as "Rapid Rural Appraisal" or "Participatory Rural Evaluation," both used often in third world countries—were too time consuming for the women with whom we work. Attending the evaluation for three half days was the most they could give because they were busy struggling for daily survival. Any one of the projects that we analyzed in a general way can be examined in further detail if and when the group decides they want to.

[19] Teresa Ujpan Pérez from the San Juan weaving group remarked that it is particularly important for mature women who have had little formal schooling to hear things repeated several times, as a form of oral learning, and to have the chance to practice.

[20] Discussing the weavers of San Antonio Polopó, Ehlers (1993) states, "My assessment of their success is that it is not based on weaving alone. Weaving is only one of the many productive strategies that they used to achieve their economic security. Each of them relies on other business ventures and their agricultural production to make it. . . . And that is the key for the rest of the town as well. Similarly, weaving has not been a miracle cure for poverty in San Antonio. Instead, it has become the latest scheme for putting some cash into the productive system" (194–95).

BRENDA ROSENBAUM

6. OF WOMEN, HOPE, AND ANGELS

FAIR TRADE AND ARTISAN PRODUCTION IN A SQUATTER SETTLEMENT IN GUATEMALA CITY

ARTISAN PRODUCTION IN A SQUATTER SETTLEMENT

Most of the articles in this volume examine the processes whereby traditional artisans working in their home communities are incorporated into regional, national, and international markets. In the following pages, I explore a different context of artisan production—namely, a cooperative organization of women living in La Esperanza, a squatter settlement in the margins of Guatemala City.

The increasing penetration of capitalist relations into rural economies, the debt crises that led to a generalized recession in the 1980s, and the neoliberal reforms and globalization of the economy have precipitated a drop in the income of rural populations with a consequent deterioration of living conditions. This situation, on the one hand, has compelled traditional artisans to intensify their production and to endeavor continuously to find new markets for their products; on the other, it has forced masses of people to emigrate to larger cities in search of jobs. Many of these immigrants, however, never find the opportunities they were hoping for. They are forced to work in the poorly remunerated activities of the informal sector and to live in self-help housing in overcrowded squatter settlements.

It is in one of these settlements that Unidas para Vivir Mejor (UPAVIM, United to Live Better) was born in the late 1980s as a cooperative project mandated to generate income for desperately poor women. In less than ten years, the women have created a development project that attends not only to the needs of its sixty members and their families but also to those of the entire community. The expansion of UPAVIM hinges mainly on the success of the production of crafts for export through fair trade enterprises and solidarity networks.[1] Women's significant economic contributions to their households from craft production as well as their growing awareness of the prevailing ideology of machismo and its damaging consequences over their lives have led to an increase in self-confidence and a struggle to transform unfair gender relations within their families.

I met Aldina and Angela, two UPAVIM women, at the Fair Trade Federation (FTF) meetings in Washington, D.C., in 1994. I was representing Mayan Hands, a fair trade project that assists Maya weavers from Guatemala in finding markets for their handwoven products. This was the first time I heard of UPAVIM. I was amazed by the enthusiasm and eloquence of the women. They referred to UPAVIM as a powerful force triggering radical changes in their lives and allowing them to hope for a better future. On a visit to the organization in Guatemala, as I saw the silhouette of UPAVIM's building at a distance, the women's words suddenly came to life. Standing in the middle of La Esperanza, UPAVIM's proud three-story building overlooked a sadly typical urban landscape: open sewers in the middle of a dirt road bordered by hundreds of tiny cardboard and wooden shacks crowded together with no running water.[2]

In my years working with Maya artisans, first as a researcher and since 1990 as a fair trader, I have focused on the ways in which weavers express an entire way of life in a plethora of symbols and aesthetic conventions. Many scholars have noted that such production connects the artisans to ancient religious ideas and values, and embodies their culture's particular ways of seeing the world as well as community, family, gender, and personal identity.[3] The embeddedness in a larger context of meaning gives traditional artisans the strength to resist invasive forces that threaten their way of life (Anderson and Garlock 1988; Eber, this volume; Nash 1993b; Otzoy 1992). Receiving an income from sales of traditional products reinforces the viability of their culture, while the artisans obtain needed cash (Rosenbaum and Goldin 1997).

I was impressed to find such vigor and optimism in women living under the difficult conditions of a squatter settlement. Their productive processes and the items that result from those processes do not carry a profound symbolic meaning or bear a connection to community, self, and culture as happens with traditional artisans. Nevertheless, by engaging in productive activities for a living, working side by side with other women, and creating a forum to express their ideas and work on their personal problems, UPAVIM women are becoming stronger, gaining control, and transforming their lives.

As an anthropologist working in fair trade, I understand my role as twofold: supporting producers and informing consumers. In the first aspect of my role, I make available to the artisans information on the U.S. market—such as trends, popular products, and motifs—to enable them to devise ways to incorporate the information into successful, new products. I also try to establish marketing contacts for their products within the fair trade or solidarity markets. The other aspect of my role consists of informing U.S. consumers about conditions of life in the third world, the meaningful contexts of traditional artisan products, and their labor-intensive nature, with the purpose of facilitating responsible purchasing choices. Consumers with an awareness of the world come to view their purchase as a political act.

Since meeting UPAVIM members in 1994, I have included this group in my fair trade project. An extensive network of people sells UPAVIM's products in the United States, providing feedback on the U.S. market as well as possibilities of new products. I have become one more person in the network. Moreover, among the topics of talks I give to groups interested in Central America, I have added a section on UPAVIM women and their struggle to beat the odds in a society where the poor, especially women, have very few options.

These women have a story to tell us. In the next few pages, I examine the general context of urban poverty in Latin America and Guatemala, and the emergence of La Esperanza. Then I discuss UPAVIM's gradual development into what it is today, highlighting the role of the production and marketing of crafts. Next, one of UPAVIM's founding members assesses how her life has been radically altered since she joined the organization. In a final note, I reflect on whether UPAVIM's model can be replicated in similar urban contexts.

THE AFFLICTIONS OF URBAN POVERTY

In September and October 1997, heavy rainfalls fell continuously over Guatemala City and loosened the ground. Slum dwellers around the city were mostly unaware of the imminent danger, as the following quotation from a newspaper article conveys: "It was 10:30 in the morning; the children were playing in the street, and the women were talking when they heard the rumbling of the sheet-metal roof falling and the screams for help. They got close to the edge of the ravine to see the stone sinks, the pots, and the recently washed clothing of their neighbors lying at the bottom of the ravine, amidst mud and stones. Then they saw how the firefighters brought up the body of the woman everybody called Elvirita" (*El Periódico* 1997b, 13).

The Flores family lived in a precarious shack made of cardboard, pieces of wood, and corrugated sheet metal on the sides of a ravine in Guatemala City not far from some of the most elegant residential areas in the city. Heavy rainfalls during the previous days had loosened the ground and precipitated a landslide. There are thirteen thousand hectares of ravines surrounding the city. About one hundred sixty thousand families live at the edge, sides, or bottom of the ravines in some 320 squatter settlements (*El Periódico* 1998, 3).

This type of living situation is not atypical in Latin American cities. Latin America is the most urbanized of the third world regions. Half of all Latin Americans live today in cities with a population of more than one hundred thousand (Angotti 1995, 14). In spite of how terrible living conditions in the cities may be with the lack of jobs, absence of basic services, and glaring inequality, they are an improvement over the oppressive conditions of the decaying countryside.[4]

Millions of Latin American people began their move into the cities after the 1940s with the advent of modernization and import-substitution industrialization—hailed as the means to sustained development—which lured peasants into urban areas with the promises of new, higher-paying jobs. Rapid population increases as a result of falling mortality rates further fueled the movement from country to city, sometimes stimulated further by natural disasters or political violence in the countryside. However, immigration and population growth in the urban areas outpaced the creation of new jobs. The gap was exacerbated during the recession of the 1980s, which led to a decline in the per capita income in most countries and added millions to the already exploding ranks of the informal sector. In the absence of safety nets and well-remunerated jobs, poor families have had no option but to engage in commerce and services that support only a very low standard of living (Gilbert 1998, 57; Sánchez Otero 1993). The poorer the country, the higher the percentage of its labor force in the informal sector. In trying to eke out a living, the poorest households place many of their members, including children, in the labor force.

Latin American cities closely resemble one another. Since their colonial past, they have followed similar development patterns. Their affluent, well-serviced suburbs, home to the elite minority, speak of the expansion of North American consumer tastes (suburbs, malls, building styles) and conspicuous consumption. These suburbs coexist side by side with a mass of poor people living precariously in ubiquitous squatter settlements, some with no infrastructure or access to basic services. Today, more than half of the population of Latin American cities live in such settlements (Gilbert 1998, 79). Many of these dwellers find it difficult to satisfy even their minimal nutritional requirements.[5]

Poor women, young people, and children bear the brunt of this situation. The prevailing gender ideology in Latin America gives women all the responsibility in caring for children and performing domestic and subsistence tasks. Their domestic obligations prevent them from having access to better-paid jobs that require working uninterruptedly for long periods of time. Their options are limited to the lowest remunerated activities in the informal sector—namely, those rejected by men. They run little shops or operate the poorest market stalls in their shantytowns, wash other people's clothes, run errands, or perform unremunerated tasks in their husbands' informal businesses. Women who work at home under contract with modern enterprises do not fare much better.[6] The cultural attitude that undervalues women's work and keeps them tied to their domestic obligations legitimizes the poor pay they obtain working in the piece-rate system (Gilbert 1998, 75; see also Benería and Roldán 1987). However hard they work, women at this level of poverty find it difficult to overcome the gender constraints imposed on them. Their smaller contribution to the household economy vis-à-vis that of men as well as the invisibility and undervaluation of household and subsistence tasks reinforce the gender hierarchy within the family.

Latin American children have carried a heavy burden in the tremendous social and economic upheaval in the region over the past fifteen years (NACLA 1994, 19). Typically, children living in poverty perform the scavenging and carrying tasks as well as a variety of unremunerated tasks in the families' economic activities. Often, they must stop their schooling because their work becomes indispensable for household survival. One of the most tragic consequences of the growing impoverishment of Latin America has been the appearance of street children, especially in larger cities, with its related horrors of child prostitution and children's involvement in drug trafficking and crime (DeCesare 1998).

Guatemala is one of the poorest countries in Latin America. The United Nations Development Program (UNDP) reports that Guatemala lags behind its Latin American neighbors in many central social indicators, such as access to drinking water, health care, and education (*Cerigua Weekly Briefs* 1998). Indeed, Guatemala has the second highest illiteracy rate in Latin America, following Haiti.[7] Although Guatemala's gross domestic product (GDP) grew more than that of its Central American neighbors, this fact obscures the levels of poverty and inequality that prevail. Statistics reveal that 80 percent of the population of the country lives in poverty; in certain rural areas, this number rises to 90 percent, with 75 percent living in extreme poverty. In Guatemala City, poverty affects 65 percent of the urban population, and extreme poverty affects 30 percent (*Prensa Libre* 1998, 2).[8] The UNDP report also notes that Guatemala's ratings fell in indexes dealing specifically with women. It dropped in the "gender empowerment scale," which measures the disparity of income between men and women and the ability of women to participate in the political and economic life of the country (*Cerigua Weekly Briefs* 1998).

The growth of poverty will continue to pose a serious threat to Guatemala's fragile democracy unless the government implements social and economic reforms to benefit the majority. While "runaway consumption" widens the gap between rich and poor, the country continues to exhibit a high population growth rate of 2.8 percent per year—a dangerous combination (Swedish 1998).[9]

Of the total population of Guatemala living in urban areas, half reside in Guatemala City's metropolitan area (Espinosa and Hidalgo 1994, 6). The great waves of immigration from the countryside took place during the period of modernization in the 1960s, after the 1976 earthquake, and in the 1980s when political violence devastated the country. The explosive growth of the city's population in the past twenty-five years has aggravated housing deficits and the delivery of public services such as education, health, transportation, potable water, and electricity. It has also worsened the problems of unemployment and underemployment.[10] The poor cannot afford to buy expansive urban housing given their low incomes, unstable jobs, and lack of credit. Due to housing shortages, rents are high, and landlords reject families with many children—which are usually the most impoverished families. Approximately two-thirds of the children born in the metropolitan area are born to poor families (Espinosa and Hidalgo 1994, 11).

The lives of struggle and deprivation that people endure at the edges of survival and the high density that characterizes poor neighborhoods tend to engender fragile families in which women and children work and, in many cases, are victims of domestic violence and exploitation. A report by the United Nations International Children's Emergency Fund (UNICEF) points out that between 20 and 25 percent of women living in precarious settlements are single mothers and that four out of ten teenagers are single and have children out of wedlock (Espinosa and Hidalgo 1994, 12). In the psychological arena, researchers detect emotional instability, apathy, and low self-esteem. It is not surprising that alcoholism, drug addiction, and gang violence thrive under those conditions (Espinosa and Hidalgo 1994, 12–13).

Surveys in two precarious settlements in Guatemala's metropolitan area, La Brigada and El Mezquital, shed light on the situation of women (FLASCO n.d., Pérez Sáinz 1990). The central findings of the surveys corroborate the Latin American data that women's domestic and subsistence responsibilities condition their participation in the labor market. In ideology and in practice, women continue to be defined mainly in terms of their reproductive tasks in the household. In both settlements, domestic and subsistence activities are defined as women's work; men's singular domestic task is to haul water. Women buy food and other necessities, cook, clean, wash clothes, and raise children. When space exists, they raise chickens or an occasional pig. They keep active the networks of reciprocity with family and friends—an indispensable resource in an environment where crises abound. Women also approach nongovernmental organizations (NGOs) and other institutions that offer ways to obtain foodstuffs or medicines for their families. Additionally, in El Mezquital, they have been the main beneficiaries of training opportunities offered by some of those institutions.

In the harsh conditions of squatter settlements, women wage an arduous battle to procure their families' subsistence. In El Mezquital and La Brigada, only a fourth and a third, respectively, of the women work compared to 60 to 70 percent of men.[11] Of the working women from El Mezquital, more than half work for a salary (primarily in shops, hotels, and restaurants), a third in the informal sector in microenterprises or in commerce, and the rest in domestic employment. But even in the category of salaried work, the majority of women (60 percent) are immersed in unregulated labor relations with high turnover ratios and no social benefits. About two-thirds of the women who work do not earn more than Q200 or U.S.$64.10 per month (Pérez Sáinz 1990, 84).[12] In La Brigada, younger unmarried women work for a salary, especially in the Korean-owned *maquila* plant located in the community. Work in the maquila is an option only for women with no family obligations because women with children are overwhelmingly involved in commerce on their own.

Thus, the traditional division of labor persists. Men continue to be considered heads of households with the responsibility of obtaining an income to support their families. Women are in charge of mobilizing a variety of resources for their families' survival. The perpetuation of this division of labor at the ideological level has damaging effects on women's educational level and on their consequent potential to enter the labor market. Moreover, it reproduces the gender hierarchy within the family and in society at large. Some parents still think that schooling is not as important for their daughters, who are destined to be future homemakers, as it is for their sons. In La Brigada and El Mezquital, the level of schooling for both adult men and women is quite low, yet the illiteracy rate is much higher for women.[13] Currently the number of girls and boys who attend school in both El Mezquital and La Brigada is approximately the same. However, girls also have to perform domestic chores, whereas most boys can devote themselves exclusively to their studies.

Households headed by women represent 23 percent of all households in El Mezquital and 20 percent in La Brigada (Pérez Sáinz 1990, 90; FLASCO n.d.). In addition to their household and family obligations, these women work for an income and usually live in family residential compounds, where they can rely on the support of relatives to help them balance their multiple responsibilities. Unequal educational opportunities have had a negative impact on the lives of these women, who must support their families on their own. Ill equipped because of their low level of education, they can barely earn a living.

A survey of La Brigada found that half of the children fourteen to seventeen years of age work (FLASCO n.d.). Both male and female working adolescents usually come from larger families than their nonworking counterparts and from families in which the heads of households have little formal education. These families must pool their members' incomes because all of them work in unstable, poorly remunerated activities. Unfortunately, adolescents in this situation are condemned to the fate of their parents, barely surviving at the lowest rungs of the socioeconomic ladder. They usually do not finish their primary education, and the majority of them (70 percent) will not continue with their studies.

With this general backdrop of the social conditions in squatter settlements, I now examine the invasions of land in which La Esperanza and four other settlements sprouted almost overnight. The squatter settlements emerged as a veritable city with large numbers of people and no infrastructure to support them.

A NEW SQUATTER SETTLEMENT

In June 1982, about ten invasions of urban lands occurred in the area of El Mezquital, southwest of Guatemala City. Nothing now remains of these early invasions because they were all dismantled by the police. Of the next wave of invasions, between March and May of 1984, only one was successful. Approximately eight hundred families claimed that they could not find a place to house their families. Moreover, they argued that the Banco Nacional de la Vivienda (BANVI, National Housing Bank) had not responded to their petitions, so the group took possession of twelve hectares of land that the BANVI had deemed unsuitable for housing. After four months, five squatter settlements appeared on this land (El Exodo, Monte de los Olivos, Tres Banderas, El Esfuerzo, and La Esperanza), supporting some forty-five thousand people.

Faced with difficult housing situations, several UPAVIM women arrived in the area after hearing on the radio that people were invading lands in El Mezquital. At the beginning, the main preoccupation of the settlers was the constant threats of being evicted, spurred by rumors that the government would send in troops to dismantle the area and force people out. The settlers' committee decided to have women and children stand guard in front of their shacks or tents, especially during the night, when they expected the troops. Carmela, an UPAVIM member, recalls when soldiers climbed the ravines, and seeing only women and children guarding the lots, they left without firing a shot. Thus, the invaders began their long task of turning the inhospitable area into their home.

Their priority was to obtain property titles to the lots and access to basic services. The area lacked even a road. In the early days after the invasion, insufficient clean drinking water caused three to five children to die daily, afflicted with typhoid fever and intestinal infections (Espinosa and Hidalgo 1994, 18). The population formed local committees that focused on two basic problems: land/housing and health. They presented their demands to the chief of state (a coup had deposed the president) at that time, and eventually government authorities took note and sounded the voice of alarm to international organizations. In 1985, the first NGOs and international organizations made their appearances. Representatives from UNICEF contacted the board of directors of La Esperanza, the poorest settlement, and trained 120 people (mostly women) to conduct a survey to determine from the settlers' points of view what the central needs of the population were. The survey requested information on environmental sanitation, drinking water, types of housing, neighborhood organization, and the settlers' sources of employment. The survey revealed that obtaining drinking water was the settlers' highest priority in light of the epidemics killing children and the high price of water sold by distribution trucks. In 1985–86, UNICEF helped La Esperanza settlers install eight faucets. It was mostly women who dug the trenches and put in the ducts. Few leaders and men participated. Soon after this, other organizations such as the National Nursing School of Guatemala, Doctors without Borders, UNICEF, and the Guatemalan Department of Health developed a preventive health program in the area, the Programa Integrado de Salud (PIS, Integral Health Program). They organized a group of health promoters whose work to assist the population and prevent diseases continues today and has been acclaimed as a model for such work in other communities. All of the settlers who attended the training program and became volunteer health promoters in their community were women (Espinosa and Hidalgo 1994, 33). A La Esperanza settler and UPAVIM member, Doña Elva, remembers the early days:

The first months in La Esperanza were very sad because we had no water. The water that the trucks brought was very expensive. First, they charged us fifty centavos for each gallon and after that one quetzal. And there were too many flies here—too much illness, especially typhoid fever. Many people died. Yes, it was very sad. Now things are organized, but before we had no light, nothing. We lived about three years with no light, only candles. We had to go all the way to the Bucaro [where the water trucks arrived]. We also went to the Bucaro to wash our clothes in a stream. There were so many flies everywhere! There were many people in La Esperanza who were in better shape; they appropriated the money that came to help the people. For example, the people in the board of directors had latrines. We didn't; we had to go to the ravine to relieve ourselves. But then, working in groups, we started building our latrines. And then they came to install our water and electricity. We worked at night. It was fun because we worked with a group whose leader, Doña Marta, was a nice person. She fought for us. She told us, "We have to work by night to install the water." We worked in shifts. I worked from ten to eleven at night. Then, from one to two in the morning. Without any light! I was afraid because there were many thieves. One day I had my *botes* [old cans] in the faucet; I was filling them up with water. Then some men came along, carrying machetes, and they took away my containers. I just stood there watching, sad and angry, while they took my botes. What could I do?[14]

A BEACON OF HOPE: UPAVIM IS BORN

In 1988, a U.S. nurse, Barbara Fenske, arrived in Guatemala and began working in the health care center in La Esperanza. She established a growth-monitoring clinic to determine early signs of infant malnutrition and other similar problems common in areas of high risk. Mothers came once a month to chart their babies' progress, and Fenske recruited volunteers among the mothers to assist her in measuring and weighing the children.

Through the Sister Parish program, La Esperanza was linked with a church in Bemidji, Minnesota. A group of people from this church visited La Esperanza, and several people from the community were invited to meet with them. Surprisingly, only women attended the meeting. Because the Sister Parish program included funding for a project in Central America, the women from La Esperanza and the visitors from Bemidji decided to develop a dental clinic in the community, a sorely needed service.

Working together with dental professionals in Guatemala, the Sister Parish group organized and built the clinic and provided initial financial and technical support. Several community women were trained to clean and extract teeth, take impressions, purchase and inventory supplies, and maintain the clinic (Littrell and Dickson 1999).

Encouraged by the success of the original project, UPAVIM has grown since then into a self-governing organization of approximately sixty women who joined to improve their lives; in other words, they have "united for a better life." In 1994, they inaugurated their three-story building constructed with funds from several international organizations. Currently, the women at UPAVIM work on five different projects: the crafts project, the Childhood Center (day care and preschool), medical clinics, lab, and scholarship programs (which includes a tutoring component for children who are having problems in school). Each program has its own board of directors comprised of UPAVIM women and separate accounting systems. In addition, each project receives its own donations and endeavors to become self-sufficient. Except for a few outside professionals—such as the doctor, nurse, accountant, lab technician, and sewing teacher—UPAVIM women perform most of the work within the organization, including cleaning the building, cooking, teaching, working in the lab and pharmacy, and manufacturing the craft products for export. The organization offers training to women to become teachers for the Montessori preschool, dental assistants, and assistant lab technicians. It maintains a sewing teacher in residence for women who want to learn or perfect sewing skills in order to participate in the crafts project.

The program and underlying philosophy of UPAVIM substantiate the view that obtaining an income is only the first step (though an essential one for people living in grinding poverty) toward a dignified life. Women at UPAVIM understand that education is the key to progress. Many of them have pursued technical training or attend school on weekends to complete their elementary and high school education. They are steadfast in their quest to give their children education and, they hope, a better future. Indeed, UPAVIM goes beyond offering its women the possibility of training to improve their skills and competence in the work place. Every year, it provides 650 scholarships for community children, which cover the costs of registration in the local public school and school supplies, so lack of resources never prevents any child from going to school. The money for the scholarships comes from donations from UPAVIM friends in the United States.

The women are making great strides in their feminist awareness. From talks given by La Leche League promoters and other feminist voices, they have begun to question and challenge the pervasive culture of machismo that limits their opportunities and submits them to male control. The awareness has translated into increased self-esteem and confidence. Many of the women argue that they do not need to tolerate abusive men or men who do not support their children. After episodes of domestic violence, some women have reported their husbands to the National Human Rights Office to place them under arrest. Women find a haven at UPAVIM, where they have a space to talk about their personal problems, vent their emotions, and support one another in their struggles for survival and autonomy. Additionally, because UPAVIM functions as a self-governing body, the entire membership meets three or four times a year to discuss matters of central importance to the organization; they meet more frequently in smaller groups to discuss issues relevant to each of the programs. These meetings encourage the women to speak their minds in a positive environment and learn basic democratic processes such as participation, discussion, problem solving, and consensus building. This invaluable training not only encourages confidence in their everyday practices at home and work, but represents a crucial building block in Guatemala's democratization.

A central tenet of UPAVIM's philosophy and practice is its communal focus. Women learn to consider carefully the needs of the community in which they live; they know they will not succeed if they remain an island in an ocean of bitterly poor and frustrated people. Many of UPAVIM's services benefit the entire Esperanza area and beyond. Working parents can bring their children to the day care and preschool facilities. People pay lower prices for lab exams, medicines, and visits to the doctor and dentist. To evidence their commitment to this communal and service spirit, women who want to join UPAVIM must begin by working as a volunteer for thirty-two hours in any of the projects, and as UPAVIM members, women donate services two hours per week to keep costs down and to benefit the group.

THE CRAFTS PROJECT

Living in La Esperanza and getting to know the mothers in the clinic, Barbara Fenske soon realized the desperate need of women for income-earning activities. Mothers checked on their children's development month after month, but they worried about how they would keep their children healthy under such distressing conditions. Thus, the idea for an income-generating program was born. A few women began to learn how to make barrettes and, if successful, to teach others. If they could find an export market for their products, the project's profits would pay for the expenses of the child-monitoring clinic. At that time, Guatemalan artisan products were very popular in the U.S. mainstream market, so the women decided to go into production of crafts.

Their first customers were people from the United States who came to visit projects run by Maryknoll nuns in the community. The nuns directed these tourists to UPAVIM, where they learned about the women's lives and work. The excited visitors returned to the United States with the women's crafts and stories. Gradually, a U.S.-based support network developed comprised of the members of the Sister Parish in Minnesota, other groups visiting the community, and long-time friends of the Fenskes. Today, people throughout the world who come to Guatemala for language programs, different church projects, or vacation are encouraged to visit UPAVIM to witness the self-help project that serves as a development model for poverty-stricken areas. Visitors react with both shock at the community's poverty and amazement at the stamina and enthusiasm of these women in their fight to improve their lives.

La Leche League of Guatemala made the first large sale, purchasing fifty barrettes to sell at a meeting in Mexico in the early in 1990s. Afterward, UPAVIM women began sending delegates to the North American Fair Trade Federation conferences and expanded their client network into the U.S. fair trade market. They love the opportunity to visit the United States and to see buyers' reactions to their products and stories. The conference seminars have taught them a great deal about quality control, color trends, pricing, and the production of catalogs.

In the crafts project, UPAVIM women produce items that have a distinctly Guatemalan look; most items are fashioned from *jaspe (ikat)* cloth purchased from a cooperative of Maya weavers. At first, they produced items already popular in the U.S. market, such as barrettes, scrunchies, padded fabric folders, backpacks, and vests. Currently they have diversified into new and original products that have found a large market in the United States because of their charm, ingenuity, and reasonable price. With Fenske's aid, the group keeps a close watch on trends in the U.S. market. They receive feedback and ideas for new products from the people in the solidarity and fair trade markets,[15] from seminars at fair trade conferences, and from foreigners visiting La Esperanza to learn about the organization. Through this feedback process, they have developed extremely popular items, such as the Angel of Hope, a chubby, cloth angel with braids and rattan wings that sells as a Christmas-tree ornament and that served as a base to develop a new cloth nativity. Among other exciting new products are a Noah's Ark bag filled with small cloth animals and a "working women's wreath" made of small, cloth Maya dolls bearing their tools of work—namely, brooms, chopping boards, and baskets. Thousands of these wreaths continue to be sold.

Today, forty-five UPAVIM women earn a living in the crafts project. Of an active list of 125 clients, 97 percent are fair traders, solidarity traders, and individuals from small and large businesses who want to contribute to the success of these remarkable women. In 1997, sales totaled $135,000; this figure is projected to increase in 1998. Working full-time in the crafts project, women can earn between Q40 and Q60 per day (roughly U.S.$6.50–$10.00).[16] Compared to other married women in La Esperanza, UPAVIM women are more financially secure and simultaneously enjoy a flexible work schedule. They work at home, or if they need to use the industrial sewing machines at UPAVIM, they do so at their convenience. The organization gives the members the possibility to combine work and domestic responsibilities in the way that best suits their individual needs.

For the UPAVIM women, traveling to the United States, receiving visitors from all over the world, and meeting so many individuals committed to their cause and to selling their products seem like miracles. Their crafts have created a bridge between two distinct worlds, and the solidarity generated in the relationships boosts the women's confidence that UPAVIM will continue to thrive. The organization uplifts them and helps them to deal with the difficult realities of their everyday lives in La Esperanza. As Angela Bailon, comanager of the crafts project, confided:

> Sometimes I'm afraid about what may happen if Barbara leaves and we have to continue by ourselves. Before I used to be more frightened thinking that we would not be able to do it, . . . but now I have realized that, thank God, we have overcome obstacles in the group, we have a great desire to succeed, and we can do it. We are so thankful for the support we get from people in the United States. Yesterday, a group came to visit us, and I was thinking, as I spoke with them, that I feel UPAVIM inside me. I am so happy and proud to say this is who I am, this is what we do, and this is UPAVIM. People listen to us and get excited and interested; they ask many questions. They are very impressed with the work of UPAVIM.

Upon her return from a trip to the United States in August 1998, Angela commented: "This time there were five of us going to Bemidji to visit our Sister Parish. It was wonderful; everybody was so good to us. . . . They took us all over. . . . Everywhere people would be wearing products made by us or had UPAVIM decorations around their homes.

People knew of our organization; 'Ah, you are from UPAVIM!' they would say. And I thought to myself how great UPAVIM really is!"

The profits from crafts sales support the Childhood Center, which provides day care and preschool facilities at an affordable price to UPAVIM members and the community. The women's visions of UPAVIM's future rely on a strong crafts project. To fulfill their immediate goal of expanding the Childhood Center into a Montessori school for elementary education, UPAVIM must increase funding from the project. The women are currently reorganizing the production process to make it more efficient.[17] They plan to systematize the product development process, rather than base it on occasional advice from customers or visitors, and hope to establish internships for design students from the United States who can keep UPAVIM women abreast of new trends and ideas. Last, they want to expand their sales network abroad and have recently opened a wholesale distribution operation in the United States to further this goal.

IN CARMELA'S WORDS

Most UPAVIM women grew up in poverty, suffering the ravages of family disintegration, domestic violence, and alcoholism. Many recount their decision to live with their boyfriends as a way to escape an unbearable family situation or to fill the longing for someone to love them. Most often, however, they found themselves trapped in the same vicious cycle of poverty and violence. Desire for change, faith in God as an ally, and love for and commitment to their children give the women the strength to cope with tough situations and the impetus to overcome them. Becoming members of UPAVIM helped them analyze their situations critically and open new paths to solve their problems.

Carmela[18] grew up an impoverished, Guatemalan village in the countryside. Her father abandoned her mother, Carmela, and two siblings. Her mother often could not work because of illness; she regularly relinquished her food ration (a common form of payment in lieu of cash in rural Guatemala) to her children, thus keeping her in a weakened state. Carmela started selling in the market at age six. She vividly remembers the times she stole edible greens from her neighbor's cornfield because there was nothing to eat at home. Before turning nine, she was taken to a nearby town to care for a baby. She earned approximately $2.50 per month. Years later, she met her husband, a construction worker in Guatemala City. Her suffering, she says, started the moment she moved in with him. He drank a great deal, beat her, and worked very little. She had one child after another and worked in the streets selling fruits and vegetables to buy some food. Now, however, she works for UPAVIM's Montessori preschool and produces items for the crafts project to earn extra money in her spare time. She supports her eight children by herself. Her eloquent words assess the way UPAVIM has affected her life:

I used to think this is my fate, and there's nothing I can do. I had not awakened; I lived in ignorance. I would let my husband beat me up, take my money, and go around with other women. I thought that's the way it was; a woman and a man together lived like that. . . . Every time I became pregnant, he would beat me up and threaten me, force me to take pills and herbs to abort my baby. But my children were born anyway. When I was pregnant with one of my youngest daughters, he said "Get it out of there; I'll make sure you do," and he beat me up for the entire nine months. But my child was born. At the time, he already had another woman in La Esperanza. I told him, "Go with her. I don't want you here. Go." I had started working with Barbara and talking with the other women. I was awakening and starting to change. I had been so ignorant; perhaps I was experienced in having many children, but I never thought of myself. The women encouraged me, "Why don't you sign up to study in the dental clinic?" So I started to go there, and he would beat me up, more and more. I had no clothes. At night I washed my dress and left it to dry on the line. Still a bit wet, I would put it on and go to study on Sundays. I couldn't even remember how to write. . . . My husband forced me to have sex with him; if I didn't want to, he would tear my clothes and rape me. . . . The women at UPAVIM, Barbara, and the doctor tried to help me: "Don't let him beat you up like that. Why don't you leave him? Look at how he treats you. Why do you put up with him?" "You are the one who brings an income to the house anyway." That's what they would say. I used to haul water in big containers from up there, for people living down here. They paid me seventy-five centavos for each [about twenty-five U.S. cents]. I spent my entire day hauling water, running errands for other people, to get some money to buy my children's food. I would leave some food for him as well because if not, he would beat me up. He worked and made some money, but he never gave me or the children any. Well, finally I kicked him out of the house. . . . I've been alone for five years, and I've changed so much. I learned about improving myself, treating my children better. I'm not the same woman I used to be. Before, I would not have dared to look into your eyes. I went about life barefooted and disheveled. I was so ignorant. I felt an obligation to be with my husband. But listening to interesting talks they came to give us, I learned that I, too, have my rights; I want to improve. I've attended talks about how women can be self-sufficient to support their family and learned that we, women, are valuable too. We started supporting one another, and they used to tell me, "Don't be stupid; don't let him beat you up; leave, hide, whatever. If you cannot defend yourself, just leave." When he noticed I was changing, he was worried. "You have another man; you're changing," he said, but it wasn't anything like that. I was trying to change for myself and my children. I realized I had dreams of being a great woman so that my children would not suffer so much. Thanks to God with my work here at UPAVIM and the example I'm setting for them, they will also try to learn and make it. My greatest dream as a child was to become a teacher. Here I had the opportunity to work at the dental clinic; I loved it. The doctors I worked with tell me, "You are such a good assistant; you are really excellent." Thanks to the program of the dental clinic I began to change. Because I never imagined that, being illiterate, I could learn to extract molars, put in fillings, and clean teeth. When a group of visitors coming from abroad would ask me, "What would you like to be?" I'd reply that "I'd like to be a dentist, but I need to study many years." A woman in one of the visiting groups told me she would try to find money so I could go to school. I also received a course in the Montessori method. I dreamed of working with children, even though I have eight and I should be bored of children. I started to devote myself then; I studied and studied. Thanks to God I learned, and I love to work with children . . . to watch the progress of each child, how they are doing when they enter our preschool and how much they progress as they move on to school. I love it.

Though the details of their lives vary, most UPAVIM women with whom I have spoken narrate similar stories of deprivation, strained marital relationships, and lack of opportunities to improve themselves and earn a living. Through their active participation in creating and developing their organization, these women have simultaneously transformed their own lives.

CAN THE SUCCESS STORY BE REPLICATED?

Unidas para Vivir Mejor has succeeded in addressing and helping to resolve some of the pivotal problems women face living in the depths of poverty in precarious settlements. It raises their awareness of their social conditions and problems, and encourages them to obtain technical training, continue formal schooling, and acquire the necessary self-assurance to take control of their lives. It gives them the opportunity to earn a good income without jeopardizing their children and neglecting other responsibilities important to them.[19] Youths who run a high risk of remaining trapped in poverty or falling into serious problems—such as prostitution, alcoholism, and drug use—are reaping the benefits of the UPAVIM organization. Their mothers go to great lengths to keep their children in school and talk with great pride about their children's desires to become secretaries, teachers, and nurses or to continue studying at the university. Some members' teenage daughters have begun making crafts at UPAVIM, provided that they keep up their grades in school. With this income, they help their families without giving up their education and begin to immerse themselves in the optimistic, self-image-boosting atmosphere of UPAVIM. Hopefully, these girls will have an easier life than that of their mothers and grandmothers.

The organization promotes development in the more comprehensive sense of the word. It goes beyond providing simply income for poor women and fostering economic growth in the community. It has empowered the women, enhanced their dignity, and greatly improved their quality of life. In a country such as Guatemala, with millions of impoverished people and a government unwilling or incapable of creating programs to benefit the majority, UPAVIM stands out as a promising example of a self-help project. Can it be replicated?

The success of UPAVIM owes much to its ability to tap resources from North American individuals and organizations. Indeed, UPAVIM's building, scholarship program, medical and dental clinic, and equipment are provided with money from U.S. donors. Though UPAVIM is working to wean itself gradually from the need of donations and to become self-sufficient, there is no doubt that these donations have been indispensable for the development of the organization.

The felicitous choice of engaging in the production of crafts (rather than a different business, such as a bakery) has had a decisive impact on UPAVIM's economic feasibility and growth. Although at the beginning Fenske drew on her own friends and acquaintances in the United States to assist UPAVIM, the network of support has grown extensively through the marketing of the crafts. In their search for markets, UPAVIM women have contacted hundreds of individuals and organizations in the United States, and the sales of crafts, along with the diffusion of the organization's story, have added hundreds of supporters to their original network. Because their products are channeled through the fair trade and solidarity markets, many clients interested in the organization are willing to contribute money or time to retail their products.

The craft sales have skyrocketed in the past few years. It is not an easy task to create a successful fair trade business, as attested by some of the articles in the present volume (see Causey, Cohen, Milgram, and M'Closkey, this volume) and by my own experience in marketing handwoven Maya textiles. What makes for the success of UPAVIM craft production?

Part of this success story has to do with the product itself. Ironically, the fact that UPAVIM women are not steeped in a culturally bound, sophisticated artisan tradition, as many Maya weavers are, works in their favor. It allows them greater flexibility in fashioning items that fit the rapidly changing fads of North American consumers. A clear example of this phenomenon may be seen in the development of products with the angel motif, which gained popularity in the United States in the 1990s. The women produce several different products that contain angels, such as pins, necklaces, Christmas-tree ornaments, a Christmas garland, and a small clay angel in a cloth bag. In most cases, they purchase many of the components for these products in a semifinished stage. For example, they purchase small Maya dolls, add a beaded halo and wings made out of ribbon, and glue a pin to the back to make the angel pins. When Maya weavers tried to devise such a product with the angel motif, they found it more difficult to accomplish because their traditional repertoire does not include this motif. The only choice open to them was to devise a way to weave an angel figure into the cloth they make. Maya women's devotion to weaving as well as the technical demands and cultural constraints of weaving technology and practice may limit their versatility. The women who work within UPAVIM have no such constraints. Keeping a close watch on consumer trends in the United States, they rapidly develop new products to fit the changing demands.

The price of UPAVIM crafts is also a decisive factor in their success. The labor-intensive nature of most artisan production results in an item that bears a relatively high price if its producer is to receive a fair return. Frequently, even consumers in the fair trade market are unable to pay a weaver a fair price for a weaving she worked on for an entire month (i.e., a price that will allow her to support her family at other than a poverty level). Either the price of the item does not cover the costs of reproduction, or the product cannot be sold because it is "too expensive."[20]

The women with UPAVIM usually design innovative products that are less labor intensive and whose components can be acquired inexpensively in the market. Indeed, producers are fully aware that one of the basic requirements for a product is a "reasonable" price. Whereas a traditional, labor-intensive product would reach the final consumer at a high price and therefore would not sell well, UPAVIM has succeeded in marketing its products to large enterprises because it has been able to keep costs lower.

Another factor in UPAVIM's craft success is its marketing network in the United States. I have discussed how this network developed and continues to grow. Many of the people who sell these crafts have a deep commitment to UPAVIM. They operate squarely within a solidarity framework. Working together, UPAVIM women and their U.S. trading partners and friends have raised awareness in both groups about the existence of one another and about the possibilities of a successful collaboration. It is exciting to realize that global connections within the fair trade and solidarity systems can produce drastically different results from those produced by the global economy and free trade.

In brief, aside from the hard work of its women, UPAVIM's accomplishments have depended on its success in drawing donations and in finding a growing market for the crafts the women produce. In this process, the presence of Barbara Fenske, UPAVIM's advisor, has been critical. She provided the initial impetus for organizing the women, making the first connections to U.S. buyers, assisting producers in different organizational areas, and "translating" the transient tastes and fads of North American consumers (Littrell and Dickson 1999). However, the organization is and has always been run by the local women. Connections with their support network and trading partners are securely established, and the women are learning the feedback process involved in creating new products and expanding their market. They are gradually taking complete charge.

The model provided by UPAVIM may not be replicative in its entirety because the combination of factors pivotal in its specific trajectory may not be present or attainable in other communities. Had UPAVIM women chosen a bakery rather than crafts project, the organization would have evolved differently. However, there are two central elements in UPAVIM's story that should encourage local NGOs to help women develop productive projects in economically depressed areas. First, the productive and transformative potential of women working together for the welfare of their families and communities is immense. And second, as global awareness and the number of socially conscious consumers increase, the possibility of mobilizing resources from the industrialized world to assist the poorest third world populations will continue to expand. The development and growth of UPAVIM attests to this hopeful possibility.

NOTES

1 As Grimes (this volume) explains, fair trade or alternative trade refers to a new way of doing business in which people, not profits, come first. In this chapter, I similarly refer to a solidarity market or network formed primarily by individuals or groups, rather than by businesses, who support third world producers. With a sense of a mission, these people make sincere efforts to buy or sell even unattractive, defective, or more expensive products because they know that the producers need the income. Many sales in churches or to groups of people with a known devotion to a specific project, ethnic group, or country fall within this category (see Eber, this volume). It is important in the future to explore the similarities between fair trade and solidarity markets, as well as their differences, respective strengths, and weaknesses.

2 This panorama has changed. The main street in La Esperanza has been paved. New cement block houses are being built to replace the cardboard, wood, and corrugated sheet metal shacks. Sewers have also been installed in the community.

3 See, for examples, Eber, this volume; Eber 1995; Eber and Rosenbaum 1993; Morris 1988; Nash 1993a; and Rosenbaum 1992, 1993.

4 In Latin America, 34 percent of city dwellers but 53 percent of rural people live in poverty.

5 Inequality grew considerably in Latin America during the 1980s. The percentage of poor people rose from 41 percent in 1980 to 44 percent in 1989, roughly 183 million of which—the majority—live in the cities (Gilbert 1998, 168–69).

6 For example, in their study of industrial home work in Mexico City, Benería and Roldán (1987) found that women who were engaged in domestic piecework subcontracted by industries received an average wage of about one-third of the minimum salary. They work on the margins of illegality and receive no type of security or benefits, nor is their work in compliance with other legislated work regulations (33, 64 ff.).

7 As the Guatemalan sociologist Edelberto Torres notes, if the population cannot gain access to education, there is no hope for Guatemala's development (*El Periódico* 1997a, 8).

8 See Lynd (this volume, note 3) for the definitions of *poverty* and *extreme poverty*.

9 Guatemala and Honduras share the highest population growth rates in the Americas.

10 In 1991, the housing deficit in the urban areas was some 350,000 houses. The number grows 35,000 to 50,000 annually in the metropolitan area. Recent calculations note that close to 1,000,000 people live in precarious settlements in the greater Guatemalan Metropolitan Area.

11 Pérez Sáinz (1990) argues that the lower levels of participation of women in El Mezquital has to do with a sample bias. The women interviewed had school-age children and were, therefore, in the procreation cycle, when it is the most difficult for women to be active in the labor market (68).

12 The average wage per month in Guatemala City was Q438 (U.S.$141 at the 1989 average exchange rate).

13 Forty percent of women are illiterate versus 20 percent of men in La Brigada, and 21 percent of women versus 4.6 percent of men are illiterate in El Mezquital (Pérez Sáinz 1990, 68).

14 I am indebted to Allyson Shelley, who generously shared some of her interviews of UPAVIM women with me.

15 Fair trade businesses, such as SERRV International, Ten Thousand Villages, and Pueblo to People before it closed (see Grimes, this volume).

16 Monthly incomes, however, average between Q500 and Q600 (U.S.$83 to $100), yearly incomes Q8,772 (U.S.$1,462) (Littrell and Dickson 1999).

17 For example, they changed from having each woman cut her own cloth to one woman cutting the cloth for everyone and are training more women to use industrial sewing machines.

18 This is a pseudonym. Throughout the text, I use this name to protect the informant's privacy.

19 The women of UPAVIM earn higher incomes than other women in the community. See Littrell and Dickson (1999) for examples of women's incomes working in private homes, in restaurants, in maquilas, or at home sewing under contract. Married women usually do not opt for these types of jobs (except part-time domestic work or piece-rate work) because of the long hours and usually long commute. Women with children most often work in the informal sector, where incomes are lower.

20 See Lynd (this volume) for ways Maya Traditions has worked to solve these problems.

B. L YNNE M ILGRAM

7. REORGANIZING TEXTILE PRODUCTION FOR THE GLOBAL MARKET

W OMEN ' S C RAFT C OOPERATIVES IN I FUGAO, U PLAND P HILIPPINES

Artisans worldwide increasingly make their living in a global marketplace. This does not mean that craftspeople abandon local customs or produce solely for commercial markets. Rather, they continually refashion personal strategies that enable them to maintain those aspects of production that they deem most important to the livelihood of their families and to their membership in the community. In some cases, artisans may consent to compromises to ensure the sale of their crafts. In no way, however, are such situations static. Individually or collectively, artisans engage in different aspects of craft production and trade to reformulate global facts into local forms (Appadurai 1996, 18).

Although changes in indigenous craft production are receiving greater attention as demand for many products grows, advocates in development continue to debate the most suitable paths for establishing successful programs for producers. Some initiatives stress securing reliable sources of raw materials, but neglect to establish ongoing markets for this production. Others succeed in exposing makers to broader markets but fail to consider how production cycles fluctuate with the availability and costs of raw materials and with the seasonal demands for labor in subsistence agriculture. Still others concentrate on product development by focusing on fast-selling souvenirs or on high-end products. The neglect of certain sectors of the production-marketing continuum has left many skilled artisans stranded. How, then, do artisans maintain control of their activities in crafts with the commoditization of their rural economies? Whereas some artisans continue to work independently, many others, particularly women, are choosing to work collectively in groups, either in a cooperative or in an association framework. Often, the formation of such collective organizations has been initiated or aided by development programs mandated to help artisans meet new consumer demands. Although these development efforts espouse a community-based participatory approach, many have failed to galvanize artisan groups into collective action that would improve the circumstances of production and marketing of crafts.

Based on my research in Banaue, Ifugao Province, northern Philippines,[1] this chapter begins an inquiry into these issues by comparing two women's weaving groups, the Northern Bannug Weaving Association and the Southern Bannug Weaving Association. I consider how group members participated in establishing self-managed weaving collectives and how they effected the transition from individual to collective production. By analyzing these projects as sites of local empowerment for women, I examine some of the factors that have contributed to their successes and failures. Whereas one weaving association—based on a preexisting, informal rotating credit group—thrives in spite of some internal problems, the other, assembled solely to gain access to development funds, is faltering. In Ifugao, women have a long history of making crafts and engaging in community and regional trade, albeit on different levels, to obtain goods not locally available (see Milgram 1997). I argue that the development projects initiated in Banaue to aid female artisans have not fully recognized the variety of women's experiences that existed before the initiatives. These projects have not considered traditional community production practices and producers' relationships to the type and design of new products. By not sufficiently considering the differences among women based on class, age, and past experience in crafts, these initiatives have failed to account for how such differences affect internal group dynamics and hence the ongoing viability of the craft association.

During my fieldwork in Banaue, I found myself increasingly in situations where artisan groups appealed to me to assist them in gaining wider exposure and markets for their products. I conclude this chapter with a discussion of my efforts to bring together the women in the Ifugao weaving associations with Philippine government departments and nongovernmental organizations (NGOs) mandated to support rural artisans in the marketing of their production. I discuss the bureaucratic roadblocks that prevent these weaving associations from taking advantage of such government-designated funds, but at the same time aid those entrepreneurs, men and women, who are already successful in craft businesses. I also examine the problems artisans face in fashioning suitable products for the Western markets without ongoing consultation on product design.

DEVELOPMENT AND THE COOPERATIVE CONTEXT FOR CLOTH PRODUCTION

My analysis of Banaue's weaving associations adopts an inductive approach to understand how development programs, such as those in crafts, differently influence poor women and how these women, in turn, effect changes in these initiatives by accepting, reconfiguring, or rejecting development aid. I dispute approaches that view informal economic activities, such as craft production, as merely a survival strategy of the poor

and that see artisans as a discrete economic group that can be released from poverty
only through Western intervention. By placing women at the center of my analysis and
acknowledging the diversity of women's lives, I illustrate in the Philippine case studies
outlined here how female artisans actively explore different alternative responses to
top-down development through their collective organization—albeit some more successfully than others. To support their production and marketing of crafts, for example,
women continue to depend on informal networks rooted in community and kinship
ties. I suggest, then, that the relations of social reproduction in many instances provide
a springboard on which to build local craft production for capitalist markets (Stephen
1991a). My study questions whether the Philippine development schemes sponsoring
the Banaue weaving cooperatives recognize this symbiotic relationship.

To meet the growing global demand for crafts more effectively, some weavers
in Banaue are turning from independent to collective production and marketing practices, as noted earlier. Under the direction of a locally based government development
agency, the Central Cordillera Agricultural Programme (CECAP), weavers have grouped
themselves into organized craft associations to maximize their access to supplies of raw
materials and to broader marketing opportunities. This chapter examines the changes
that occur in the relations of production and trade when the locus of commercial craft
activities shifts from a household to a collective context. How have association members been able to use their cooperatives to make their voices heard locally, regionally,
and nationally, and to increase their potential income-generating opportunities? Given
that women's interests and positions often conflict, what does collective organization
tell us about the exploitation of producers that comes with craft commercialization?

COOPERATIVE IDEOLOGY VERSUS
COOPERATIVE PRACTICE

The debates on how participation in cooperatives empowers women center around
the interplay of cooperative ideology and cooperative practice (see also Attwood 1989,
Attwood and Baviskar 1988, Cetina 1998). With regard to a cooperative ideology that
represents a commitment to individual empowerment, the principle of democratic control and the concept of shared ownership are key. Democratic control, the right of every member to vote equally, is integral to legal cooperative organizations. Although
many women's organizations are more commonly classified as collectives, such as the
women's craft organizations I discuss here, the mandate remains that each member has

the opportunity to participate equally. The degree to which cooperatives devote their energy to realizing this ideal goal often determines the organization's success and the real benefits to members (see also Attwood and Baviskar 1988, Attwood and Hanley 1996). Especially in cases where women's authority does not extend beyond the family's household, shared ownership that provides the opportunity for women to participate equally and to set up the workplace on their own terms is in itself an important entitlement for women (AWCF and NATCCO 1995).

We must, however, consider the broader picture—namely, how women's membership in cooperative organizations can enhance their access to broader socioeconomic and political networks. If cooperatives remain marginal endeavors or islands of cooperation in a sea of capitalist competition, working collectively does little to enhance women's positions. To realize the potential of collective production and trade of crafts, for example, members must participate in regional and national networks that facilitate and mobilize support, and coordinate efforts for their advancement. The cooperative sector in the Philippines comprises an impressive network that reaches into the social and economic structure of the country. Access to these connections would greatly assist female artisans, who may not have been part of the formal (or sometimes the informal) economy. Because women's craft collectives in Banaue are not legally registered as cooperatives, however, their access to the resources offered by the extensive Philippine cooperative system is limited. At the conclusion of this chapter, I discuss how my applied work has attempted to facilitate this connection and the obstacles that impede achieving such interfaces at the local-to-national-to-global levels.

The potential of the cooperative model to support women's collective action and objectives and to empower women as individuals and as a group is often not realized. Why the dissonance between intent and results? Western development models, for example, rely widely on the cooperative format as a vehicle to empower women, but cooperative-sector practice often mirrors the dominant culture's attitude toward women, which disempowers them as cooperative members. For example, the role of women as the primary caregivers in raising children hinders their involvement in leadership roles beyond a certain point. The provision of child care within the cooperative is often necessary to enable more members to participate equally, as evidenced in the following Ifugao case studies. Also, how is the operation of the cooperative positioned to effect broader social and economic change? Unless the cooperative, aided by development agency support, promotes systemic change in the structure of craft marketing, producers, especially women, cannot assume control of wider distribution networks to enhance their personal positions and those of their families (see also AWCF and NATCCO 1995, Cohen 1998).[2]

Recent studies on women and community development in crafts analyze the channels of collective organization that rural women are increasingly pursuing. Karen Tice's (1995) important study of *mola* production in the San Blas Islands illustrates that the increased global trade of molas has contributed to social differentiation between men and women as well as among women of differing communities. She analyzes three women's craft cooperatives to argue that although women have gained local control over and more equitable distribution of income from mola sales through their collective action, their roles still largely revolve around production. The women active as traders are usually "better-off" landowners, and men still dominate the majority of mola trade because they can more easily travel to urban centers.

Charting the rise of textile cooperatives in Guatemala that have succeeded in the market for designer goods, Morris (1996), like Ehlers (1993), questions whether the cultural shift involved in gearing oneself totally to "adapt to 'the other'" justifies the economic gain (137). He points out that in such market-directed production, individual artisans often have no direct control over or relationship with their clients. They depend on professional intermediaries—exporters, importers, and designers who keep up with fashion trends. Not only do artisans sell to foreigners, but "foreigners are their trainers" and supervisors (Morris 1996, 137).[3] Although contacts between artisans and outsiders can be mutually beneficial, as outlined by Nash (1993a, 12), the power this latter type of market gives to a few individuals who are not members of the organization can lead to irresolvable conflicts (Morris 1996, 137; see also Cohen 1998).

Women who can increase their involvement in marketing their products by joining craft cooperatives inevitably open avenues to pursuing broader social purposes (Morris 1996, 140). Simply the opportunity to increase earnings and to associate with other women in meetings and in skill-training workshops gives members of many cooperatives a new independence, as discussed by both Lynd and MacHenry (this volume). Change is more subtle in regions such as the upland Philippines, where women are an accepted part of the work force. Indeed, in regions such as Ifugao, women can access different marketing options (e.g., selling fresh produce) to achieve upward economic mobility, but because craft production is ongoing in many rural areas and because many women are artisans, this sphere of work is often the most accessible option open to them.

These studies of craft cooperatives point out the tensions between the myth of egalitarian relationships postulated by development practitioners advocating cooperative efforts and the reality of how members achieve a collaborative, group work environment. Cooperatives often benefit the more affluent weavers and traders—the "not so poor," those already engaged in trade who usually have enough land to feed their families and can devote more time to cooperative activities. As the case studies discussed here illustrate, joining collective production and marketing associations does not automatically offer power to all women because different women are able to pursue different channels in their efforts to maximize collaborative opportunities.

CRAFTS AND COMMODITIZATION IN BANAUE, IFUGAO

The Ifugao live on the eastern side of the Gran Cordillera Central mountain range, which extends through the center of northern Luzon, Philippines. This study focuses on the village of Bannug,[4] one of Banaue's seventeen villages known for its crafts. The main economic activities in Banaue, as throughout the Cordillera, are cultivating wet rice and raising pigs for ritual and domestic use. Women also grow vegetables for household needs. Located at an altitude of fifteen hundred meters, Banaue's cool upland climate limits cultivation to one rice crop per year so that most households can grow enough rice to feed themselves for only two to six months. With no mixed agricultural production base and no agricultural surplus for commercial sale, cultivators must seek alternatives to earn cash. Building on their history of bartering crafts for products not locally available, artisans currently produce and sell weavings and wood carvings to the growing number of tourists visiting Banaue to view the region's spectacular mountain rice terraces. In Bannug, 60 percent of the village's approximately 250 households have at least one member involved in handicraft production or trade.

As the ownership of irrigated rice land and personal reserves of upland rice continue to symbolize wealth and prestige, any surplus of upland rice is never sold. Rather, it is stored for later distribution to family and community members on special ritual occasions. Hence, those involved in handicraft production and trade do not easily abandon their association with rice cultivation. Instead, they integrate their production and trade of crafts with their agricultural activities as cultivators and landowners.

The region of the Gran Cordillera Central resisted Spanish domination for three hundred years (1565–1898). It became part of the Philippine state through negotiation rather than conquest during the U.S. colonial period, 1898–1946 (Fry 1983). Early U.S. policy in this region stressed local control over local economy and resources.

Although this policy was later reversed, it set the precedent for the autonomy of the indigenous population (Fry 1983, Jenista 1987) and for the continuance of local customs. For example, Ifugao kinship ties, reckoned equally through one's parents to both lines of blood kin, comprise the foremost network of social relations on which people draw first for assistance in agriculture and craft activities. Many of the socioeconomic and political elements of the local culture have remained dynamic and have provided the basis of unique local development.

COMMERCIALIZATION OF THE RURAL ECONOMY

The rapid monetization of the lowland Philippine economy that took place during the 1800s did not occur in the Cordillera highlands; thus, upland artisans continued to produce goods for themselves, for fellow villagers, and for trade in regional markets. Currently in Ifugao, craft production is largely practiced at the household level by independent home producers.[5] Independent household industry, however, coexists with a commercial market economy that was introduced by the U.S. colonial administration in the early 1900s and that has accelerated since the Second World War.

The postindependence period (after 1946) opened the way for the commercialization of some rural crafts, such as wood carving, for which the Ifugao are renowned (Aguilar and Miralao 1984, 6–7). Carvers who left Ifugao to work on the U.S. government road-building projects in Benguet Province to the south found a ready market for their carvings in the U.S. servicemen and other visiting foreigners working in the region. Although the demand for textiles never reached the national and international popularity of wood carvings, weaving in Banaue has undergone its own unique transformation. Some weavers continue to produce Banaue's distinctive striped textiles, which are used as gifts in ritual exchanges and worn as markers of ethnic identity, whereas others focus on making market-driven weavings (see Milgram 1999). In response to the increase in local tourism after the mid-1970s, Banaue weavers have built on their history of producing and marketing crafts for local and regional markets by developing a line of commercial textiles designed specifically for sale to visitors.

The woven table runner (three hundred centimeters long by thirty centimeters wide) has emerged as the main product weavers sell to tourist markets. It is sold as yardage or sewn into a variety of functional items, such as purses, bags, backpacks, and vests. The woven table runner is not tied to the conventions of patterning of Banaue's traditionally striped cloths, so it can be woven in a number of colors and designs in response to changing consumer tastes. This study focuses on the production and sale of these market-driven textiles because these textiles are the focus of cloth production in the women's weaving associations.

The demand for commercial textile production, however, is tempered by the seasonal cycle of tourism, which in turn partially determines whether women decide to work in cultivation or in crafts. As I have discussed in more detail elsewhere (Milgram 1998), craft sales are highest during the dry, hot months from March through May, when most foreign tourists and Philippine nationals visit Banaue. During these months, weavers capitalize on the steady demand for their crafts by devoting most of their time to cloth production. Conversely, during the harvest season, June through August, the majority of weavers work in their rice fields and spend little time at their looms. Because this is the rainy and nontourist season, demand for their products is low. Producers want to work in cultivation at this time not only because harvesting renews community ties, but also because it presents opportunities to earn upland rice and extra cash from landowners who must harvest their crop as soon as possible after it ripens. During the part of the rainy season that extends through planting time from December to February, few tourists visit Banaue. In these months, weavers divide their time between cloth production and farming; the time spent in each activity is an individual decision. The success of Banaue's current-day weavers, then, is "tied to [their] ability ... to take advantage of existing marketing networks and skills when tourist and export markets [open] up for their craft products" (Stephen 1996, 382).

By working with women in the Northern Bannug Weaving Association and the Southern Bannug Weaving Association, I learned about members' successes and goals, their concerns and problems, and the ways they handled the shift from independent to collective production and marketing. Members explained why and how they formed their groups. They discussed the bonds holding them together and reflected on the extent to which group structure is rooted in preexisting community frameworks. In the following section, I analyze the operation of these two groups within the development framework that sponsored them, and I question the potential of these initiatives to lay the groundwork for change for women.

TWO CASE STUDIES

In the early 1990s, the Central Cordillera Agricultural Programme, a development agency jointly funded by the European Union and the Philippine government and operating in the Cordillera provinces of northern Luzon, extended its mandate to include crafts, in addition to agriculture, in its financial assistance programs (CECAP 1995). In 1994, two groups of women from Bannug, a village known for its weaving, organized themselves to access the CECAP loans.

The Northern Bannug Weaving Association

When Norma Tayadan, a weaver and fledgling entrepreneur, learned of the CECAP loan project, she organized twelve Bannug weavers who were relatives and close neighbors into a group and requested a CECAP loan to purchase raw materials for cloth production. The weavers have repeatedly explained to me, "We do not have the capital to buy thread," and they have identified this factor as the main reason they cannot always engage in cloth production even when demand is high. Responding to producers' pleas, CECAP targeted their loan to the Northern Bannug Weaving Association to purchase yarns and gave the group a loan of twenty-five thousand pesos (one thousand U.S. dollars) at 12 percent interest per year; repayment was based on a schedule of semiannual payments spread over two years.[6] With this loan, weavers could buy yarns at wholesale prices. The repayment schedule was intended to enable members to retain part of their earnings for the six-month period as a revolving fund to reinvest in buying yarns; the other part of their earnings would be devoted to repaying the loan. Because the loan was group owned but individually managed, each weaver was responsible for repaying her share of the loan, the exact amount determined by the value of the yarn that she used.

To build up the working capital of the group, CECAP encouraged members to meet monthly and at this time to contribute fifty pesos to their bank account. If members did not have cash each month, Norma, the group chair at the time, suggested that they sell her one woven table runner, from which the producer's profit of approximately fifty pesos could then be given to the group account. This initiative, however, did not materialize. Weavers did not always want to sell their weavings to Norma, who often did not pay them the current price of one hundred pesos per runner, nor did they always have runners to sell if they had been working in their rice fields.

Officials within CECAP concede that they, rather than the members, chose Norma as chair of the group because her house is conveniently located on the road at the entrance to the path leading to the village. The Ifugao do not live in nucleated settlements, but rather in individual houses dispersed throughout their rice fields, so Norma's house would be most appropriate as the central meeting place for the group

and as the storehouse for the yarns. Because Norma's family owns rice land and because she had been active in trading weavings, many members felt too intimidated to
offer objections to her appointment.[7] In their decision to appoint Norma, the CECAP
officials did not consider the preexisting differences in status among women and how
the appointment would further accentuate this division.

In the northern Bannug group, other problems arose over the manner in which
the loan was used to purchase the raw materials. Traveling often to Manila, Norma
assumed the responsibility of purchasing the yarns. Because the amount she was buying was still small by Manila factory standards, her purchases were restricted to the
supplies that remained after large wholesale orders had been filled. Thus, the quality of
the yarns available to group members was uneven. In addition, by purchasing all of the
thread in one order to save the cost of returning to Manila, Norma did not account for
the variety of colors and types of thread that weavers require to fill shop owners' orders
for variety in their products. The northern Bannug group quickly encountered problems because their stock held too much of one color and yarn type, and not enough of
others. Stocks of particular yarns were quickly depleted, and weavers turned to other
suppliers to obtain the yarns they needed for specific orders. Purchasing their yarn
from outside sellers at the full retail price reduced the funds they had available to repay
their loan. Within the first year of operation, weavers in the group fell behind on their
loan repayments because many members objected to paying for yarns they were not
using.

In the meantime, Norma decided to stop weaving because she could earn
more income by sewing runners into functional items. She sold her products to craft
shops in larger urban centers or gave them on consignment to local traders who made
the trip. When I returned to Banaue in 1998, I learned that Norma had taken further
advantage of having the yarns stocked in her house. She had made selling the group's
leftover yarn to nonmembers her personal priority; she would often arrange to buy
runners made with that yarn from the nonmembers and then sew them into saleable
products. Although Norma insists that she deposited the profits from the yarn sales
back into the group's bank account, the account could not be reconciled, and the first
two loan repayments were incomplete. Members explain that they often could not devote their attention to the operation of the group because their time and resources were
required in rice cultivation. Group meetings were infrequent and often canceled at the
last moment when Norma repeatedly failed to attend, so feelings of mistrust developed
among group members, and the group had largely disbanded by early 1998.

The Southern Bannug Weaving Association

In availing itself of the CECAP loan program, the Southern Bannug Weaving Association has been more successful in sustaining group solidarity, although it has also experienced internal problems with member dissension. One of the major differences between the northern association and the southern association is that some of the members of the latter group are also participants in a rotating savings and loan group that has been operating since 1990. Helen Sadamo, a weaver and active community church member, assembled a group of ten neighbors and relatives into a loosely organized association that members termed the Bannug Rural Improvement Club (BARIC). Consisting of both farmers and weavers, this group of women seek more control over their economic earnings. By pooling their savings, they can apply larger lump sums to their production activities to better utilize their earnings. Three members are full-time rice farmers; three women are sewers who manufacture locally woven runners into functional items for commercial sale; and the remainder are weavers.

In late 1993, with the Ramos administration's establishment of the National Economic Enterprises Development Program designed to "fast-track the development of the countryside" (Bunolna 1993, 2), the BARIC group secured an interest-free loan of ten thousand pesos (four hundred U.S. dollars) from the Department of Social Work and Development, targeted to promote livelihood enterprises. Each member received one thousand pesos, and Helen assumed responsibility for members' repayments, which were due in monthly installments over two years. The farmers used the money to hire laborers to cultivate their fields or to purchase seedlings for vegetable gardening; weavers applied the funds to the purchase of thread; and sewers used the money to stockpile and manufacture woven runners. This initiative gave BARIC members access to small amounts of capital, with repayment based on neighborhood peer pressure. Many of the farmers work together in labor exchanges in rice cultivation,[8] and some farmers and weavers have organized an arrangement in which a half-day's labor setting up the loom, a two-person task, is exchanged for half-day's labor in the fields. As BARIC continues to operate, members are considering contributing fifty pesos to a group fund, in a schedule yet to be decided, in order to accumulate the two thousand pesos needed to register as a formal cooperative.

In 1994, CECAP officers identified the weavers and sewers in the BARIC group who would qualify for their loan program to artisans. Because the farmers could not participate in this project, additional artisans were approached to join this new group to bring the membership to twelve. The members of this artisan-based group, formed to access the CECAP loan, called themselves the Southern Bannug Weaving Association. As BARIC continues to operate, some of these artisans are simultaneously members in both groups. In an effort not to repeat the problems encountered with the Northern Bannug Weaving Association, CECAP officers decided to allot the low-interest loans on an individual basis. They based the loan amount on individual interviews in which members were asked to calculate their average monthly income from weaving. Weavers admit that this calculation is of limited use because they do not factor in the cost of their labor time. In addition, such an approach does not take into account the seasonal demand for craft products and the time artisans devote to family responsibilities and to cultivation. Thus, because the loan to each individual was tied to her net income, different members received different amounts.

Group members express varied opinions about how CECAP allocated their development funds. For many of the weavers in the group, the CECAP loan was appropriate, supplying them with sufficient capital to purchase thread for their cloth production. The weavers explain, "A loan of one thousand to two thousand pesos enables us to buy eight kilos of mercerized cotton to weave the best-quality runners. With this amount we can produce enough runners to fill craft shop owners' large orders during the busy season." Some weavers emphasize that they hesitate to borrow more money, uncertain of their ability to repay the loan on time, whereas others complain that the funds are not enough to make a real difference to their production.

Betty Inay, for example, a sewer who manufactures woven runners and sells her products locally to Banaue craft shop owners and regionally to Baguio City tourist markets, is pleased that the loans have been calculated on an individual basis. She explains:

> With the CECAP loan, I feel responsible only for my share. I can concentrate on what I can manage personally. I am used to working on my own, so this arrangement does not require me to change the way I do business. Before, I was happy to receive our group's initial loan of one thousand pesos, which I could use for six months. But as I am trying to expand my business, I need more capital to substantially increase my sales. With one thousand pesos, I could buy only ten additional (one hundred pesos each) woven runners. With the larger CECAP loan of six thousand pesos, I can purchase more runners and have this stock to sell when the demand is high in Baguio City.

Helen Sadamo, the chair of the group, received the largest loan because she had secured a large order from a Baguio City craft shop owner. The development program used this order as collateral for giving her a thirteen-thousand-peso loan.[9] Helen spent ten thousand pesos on the yarn that she would weave on her upright floor loom and saved three thousand pesos to cover other expenses. She had woven one-half of the order when she learned that the buyer reduced the number of items she wanted. Helen's distance from Baguio City and her lack of funds to pay for legal counsel prevented her from challenging the urban buyer (see Milgram in press). Helen was left with a stock of similarly patterned and colored yardage, and thus had to borrow money from family members to purchase the variety of yarns requested by local buyers. She returned to weaving on her backstrap loom but experienced difficulty keeping up with her payments. Some members of the group resent that Helen received a larger loan, but hesitate to object because she was instrumental in organizing the initiative and continues to be very supportive of other group functions.

Although the members of the Southern Bannug Weaving Association are behind in their overall loan repayment, they have been able to submit regular repayments, with Helen's insistence, although the amounts submitted are below the minimum CECAP originally required. In 1998, Helen was still struggling with her double debt, but members were continuing to meet and were contributing individually what they could afford to pay on their loans.

HOW USEFUL ARE CECAP'S DEVELOPMENT LOANS TO ARTISAN GROUPS?

The Southern Bannug Weaving Association is a stronger women's craft collective because of the preexisting social relationships the members had established in their rotating local credit activities as part of BARIC. This strength of the group, however, is potentially threatened by CECAP's policy in which group loans are individually owned and managed. This practice of loan allocation could, in some cases, undermine individual members' impetus to work together to repay the loan as a whole. Although CECAP's policy of individually allotted loans to the southern Bannug group supports the regional ideology of individualism or *kanya kanya,* it also favors the enterprises of those already established in trading, such as Helen and Betty, by giving them larger capital loans.

Moreover, group members remain dependent on one person's leadership. When Helen Sadamo became embroiled in personal debts, the cohesiveness of the group temporarily faltered until she, with family support, again devoted her time to the group. As with the Northern Bannug Weaving Association, the majority of the members of the southern group have not been sufficiently encouraged or trained to develop leadership skills and responsibilities that would facilitate transferring positions of power within the group.

In the Northern Bannug Weaving Association, the failure of members to assume shared responsibilities and to identify group goals with their personal goals further accentuated an unstable situation in which the chair was driven by personal self-interest. Failure of CECAP staff to consider the differences among women in the group and to intervene when it became evident that the appointment of the chair was problematic contributed to the failure of this group to sustain operations. As an emerging trader in weavings, Norma Tayadan employed individual business strategies, which often conflicted with those of other traders and producers in her group. The manner in which female traders choose to conduct their businesses, like that of men, may involve deceit and secrecy, and may depend on comparative advantage over other women, as evidenced by Norma's practices. Their trading strategies can also often rely on paying low wages to their female laborers. Artisan-producers feel too intimidated to protest against the behavior of elected group representatives such as Norma because the latter have been able to translate their positions as new craft traders into membership in the business elite. As Susan Russell (1987) points out, "Status-based restrictions inhibit small, relatively isolated producers from pressing demands or complaints in a straightforward manner, and these inhibitions are increased by the greater knowledge middlemen have about the wider society" (152). Norma's practices illustrate the complexity of the relationships between traders and producers, here made more pronounced because both are participants in the same craft group.

The efforts of CECAP to aid artisans have addressed only one-half of the equation of craft production and trade. Because CECAP did not balance artisans' increased accessibility to production materials with a cohesive marketing plan for their products, weaving sales are still slow or irregular in times other than those of the busy tourist season. Increased accessibility to raw materials does little to challenge the marginalization of crafts in broader marketing processes.

Rather than promoting the advocacy of group members to challenge the preexisting parameters of marketing and the tensions of producer-trader relations integral to the local craft industry, CECAP's program adopts a welfare-oriented approach that targets only the economic factors affecting production. It has not developed noneconomic support systems for women, both inter- or intragroup services, that would facilitate their craft production by providing assistance with their domestic responsibilities (e.g., laundry, shopping, child care).

Members of both the northern and southern associations continue to devote much of their energy to the internal dynamics of their groups. By not providing artisan groups with sufficient management-skills training and by not developing producers' potential to market their own products through linkages with broader craft-marketing networks in the Philippines, CECAP policies have, in effect, done little to fulfill its mandate to empower local artisans. The perception of Banaue's female producers as poor and oppressed constructs a monolithic entity that practitioners believe can be released from poverty only through Western intervention. The program's approach to development needs to give attention to the different socioeconomic and cultural contexts of peoples' lives (Mohanty 1991). Rather than one factor, a multitude of relations—including those of class and ethnicity as well as those between people and their material environment—shapes the lives of Ifugao women, as evidenced in these case studies.

In late 1996, CECAP initiated Phase II of its program. Part of their mandate includes revisiting the shortcomings of Phase I projects, such as the initiatives with the Bannug weaving associations. My current research charts CECAP's efforts to revitalize these projects. I particularly focus on the extent to which their revised approach acknowledges the diversity of women's lived experiences and the differentials that exist between women before project implementation. I also examine the extent to which CECAP policies recognize the imperative to facilitate local-to-national-to-global connections. The following section addresses my own efforts in this direction.

LINKING THE LOCAL TO THE GLOBAL: FACILITATING BROADER MARKETS FOR IFUGAO WOMEN'S CRAFTS

During my research in Ifugao in 1995, I found myself in situations with craftspeople that made me reevaluate my role as a researcher and question my relationship with the Banaue craft community. At seven o'clock one morning just before harvest season, two weavers from the Northern Bannug Weaving Association arrived at my house asking me to purchase some of their woven textiles. Maria had woven a large blanket, and Karen had made two table runners, all of which they promptly spread out and displayed on the ground in front of me. They explained, "Until we are able to work in the harvest to secure supplies of rice or cash income, we do not have enough money to buy our families' needs; we are looking for rice. . . . We are always running after rice." I promptly bought the two table runners from Karen and arranged for one of the CECAP staff to purchase the blanket. A few weeks later at the Saturday morning market in Banaue, I encountered the same artisans making the rounds to craft shop owners to sell their weavings. Without hesitation, I purchased another two woven runners.

For people like me who stand in the marketplace wondering what to do next, there seems little choice but to get involved. Weavers explain, "We must continue to sell our textiles to you so that our families can continue to eat." To achieve some practical alternatives for weavers, I decided to focus on the market to put artisans in touch with groups that can potentially help them sell their products (see Morris 1996, 137; Eber and Causey, this volume). My limited efforts thus far anticipate the work that needs to be done.

When I returned to Canada in 1995, I brought with me a variety of types of woven table runners, which I left on consignment in the gift shop of Toronto's Museum for Textiles. Because I was consumed at this time with writing my doctoral dissertation, my primary purpose was simply to keep in touch with Banaue weavers by purchasing and selling a small but steady flow of their textiles. I kept the price of these pieces low by recovering only my basic costs. I composed detailed labels for the pieces displayed in the museum shop, describing the technology of the weaving and dyeing used in creating each piece and indicating the name of the weaver. I also assembled photo documentation of the cloth production process. Sales, however, were slow. Museum visitors hesitated to purchase the runners, explaining that they were uncertain about how to use them if, for example, they already had a runner for their dining room table or for other pieces of furniture. I could not continue to repeatedly press my colleagues and friends to purchase yet another weaving from me to help me cover the cost of ordering more pieces. I needed to pursue another direction if I wanted to promote Banaue's weavers.

My research assistant in Banaue, with whom I keep up correspondence, agreed to help me organize a limited line of manufactured items. Drawing on my experience as a weaver, I designed small cases sewn from the wide variety of artisans' woven table runners to hold computer disks and letter- and legal-size carrying envelopes. The shop at the Museum for Textiles agreed to carry these items, which continue to sell slowly.

However, I ended up giving away more of these items as gifts. The time I had to devote to this endeavor was limited. On my return to the Philippines in 1998, I pursued the possibility of connecting producer groups, such as the Bannug weaving associations, with broader networks that could make a real difference to artisans' marketing options.

The Philippines supports a well-developed network of government and non-government organizations mandated to assist producer groups, both in crafts and in agriculture, that are organized and registered as cooperatives. To formally register, groups must elect a board of directors, formulate by-laws, compile a financial statement, and pay the two-thousand-peso (fifty U.S. dollars in 1998) fee to register these documents with the Securities Commission. Not only is the two-thousand-peso registry fee prohibitive for most associations, but the skills required to put into effect such cooperative structures are often beyond what group members can accomplish without professional training and initial financial assistance. Because CECAP's Phase I projects with the Northern Bannug Weaving Association and the Southern Bannug Weaving Association did not result in either group attaining cooperative status, these collectives are largely precluded from receiving the training and financial aid available from professional cooperative-help agencies. For example, these groups did not qualify for aid from the Northern Luzon Federation of Cooperatives and Development Center (NORLU), which offers technical training in marketing, financing, and service delivery for a wide variety of formally registered cooperatives (NORLU 1992, 1998).

While in Manila, I contacted the Community Crafts Association of the Philippines (CCAP), a nonprofit development NGO established in the late 1970s to promote the export of Philippine handicrafts. I understood from my correspondence with CECAP staff that they intended to continue working with the Bannug weaving associations, and I hoped to facilitate a dialogue between these weaving groups and CCAP. A fair trade organization, CCAP actively supports equitable business practices for small handicraft groups throughout the Philippines. Similar to the fair trade organizations described by Grimes (this volume), CCAP seeks to eliminate the exploitative marketing structures in the craft industry by eliminating the layers of middlepeople between producers and final buyers (CCAP 1997). Under the innovative leadership of their newly elected director in 1996, CCAP has heightened their profile by mounting a website on Peoplink (see Grimes, this volume) and by expanding their mandate to encompass reliable producer groups whether or not the artisan organizations are formally registered as cooperatives. In addition, CCAP is coordinating with the Department of Trade and Industry's (DTI) Product Development and Design Center. The latter organization is a technical agency of DTI mandated to develop the quality and competitiveness of Philippine craft products for global marketing.

When I first visited CCAP, the director took me through its newly renovated building and warehouse space that houses the crafts arriving from rural artisan groups. A permanent showroom displays the different types of products available; each one is identified with the product's origin, type, and price. Beside the showroom is a large illustrated map locating each of the producer groups with which CCAP conducts business. All groups are located in the central (Visayas) and southern Philippines (Mindanao). No groups are "pinpointed" in the northern Luzon section of the map. The CCAP director explained that she was at that time unable to identify producer groups in this area with whom her organization could work. Although craft groups do not have to be registered as cooperatives, the CCAP director explained that in order to maximize the efforts of a small staff, "CCAP works only with producer groups who have proven themselves to be viable community-based enterprises that are effectively organized and self-reliant. Artisan groups must ensure reliable and timely delivery of their products, and goods must display consistent quality in order for us [CCAP] to meet our guarantees to our foreign buyers." These factors remain problematic for Banaue artisans. Communication between Manila and Banaue is often difficult due to very limited telephone and fax facilities, and the road, the sole mode of transportation, is often impassable because of the numerous mud slides that occur in the long rainy season. However, because many of CCAP's artisan groups produce baskets, the director expressed keen interest in obtaining examples of the Banaue weavings that I showed to her. In my discussions with her, I learned that CCAP had not been approached by any development agencies working in northern Luzon or by any of the region's producers asking the Manila-based agency to manage handicrafts from the Cordillera provinces.

When I returned to Banaue in early 1998, I met with CECAP management staff and with members of the Bannug weaving associations to inform them of the new CCAP initiatives and to encourage both the agency and individual groups to develop this connection. The prospect of obtaining viable marketing options for Banaue producer groups as well as noneconomic support necessary for women's daily production could provide part of the impetus for members to reconsolidate their groups and reformulate marketing strategies.

CONCLUSIONS: CRAFTS, COOPERATIVES, AND RURAL SUSTAINABILITY

In their efforts to improve the social and economic conditions of production and to overcome vacillating market conditions, some female artisans in Banaue have moved the locus of craft production and trade from their household-based enterprises to collective organizations, such as the Northern Bannug Weaving Association and the Southern Bannug Weaving Association. In so doing, they have contributed to the potential of their craftwork to function as a source of rural sustainability, laying the groundwork for the region's economic development. Given the dynamics of Banaue's competitive trade in crafts, securing more stable and widespread markets for products appears to be the most viable way to improve the prices producers receive for their crafts and, hence, the security of their positions (Pye 1988, 94–121; Rutten 1993, 248). Other communities looking to improve artisans' livelihoods have also established craft cooperatives, often under the auspicious of development agency guidance. Tice (1995) argues that production and marketing cooperatives can allow more women control over the sale of their products and emphasizes that the most successful cooperatives are those based on preexisting collaborative forms of socially organized labor (188; see also Stephen 1991a). The Banaue case studies similarly demonstrate that if a cooperative project is to succeed, its organization must be built on the everyday work and values of participants. To take advantage of women's knowledge of crafts and to realize their potential contributions to the economy, any action facilitated by development programs needs to be initiated and "interpreted through indigenous logic and not through management logic" (Van Esterik 1995, 257).

My findings suggest that development agencies, such as CECAP, who seek to establish viable cooperatives need to adopt an inductive approach (Kabeer 1994) and consult with women particularly in the planning and implementation of projects so that the cooperatives are participant managed and operate as sites of local empowerment for members. The differences in the operation of the northern and southern associations deconstructs the homogeneous image of oppressed "third world women" to demonstrate that women's positions as artisans and traders are crosscut by factors such as age, class, and individual differences. Future development initiatives need to consider these preexisting inequalities among women as well as the differences that have arisen in Banaue's contemporary craft industry from women's unequal control over production and exchange relations.

Working with fair trade organizations, such as CCAP, offers an option for co-operatives to pursue in a competitive market where price undercutting keeps prices for products low (Pye 1988, 118). In their efforts to connect artisans to reliable national and international buyers, CCAP encourages artisan groups to develop high-quality products instead of engaging in mass production in which large quantities are made to off-set low markups. Artisans in Banaue are capable of producing high-quality crafts, as evidenced by the fine weavings that I saw during my Ifugao research. The extent to which women's crafts in Banaue will emerge as viable forms of rural sustainability will be played out in the twenty-first century.

NOTES

[1] Fieldwork for this essay was conducted from 1994 to 1995 and from January to July 1998 in afflliation with the Cordillera Studies Center, University of the Philippines College–Baguio. Financial support was provided by the Social Sciences and Humanities Research Council of Canada Doctoral Fellowship and Post-Doctoral Fellowship and by the Canada ASEAN Centre. I thank CECAP management and field staff for their assistance with and support of this research. To the people of Banaue, I owe a debt of gratitude.

[2] In his analysis of an artisan's cooperative in Oaxaca, Mexico, Cohen (1998 and this volume) points out that to understand the determinants of an organization's success, we must look not only at the internal dynamics of local cooperatives, but also at how they are positioned with regard to their access to and knowledge of market trends and export networks.

[3] Lynn Stephen (1996) similarly demonstrates that Zapotec merchant households gain more than weaving households with the commercialization of weaving in southern Mexico.

[4] The village name is a pseudonym, as are the names of the individuals and the names of the local associations identified in this chapter.

[5] Indeed, Aguilar and Miralao (1984) confirm that the "cultural communities in the hinterlands of Northern Luzon . . . certainly resisted the offensives of colonialism in both cultural and economic senses, and many have successfully retained their crafts of cloth weaving, basket-making and other indigenous industries" (5).

[6] In response to their request, CECAP conducted a simple feasibility study on circumstances of cloth production and marketing in Banaue and led an information session for members to acquaint them with the terms of the loan. The group then opened a bank account at the local Multipurpose Cooperative, with each member contributing fifty pesos to cover their initial share capital and the banking co-op membership fee. The CECAP loan and the future loan repayments would be funneled through this account. Each member, including anyone who did not read or write, then signed a Memorandum of Agreement to acknowledge the terms of the loan. The Cordillera development program also organized one- and two-day workshops on basic bookkeeping and leadership skills, but not all members attended, or they attended for only part of the sessions. Many participants complain that they did not understand the material being taught. Indeed, part of the group's current problem stems from the fact that neither the chair nor the treasurer has been able to maintain accurate books.

In 1995, the official exchange rate was one U.S. dollar equaled twenty-five Philippine pesos. In 1998, the rate changed to one U.S. dollar equaling forty-two pesos. The U.S. equivalents cited reflect these two rates depending on the year in which the data was collected.

7   Officers in CECAP face the problem of supervising different programs in widely dispersed settlements, where visits to association members could mean a thirty- to ninety-minute walk between members' houses. The two field officers handling this program explain that they feel pressed between the demands to expand their program and the need to provide quality follow-up services to ensure the strength of existing groups. Their compromise was the appointment of Norma as chair because of her roadside location.

8   Women characteristically engage in labor exchanges in rice cultivation. In this arrangement, a day's labor is exchanged for a day's labor, most often within the same agricultural cycle.

9   After the devastating earthquake in northern Luzon in 1990, DTI distributed upright floor looms as a grant to eight weavers living along the road. Helen Sadamo received one of these looms and alternated weaving on her backstrap loom for small orders and on the upright floor loom for large orders that required the same color and pattern arrangements.

JEFFREY H. COHEN

8. TEXTILE PRODUCTION IN RURAL OAXACA, MEXICO

THE COMPLEXITIES OF THE GLOBAL MARKET FOR HANDMADE CRAFTS

Woolen textiles produced by indigenous Mexicans in the central valley of Oaxaca, Mexico, are an important feature of the local tourist and export market for handmade crafts. The production of woolen textiles in central Oaxaca is dominated by weavers from two Zapotec communities, Teotitlán del Valle and Santa Ana del Valle. Since the 1940s, weaving in the area has changed from a part-time vocation, done largely for local markets, to full-time work for international markets. Gallery owners and exporters present the textiles as the product of Oaxaca's pre-Columbian history, archaic technology (looms introduced in the early seventeenth century and natural dye sources), and romantic images of contemporary indigenous life and culture. In reality, craft production is difficult work that is often done in less than optimal settings with little light or ventilation and that typically leads to chronic back pain. In addition, the historical roots of production and design are problematic at best. Although weaving is part of the region's indigenous past, contemporary textile production reflects the demands of international markets and exporters rather than native motifs and traditional cultural practices (see Nash 1993a, 1994b).

This chapter explores the complicated nature of textile production in Oaxaca and focuses specifically on contests between weavers in Santa Ana and Teotitlán as they compete for shares of the international market for woven goods. After outlining the structure of textile production and competition between Teotitlán (the dominant of the weaving villages and home to most middlemen and women) and Santa Ana (a community characterized largely by contract weavers who produce for Teotiteco buyers), I turn to a discussion of some of the ways in which Santañero weavers have organized to meet the challenge of participation in the global handicraft market. Craft production can be an effective means for a community to develop its economy, to protect and document patrimony, and to organize for participation in global market systems (Nash 1993a, Stephen 1987, Tice 1995). Nevertheless, the rivalry that exists between Teotitlán and Santa Ana (not to mention the contests that often pose households against each other in local competition) as well as the many attempts made by Santañeros to deal with their growing involvement with the global market and tourism indicate the complex and conflictive nature of craft production (see Cohen 1998). An additional point of importance in the dynamics of craft production is the role outsiders (including anthropologists) play in the support and exploitation of rural producers. Often, the construction of "authentic" or "native" and quality goods for the marketplace is largely defined by outsiders who sit in judgment of local producers (Nash 1993a). Thus, the final section of this essay examines the role of outsiders (the exporter, governmental official, and anthropologist) not as passive observers but as active participants in the construction of meaning in this changing system.

TEXTILE PRODUCTION IN RURAL OAXACA

Teotitlán del Valle and Santa Ana del Valle are two of four rural Zapotec villages well known for their production of woolen textiles and blankets (collectively called *tapetes*) for Mexico's tourist market and for export. The other communities involved in production are the neighboring villages of Diaz Ordaz and San Miguel (see Bailón Corres 1979, Cohen 1999, Stephen 1991b). Weaving in the area originated with the production of cotton goods on backstrap looms and was largely the work of women (for contemporary examples, see Clements 1990, Hendrickson 1995).[1] Contemporary production is rooted in technology, materials, and production strategies introduced by Dominicans to the area following the conquest—including wool as well as two-harness and free-standing looms. Men also became primary textile producers, although both men and women typically weave today (Gay 1986, Stephen 1991b, Vásquez and Vásquez Dávila 1992).

Textile production for sale beyond local markets and as more than a supplement to subsistence agriculture commenced following the completion of the pan-American highway (Cook 1993, Stephen 1993). The contemporary structure of the local textile industry developed during the economic crises of the 1980s and in particular during the collapse of the peso and the parallel increase in U.S. and European tourism to Mexico. The boom in the North American market for folk crafts also stimulated the industry. Much of the popularity surrounding today's weaving developed from an interest in "things Indian" in the United States (see Wood 1995 and M'Closkey, this volume).

Local demand for new goods and services brought textile producers and their communities into new economic relationships. Villagers needed to earn cash to meet household demand for goods (whether prepared foods, consumer items, clothing, or building materials) and services (from electricity and access to piped water to entertainment and education). Local demand further stimulated the movement away from subsistence-based agriculture and toward textile production, wage labor, and migration (see Alarcón 1992, Cohen 1998).

The production, sale, and export of woolen textiles have dominated the local economies of Teotitlán and Santa Ana since the late 1970s. Looms are present in nearly all households, and entire families typically invest at least a portion of their labor power into the production of textiles (see Stephen 1991b). And although sales made directly to tourists visiting the region are often highlighted in discussions with local producers, it is the export market for tapetes or rugs that is the most important source of sales. Millions of dollars in textiles are exported annually and make their way to galleries throughout Mexico, the United States, Europe, and Asia. However, weaving is a highly elastic business that rises and falls with changing tastes and the economic well-being of export markets. The strength of the market for textiles cannot be overestimated. Even with the growth of tourism and the expansion of the local and export markets, weaving remains difficult work, and only a minority of households in the industry make more than a slim profit (see Acheson 1972).[2]

Weavers in Teotitlán and Santa Ana employ three basic production strategies: dependent or contract production, independent production, and independent production supplemented with work as a buyer-vendor of textiles. Contract work or *mano de obra* (handwork) follows the pattern of a classic putting-out system (see Littlefield 1978). Weavers receive raw materials and design specifications from a *patrón* (typically a shop owner or middleman/woman from Teotitlán del Valle), and in exchange for their finished pieces, they receive a set wage. Payment is by piece, not by the hour, and weavers have little input concerning color, design, or size of their work. The mano de obra household does not invest its capital in raw materials or its time in the search for a market. There is a guaranteed return on work completed, although patrones have been known to shortchange weavers. Contracted households save money on raw materials and have the benefit of regular markets for their finished goods. However, patrones pay as little as possible for finished work in an effort to maintain tight control of client household labor and production. Thus, although mano de obra remains an option for poor households, it also tends to limit the movement of contractees toward independent production and more direct control of their labor power.

Independent textile producers tend to pool efforts and resources to avoid the controls of patrones and contract work. The independent household invests in raw materials, covers all of the costs of production, and sells directly to consumers and buyers (tourists, intermediaries, and exporters). Typically, an independent household has more working-age members than the contract household. The members of the independent household combine their labor (some members weave; others prepare raw materials or complete finished pieces; still other members, typically older adults, involve themselves in the search for buyers) or various economic strategies (i.e., migration, wage labor, and weaving) to meet household expenses.

The third strategy employed by households in Santa Ana and Teotitlán is the combination of textile production and the direct marketing of weavings to exporters and tourists. This strategy may mean nothing more than stockpiling textiles for extended family members or neighboring households and keeping a percentage of the profits when a sale is completed. Other households, particularly in Teotitlán, function as nearly full-time buyers and middlemen/women for the export market (Stephen 1991b, 1996). There are also households that own market stalls in Oaxaca City and run galleries for the direct sale of textiles to visiting tourists.[3]

When combined with other strategies (migration, agriculture, and limited wage labor), textile production sustains most area families (see Cohen 1999, Stephen 1991b). However, all households are not equal, and conflicts exist both within each community and between Teotitlán and Santa Ana. First, households are in competition with one another for a share of the local and export markets for textiles (Cohen 1998, Stephen 1991b). Second, the market is itself in a constant state of flux as tastes and styles change among buyers (Wood 1996). Third, jealousies abound between the villages and households and among members of the same family (see El-Guindi and Selby 1976). Jealousy is rooted in any number of factors, most important of which is the fact that not all weavers are able to produce the same quality of finished work. Whereas some weavers are limited because they lack the resources (larger looms and the money to cover raw materials) to weave high-quality tapetes, others simply lack the skill to produce for the high end. Fourth, the contracted worker does not control his or her schedule, or manage his or her time as freely as the independent producer and therefore is often restricted from participating in development projects like the cooperatives discussed below. Fifth and finally, economic competition exists as only one aspect of daily life and is paralleled by contests for social status and prestige (Cohen 1999). Craft production in the central valley is a complex process, one that is tied to global market trends as well as local jealousies, the push and pull of competing weavers, and the problematic relationships that exist among the various weaving communities.

UNCERTAINTY, COMPETITION, AND THE MARKET

An unbalanced and unequal relationship exists between Teotitlán and Santa Ana. A combination of geography, economy, and history has left Santañero textile producers at a disadvantage to their neighbors in Teotitlán. Santa Ana's location a bit farther from the city of Oaxaca and the lack of direct access by bus conspire to limit the number of tourists who will venture to the village. In contrast, Teotitlán's position nearer the city and the availability of regular bus and taxi service facilitate tourist and buyer access. Teotitlán's history as a population and political center throughout the colonial period and since independence has also contributed to its higher profile. Teotitlán and Teotiteco middlemen and women dominate the local industry, controlling access to the market (Stephen 1991a, 1993). Most Santañeros cannot compete equally for business.[4] According to Santañeros, Teotiteco middlemen and women regularly pay or bribe tour guides and taxi drivers, and promise a percentage of sales if they will avoid Santa Ana.

Teotitecos and Santañeros compete with each other (within and between the communities) for market shares, links to exporters, and tourist dollars. If the option is available, households respond by moving into independent production and by establishing direct ties to exporters in the United States. Those weavers with limited skill and capital look for the best patrones and the most advantageous contracts. Other producers respond by organizing cooperatives or associations to spread risk and better meet market demand (see Stephen 1991a). A group of Santañeros (largely made up of successful independent producers) organized the Artisans' Society of Santa Ana del Valle and work directly with the Instituto Nacional Indigenista (INI, National Indigenous Institute) and the Instituto Nacional de Antropologia e Historia (INAH, National Institute for Anthropology and History) in efforts to circumvent Teotitlán's market control (Cohen 1998).

THE ARTISANS' SOCIETY

Santañeros established the Artisans' Society of Santa Ana del Valle in 1987 with three goals: first, to develop access to the export market for local textiles; second, to gain experience and training in management; and third, to expand the local market for textiles with the development of the village museum and gallery.[5] The society accomplished most of its objectives by 1992, although with limited market success. Unfortunately, during the intervening years, membership in the society has declined in response to poor sales from nearly one hundred active participants representing more than fifteen families at its founding in 1987 to only about a dozen individuals from four families by late 1993. Although the decline of the society remains a concern for the membership, the group has used the society to increase local control of production and sales and to circumvent some of Teotitlán's market control of raw materials as well as finished textiles (see Cohen 1998).

The society was founded to market locally made textiles in a more successful way. Society members quickly established a small retail market area on the western side of the village plaza to sell weavings in 1988. The price of all goods included a 5 percent markup to cover society expenses (rent of space and the cost of utilities). Any extra funds were put into the development of a color brochure, which the society hoped to publish to advertise local weavers, and into the purchase of bulk yarns, dyes, and cotton warp thread. The market was run in a cooperative fashion. Each society member or someone from the member's family spent a day watching the market once every two weeks. Most members freed their schedules by removing their children from school and leaving them to watch the market for the day. There were weeks when no one visited the society's market, though. A typical Sunday included at least one small tour bus visiting the community's museum (usually after a stop at Tlacolula's Sunday market), however, and tourists inevitably stopped to purchase tapetes at the society's market.

The society purchased two trucks to facilitate marketing and opened a new store by converting an abandoned home abutting the pan-American highway and just west of Tlacolula in November 1995. The society's families contributed time and effort to decorate the new building, landscape the grounds, and stock the shelves. They donated examples of natural dye sources, raw materials, and various finished weavings for sale and display. Unaffiliated families who wanted to participate in the store objected that they could not trust the society to sell their wares. In response, society members argued that the store was primarily for those invested in the group's well-being. The situation became quite tense and was never settled. However, as the store opened, members were inclusive rather than exclusive in their organization of stock to sell and decided collectively to accept work from any interested weavers in the village.

Society members planned to operate a café in their shop without the managerial or financial support (and what informants described as "meddling") of Union de

Organizaciones de Pueblos Indígenas (UOPI, Union of Indian Village Organizations) or INI. Unfortunately, although many society members had worked in restaurants as emigrants to the United States, the café demanded a great deal more experience, time, and energy than anyone had anticipated. It also demanded more capital than society members had on hand. With no outside backers to fund the purchase of quality appliances and new fixtures, it was never successfully opened. The gallery closed two months after its formal opening in November, leaving a poorly organized space and a legacy of only a small handful of visitors who had entered the shop. The society hoped to reorganize the gallery and café in 1996 with INI support. The café was turned over to an independent restaurateur, and a full-time sales staff was hired to manage the store and free weavers to pursue their craft.

Attracting potential buyers and the typical day-trippers to a village is not enough to stimulate the local economy. The largest source of income for area weavers is the sale of tapetes to exporters (Bailón Corres 1979). To expand local opportunity and move into the broader market for a variety of textiles (from high-priced one-of-a-kind items to low-priced "tourist" designs) and to compete with wealthier weavers and merchants in Teotitlán, the society petitioned state organizations, such as Fondo Nacional para el Fomento de las Artesanías (FONART), for loans to improve the local production and increase access to lower-priced materials. Funds granted by FONART went to the purchase of large looms for village weavers.[6]

The society used the funds to purchase new looms for weavers on a first come, first served basis. An early problem for the group was that the demand for funds outpaced available funds. The society coped with the problem by defining the need of prospective weavers. However, the funds tended to go to families already involved in independent production and to weavers who already had informal ties to exporters in the market for larger textiles.[7] More successful for the society was the use of loans to purchase prespun and predyed yarns in bulk. Buying wool directly helped Santañeros avoid the *fabrica* in Teotitlán and its price markup. Nevertheless, families who maintained mano de obra relationships with patrones in Teotitlán did not partake as fully of this support as independent weavers. The society also began to use FONART stores and Artesanías Industrias Populares del Estado de Oaxaca (ARIPO, Crafts and Popular Industries of Oaxaca) galleries to sell textiles in Oaxaca City and throughout the country. Finally, and perhaps most successfully, society members established direct export relationships with two gallery owners in the United States (one in San Marcos, Texas, the other in Denver, Colorado). These ties developed as exporters came to Santa Ana in search of new sources for woven goods. The exporters were looking for new weaving sources and, according to one buyer, a way to avoid Teotiteco middlemen and women who were asking higher prices than their Santañero counterparts.

THE MUSEUM

A second project that also has importance for the production and sale of local textiles is the Shan-Dany Museum founded in 1986. The museum was established through the collective efforts of INAH and the local community. Originally organized to document the pre-Colombian history of the area, the Shan-Dany quickly grew to become a center for the documentation of contemporary history, ritual practice, and craft production (CMSD 1992, Morales Lersch and Camarena Ocampo 1987).

The museum was founded to house artifacts encountered during the renovation of Santa Ana's plaza. Modeled after the rural museum established by INAH at San Jose el Mogote (in the northern or Etla arm of the central valley of Oaxaca), the Shan-Dany was to be little more than a storage site for the remains of two burials and other artifacts from local sites. At about the same time, INAH officials began to organize a community museum program based on Soviet and French models that aimed to build state society and document local traditions (Vázquez Rojas 1991). The institute had originally approached leaders in Teotitlán to discuss their village as a probable site for a community museum. Infighting, mistrust, and a lack of interest on the part of the community led INAH to shift to Santa Ana, where connections to political leaders eased the way for the project's early success (Morales Lersch and Camarena Ocampo 1987, 1991).[8] The mission of the museum was expanded in consultations between local leaders, INAH officials, and the local population. The museum was reorganized not only to document the past, but to act as a center for education, protection of local traditions, and the active promotion of local crafts (Morales Lersch and Camarena Ocampo 1991).

The village was involved in all phases of the museum's organization, and a five-member committee (that became an officially sanctioned community committee and part of the village's secular *cargo* system) was created. Three galleries were established (again in cooperation between the village and INAH) to document the pre-Colombian roots of the village, the Mexican Revolution and Santa Ana's role in the revolution, and the weaving traditions of the village. The society took an active role in the museum and participated in the organization of the gallery documenting textile production. Promoters were brought in from INI to train the staff and to instruct in the basic management skills needed to succeed in the textile market. Over the years, additional galleries have been added. In 1992, a special display of unique or family artifacts and heirlooms was established (the display is called "the piece of the month"); a display documenting local traditional ritual dance was organized; and a gallery for school-age children to display museum-related work was opened.

The museum is an important resource for the community and a place where village pride and communal identity are highlighted. It has also played a minor role in the local economy. First, it confers an institutional sense of authenticity to local weaving. The history of Santañero textile production is carefully documented to meet the often heard criticisms of Teotiteco merchants, who describe Santa Ana as a second-rate town. Second, the museum has participated in extensive exchanges throughout the state, the country, and the world, opening the door to new markets. Third, it is a place where Santañeros celebrate themselves and create a powerful image of what it means to be Santañero and where younger members of the community have taken an active role in the documentation of their past (see Cohen 1997, Lavine 1992). Finally, it is a venue where contradictory viewpoints concerning the village and its future are voiced (see, for example, Gaither 1992). In this respect, the Shan-Dany is a place where women voice their concerns over the rise in immigration and where the tense relationship with state authority is mediated through dialogue and cooperation (also see Kaplan 1993).

ANTHROPOLOGY, OUTSIDERS, AND THE MARKET FOR OAXACAN TEXTILES

An additional factor in the structure of the local economy for Oaxacan textiles is the outsider who participates in the selling, promotion, and study of Zapotec weavings. Many of these outsiders are dealers who have little regard for the well-being of local producers and instead see the villages of Teotitlán and Santa Ana as little more than *maquiladoras* or factories that serve an external market (Wood 1996). Other dealers work closely with local producers in more and less exploitative ways to make a living while enhancing the economic well-being of local producers (see Stephen 1993).[9]

In addition, INI and INAH officials and promoters have also worked closely with the communities and various groups within each community to build managerial and commercial skills. Programs begun by INI were aimed at "rationalizing" the local textile economy. The goal was to train weavers to manage household finances better, to begin to quantify better the efforts spent in production, and finally to have an idea of the costs of weaving (from the costs of raw materials to time invested in production). The outcome of these sessions was that weavers began to think more carefully about the price asked for their finished pieces. Officials in INAH were less interested in the economics of production and more concerned with the culture of weaving. They worked closely with weavers and the Shan-Dany Museum to tell the story of Oaxaca's woven arts, in part to wrap the weavings coming out of Santa Ana and other villages in an aura of authenticity and historical process (see Casteñeda 1997, Cohen 1990, Kaplan 1993, Wood 1995).

Working against INI projects were the mistrust locals felt for most governmental programs; the mismatch of young, female promoters with older, male textile producers; and the belief—particularly among younger, independent weavers in Santa Ana—that the best way to gain market share was by undercutting (at nearly any cost) Teotitlán's prices. Weavers believed tourists would always choose to pay less. (I suggested to them that tourists shop not simply for price, but also for quality. Pricing a finished work too low risked alienating tourists, who would doubt the quality and craftsmanship of Santañero tapetes.) In addition, the stories created by the museum and told by Santañeros to visiting tourists and dealers were regularly challenged in Teotitlán. Teotiteco middlemen and women described Santañeros as less-able weavers, as producers of inferior goods, and as a group lacking in the innovative designs and motifs that make for high-quality textiles. Unfortunately, Santañeros do tend to produce a larger portion of average to low-quality textiles, which, however, is largely because of patron-client relationships and the overwhelming number of contract weavers present in the village. Thus, economic need trumps artistic ability, and fewer Santañeros are able to weave high-end goods. Furthermore, poorly made tapetes in Teotitlán are often described as coming from Santa Ana, reinforcing the negative image of the village.

Into this fray anthropologists venture, but only with great care. My own role in the production, sale, and promotion of weavings was low key at best. I took a larger role in the village museum, where I worked closely with its committee and programs (see Cohen 1997). Nevertheless, I tried to move weavers away from underselling themselves in the name of competition with Teotitlán. I also made a concerted effort to get tourists to the villages, particularly Santa Ana if they planned a visit to Oaxaca. It is an uneasy situation. I have worked in one fashion or another with approximately one hundred households in Santa Ana—conducting interviews, surveys, and so forth. Nevertheless, it is impossible to promote every home to visitors. Instead, I have suggested that visitors patronize the society's marketplace or visit those families with whom I have established close relationships. These meetings do not always work, and more than once Santañeros have been angry with me for sending visitors who did not purchase textiles. Additionally, I have been careful to tell the people I send to the villages not to expect a special discount, and I encourage villagers not to drop prices on my account; rather, I typically suggest they should charge more.

Working with the Shan-Dany is less problematic, and the museum is a less divisive resource for the community. My role in the museum has included acting as an impromptu guide for visiting tourists who speak only English, translating museum materials, and aiding in village documentary projects. Most of my photographs from research are housed in the museum, and copies of all of my work are also stored there. In the future, I hope to continue this relationship and build on my role in the preservation and reproduction of village traditions and society.

CONCLUSIONS

Textile production in Teotitlán and Santa Ana is big business. Thousands of finished weavings are sold locally and exported to markets around the world. Income, although difficult to estimate, is likely in the millions of dollars annually (Stephen 1993). It should come as little surprise that weavers compete to gain advantage in an ever-changing market. They cooperate with each other, depend on the unpaid labor of children, and organize into more and less formal groups to improve their standing (Cook and Binford 1990). Santañeros and Teotitecos use the cooperatives to spread risk and better control the costs of production and the prices of finished goods (Esman and Uphoff 1984). Community museums (particularly the Shan-Dany) also play an important role in the ways handmade Zapotec textiles are packaged for sale and consumption (Kaplan 1993). Finally, the state becomes involved in Teotiteco and Santañero business practices through INI, INAH, and various other state-run agencies that hope to promote local economic development and capitalize on the continued importance of international tourism.

In the analysis of craft production, specialists as well as local producers often look for "silver bullets"—in other words, the project or market strategy that will bring an advantage, gain market shares, or reduce risk. There is a desire among activists and often a need among locals that a project such as the Artisans' Society of Santa Ana del Valle will solve many of the problems facing the indigenous community. And certainly, the society benefits those households that are able to participate. Indigenous society, like any dynamic group, is involved in a constant struggle for power and responds (sometimes well, sometimes not so well) to external market forces and economic pressures (see Cohen 1998). However, the challenge remains, first, how to aid groups such as the society, while not ignoring those members of a community who cannot afford the social and economic costs of participation (in Santa Ana, this includes many contract weavers), and second, how to foster market access and in the process encourage a community's continued economic growth.

NOTES

[1] There is little evidence of weaving in the pre-Columbian record for Santa Ana. However, early colonial records note the production of cotton goods in the village (Vásquez Dávila, Vásquez, and Solís 1992).

[2] Data from the 1970s indicates that the local sale of textiles accounted for only 10 percent of the total income generated through weaving (Bailón Corres 1979, 100). In 1990, there were 344 weavers working as independent producers, contract weavers (following mano de obra), and employees in Santa Ana. Surveys in 1993 indicated an average income of approximately U.S.$60 per week per weaver (or just more than U.S.$3,000 annually) in the village. Thus, textile production generated a total income of more than U.S.$1,030,000 for the village. Nevertheless, weaving is typically described as a way to secure a living, not to expand one's household income or increase economic standing.

[3] Stephen (1987) estimates as much as one-third of the households in Teotitlán are active in some type of middlemen activities.

[4] Scott Cook and Leigh Binford (1990) give two reasons for Santa Ana's subordinate position to Teotitlán (89). Their first argument, which is unfounded, suggests that weaving has a longer tradition in Teotitlán than it does in Santa Ana. Even if this is true, which is difficult to prove, Santañeros have been weaving for much of the century, and the technique is not difficult to master. Their second reason, that Santañeros are involved in mano de obra relationships with merchants in Teotitlán, is more significant. As noted above, most Santañeros lack the capital to invest in the production of high-quality, one-of-a-kind weavings that attract high prices. It is also important to recognize that weavings produced in Santa Ana are never identified as such in Teotitlán. Tourists want to buy handmade goods directly from the artisan, and the Teotiteco merchants present the goods from Santa Ana as if they were made at home by a member of one of the merchants' families (see Wood 1995). Alternatively, they regularly describe poor-quality weavings, no matter the source, as the product of Santañero producers. Winn (1976) uses the example of small-scale textiles producers in Chile to argue that nongovernmental organization and state-based training programs can be important settings through which local producers learn managerial skills and develop an understanding of market economics.

[5] Building worker participation and enfranchising local producers into market systems are difficult goals in the best of situations. Nevertheless, when programs work, they can lead to the rethinking of local industry. Based on his work on the Chilean textile industry during the Allende administration, Winn (1976) notes that programs successfully included worker, management, union, and government participation and led quickly to improved conditions on factory floors, increased pay, and a lessening of social inequality among workers and between workers and management.

6   Looms in the community typically measure from 180 to 200 centimeters wide. The new looms measure up to 600 centimeters wide. In the past, a tapete of more than a standard width was made by stitching together separate tapetes. However, consumers in the market for area rugs do not want a thick seam on the floor, and the larger looms allow weavers to complete tapetes that lay flat, are larger, and bring a higher price.

7   This highlights what Black (1991), among others, identifies as one key problem of cooperatives: they tend to assist people who are in a fairly strong economic position, or, in other words, the poorest sectors of the community tend to gain little from such projects. Society members argued it made little sense to give money to unproven weavers who would not invest wisely or fail to gain any economic advantage.

8   Teotitlán did open its own museum in 1994 at the site of its "progresso" market (a textile market found on the village's plaza). The museum presents Teotitlán's history, traditional culture, and weaving, much like its Santañero counterpart.

9   Many exporters treat local weavers with little more than contempt and will abuse social relationships with producers to increase profits. On the other hand, there are dealers who are genuinely concerned with the well-being of Santañero and Teotiteco weavers, and will go out of their way to aid the communities in the practice of "fair trade" (see, for example, Grimes, this volume). Finally, there is nothing that says local cannot abuse local. Middlemen and women living in Santa Ana and Teotitlán have also been known to become quite abusive of the weavers with whom they work. Certain patrones had reputations as less than honest in Santa Ana. One part-time buyer in Santa Ana was typically described as a "last resort" because of the low prices he paid for finished goods. He was a person to whom a producer would sell only when all other avenues were exhausted or a family was desperate for pesos.

KATHY M'CLOSKEY

9. "PART-TIME FOR PIN MONEY"

THE LEGACY OF NAVAJO WOMEN'S CRAFT PRODUCTION

The challenges posed by globalization and free trade unite the authors of this volume in their concerns for the peoples they have encountered in their research. Through my work with the Navajo, I have also discovered evidence of these dual threats. This is not a recent phenomenon for them but an unwritten story that goes back to the formation of the reservation by the U.S. government in 1868. Witherspoon (1987) conservatively estimates that one hundred thousand Navajo women wove more than one million blankets and rugs over the past two centuries (41). My research arose from the need to explain the gap between the wealth of production and the dearth of knowledge concerning the conditions under which these women labored.[1]

Looking to anthropology for answers, I discovered that weavers are missing from history. Many publications typically highlight historic collections owned by individuals or museums. Weavers' hidden history is all the more remarkable because the Navajo comprise the largest indigenous population north of the Rio Grande (250,000 with some 30,000 weavers) and are considered to be one of the most intensely studied peoples. Not only have women's economic contributions been airbrushed from history, but few scholars until very recently acknowledged the critical role that weaving played in relation to cultural survival (Witherspoon 1987). Concerned with unearthing this convoluted story, I reveal in this chapter how thousands of Navajo weavers were sacrificed to free trade over a century ago as their prodigious production became a lucrative buffer for reservation traders faced with volatile oscillations in the international wool markets after 1870. The ideology of Navajo weavers' work as primarily "domestic" has masked the relations that link their labor to economic policies legislated by the nation-state.

My research links microlevel relations to macrolevel commodity markets and reveals how I made the shift from simply being engrossed as a weaver with counting warp threads to realizing that the multiple appropriations Navajo weavers have endured for more than a century concern social justice. The Navajo occupy the bottom rung of the rural poor in the United States (Drummond 1998), and the treatment of women's textile production as an alternative way to market wool contributed to their sustained impoverishment. Today, contemporary Navajo weaving is in crisis, but it is a silent crisis. The theme of this book provides a forum to critique the construction of

Navajo textile history. My chapter explores the consequences of the significant silences from the academy in response to multiple appropriations of weavers' patterns and production, and reveals the harmful effects of those appropriations on contemporary weavers. Although thousands of Navajo face the same constraints as most producers in developing areas, the oversize coffee table publications on Navajo textiles provide a false sense of economic well-being that is unsupported by primary evidence. The information in this chapter critiques this myth of prosperity and reveals how the personal became political. The latter part of the chapter highlights my proactive stance to counter the inimical effects of the silence.

Several years ago, a friend forwarded a Sotheby's 1991 catalog containing a valuable collection of historic Navajo weaving appraised at more than one million dollars. One pair of portieres (drapes used in a doorway to divide two rooms) was estimated at forty thousand dollars. They had been woven nearly a century ago by the ancestors of today's Navajo, as described by Montoya (1996):

> In winter and summer, the scene is often the same. Inside dirt floor hogans small
> children struggle against illness that comes with life on this vast and lonely Res-
> ervation. . . . Many need medical care and it is hard to avoid sickness when four
> generations live together in one room with no plumbing or electricity and only
> small wood stoves for heat. . . . Poverty, hunger, untreated sickness, poor living
> conditions, severe winter weather—it all adds up to young lives taken before they
> are lived. Our doctors and nurses see advanced cases of disease almost unheard
> of outside the Reservation. Strep throat, measles, dysentery, hepatitis, respira-
> tory ailments, and TB occur with alarming frequency. We need your help to re-
> duce infant mortality and improve life expectancy. (1)

In this chapter, I explore the connection between the value of old textiles and current poverty levels, and compare this relationship with that of the Zapotec, another group of North American weavers: "most of the new homes being built have bathrooms, kitchens and brick floors. Many have televisions. A large number of families now own automobiles and some have traveled throughout the US to Europe and elsewhere" (Jones 1994, 22).

Both groups of weavers have been differentially affected by globalization. The Montoya quote was extracted from a letter soliciting funds to alleviate diseases aggravated by the poverty on the Navajo Reservation. The Jones quote describes the financial success of a number of Zapotec weavers of Teotitlán del Valle, currently deemed the most economically successful weavers anywhere (Jones 1994, 22; Stephen 1987; Stephen 1996).[2] This chapter explores the linkages between the sustained impoverishment of many Navajo, who live within the borders of the wealthiest country in the world, while entrepreneurs and a select group of third world weavers enjoy material rewards that are the fruits of appropriation. My chapter draws on unpublished historical evidence in tandem with recent interviews to contextualize this information, thereby enabling readers to understand the threats.

HISTORICAL CONTEXT

The Navajo, or Diné, currently occupy a seventeen-million-acre reservation in the southwestern United States. As pastoralists since the sixteenth century, they have subsisted mainly through weaving, wool production, and horticulture. By 1800, the Navajo blanket had become the most valuable commodity in intertribal trade in the Southwest (Dockstader 1976, van Valkenburgh and McPhee 1974). After formation of the reservation in 1868, Navajo self-sufficiency was undermined in part because government-licensed traders fostered a dependence on expendable commodities. By 1890, Navajo flocks produced two million pounds of wool, and wool production more than doubled during the following two decades. Between 1885 and 1915, the Navajo population increased nearly 50 percent, from fifteen thousand to twenty-two thousand (Johnston 1966, 136), yet textile production escalated more than 800 percent. Reservation traders' annual reports to the commissioner of Indian Affairs confirm the escalation in the value of production (no weights are provided), by noting that $24,000 worth of weaving was shipped from the reservation in 1890, and that amount increased to $700,000 by 1910 (Amsden 1975, 182).[3] Baskets created by the Pima rank second in cash valuation at $14,500, confirming government reports that textile production by the Navajo was "the most profitable of the native industries . . . and is done by women in their spare time" (Sells 1913, 36).

Expansion of textile production in the form of rugs increasingly bound weavers to individual traders. Large accounts were drawn against weavers' production, thus assuring a continuing supply of rugs while destroying their bargaining position (Hubbell Papers 1875–1965, M'Closkey 1996b). Traders reaped double benefits from two-way commodity trade as they engaged in "credit saturation" facilitated by geographic isolation and territorial monopoly. For decades, the per capita income of the Navajo has remained at 20 percent of the national average (Downer and Klesert 1990, 201). The dearth of information on the escalation in Navajo textile production, which has far outstripped the productivity of all other Native American groups combined in "craft" and "renewable resource" categories, is all the more remarkable given the fact that the products of the Navajo loom were valued at one million dollars annually by 1930. This dollar amount translates to an estimated thirty million dollars today (Derks 1990). It seems highly unlikely that discussion of such productivity would remain absent from contemporary publications on indigenous peoples. Indeed, one could argue that such productivity in tandem with sustained impoverishment may be the North American equivalent to the situation of the lacemakers of Narsapur (Mies 1982). The wool produced by the Navajo *churro* sheep met direct competition from carpet-grade wool imported duty-free from abroad. Navajo women's textile production provided a lucrative means for traders to buffer the fluctuations in unstable wool markets internationally.

Navajo weavers were visibly present throughout the country because they were frequently depicted in well-publicized photographs and postcards facilitating the burgeoning tourist market. Indeed, they became the archetype of industrious Indian womanhood. The weavers, however, remained substantively absent from the political economy literature. Traders, such as Lorenzo Hubbell of Ganado, Arizona, are acknowledged as having rescued weaving from decline as they developed off-reservation markets. The Navajo wearing blanket was transformed into a rug as trade blanket manufacturers appropriated the form, materials, and designs. Through traders, these commercial enterprises sold thousands of manufactured blankets to Native Americans formerly provisioned by Navajo weavers. The "golden age" of the American Indian trade blanket reigned from 1880 to 1930 and ironically parallels the precipitous decline in economic returns to Navajo weavers (Kapoun 1992, M'Closkey 1996b).

DOUBLE JEOPARDY

Unlike the produce of peasants in underdeveloped regions, which is consumed shortly after harvest, the prodigious production by Navajo women historically has come back to haunt contemporary producers. Textiles woven after 1870 were originally acquired from weavers by weight for nearly a century (Hubbell Papers 1875–1965). Today they are continually being recycled in the collectors' and investors' markets, depressing the demand for contemporary textiles. Millions of dollars of historic weaving have sold over the past three decades, initially spurred by the international tour of nineteenth-century textiles culled from the collections of famous painters (*American Indian Art*

Magazine 1972–98, Kahlenberg and Berlant 1972, Smith 1989). Classic Navajo blankets woven prior to 1870 are now beyond the reach of the average investor; it is truly a fine arts market. Investors are lured by advertisements in *American Indian Art Magazine,* periodic auctions at Sotheby's and Christie's, and ethnographic antiquities markets in Santa Fe, New Mexico, and elsewhere.

Thousands of Navajo weavers are faced with dual threats, however. It was fortuitous that the arts and crafts movement of a century ago coincided with the transition from blanket to rug when Navajo weaving was popularized by reservation traders. The most recent resurgence in popularity, which occurred during the early 1970s, planted the seeds of the present predicament. The southwestern look became the rage. Because no cooperatives existed to help weavers, rugs sold almost exclusively through traders and retailers.[4] Markups typically ranged from 300 to 500 percent.

In 1987, Gloria Duus, director of the Office of Navajo Women and Families in Window Rock, Arizona, distributed a questionnaire that surveyed the feasibility of organizing weaving cooperatives on the reservation. Four hundred copies of the lengthy questionnaire were distributed to weavers living in ten areas. Only 4 percent of the weavers surveyed had received more than $2,500 in cash or goods for their weavings the previous year. More than 70 percent of the weavers who responded "earned" $600 or less. Sixty percent of the women used wool from their flocks, and more than 90 percent made their own tools (or family members made them). Nearly two hundred women had been weaving for more than fifteen years (and were thus experienced weavers), and 65 percent of these women were older than thirty-six years of age. Nearly 75 percent of the women still took their rugs to the trading post. The picture of the situation presented in *Harmony by Hand: Art of the Southwest Indians,* published the same year, provides a striking contrast to Duus's unpublished study. Author Sarah Nestor (1987) comments on how contemporary Navajo weavers had difficulty meeting the demands of collectors and how the prices of their textiles continued to rise in consequence (58).

TRACKING THE DROP IN DEMAND

Within the last ten years, I have noted the similarity between prices for early-twentieth-century Navajo textiles and contemporary weavings at southwestern retail outlets and trading posts. This overlap in prices means that current Navajo weavers face competition not only from fellow weavers, but also from their ancestors. Collectors frequently choose older weavings over new rugs because they are attracted by the nostalgia associated with owning a piece of "history." Concerned about the economic repercussions for contemporary weavers, I interviewed thirty women on the Navajo Reservation during 1992. Several weavers were very candid, noting that collectors and dealers were paying them approximately 40 percent less than they had received five years previously for the same quality textile. However, the market had been very strong during the late 1970s and early 1980s. In 1981, Lea Lundburg published "Threads of Tradition" in *Arizona Living* magazine. She interviewed southwestern retailers who claimed to have the largest selection of Navajo rugs in the world. The cost of rugs was increasing at approximately 20 percent annually: "prices have doubled in the last five years" (17). This price increase followed on the publication of a special issue of the popular *Arizona Highways* magazine. Published during the gasoline shortages of the early 1970s, the 1974 issue featured contemporary Navajo weaving. Other issues that year featured Indian pottery, baskets, and jewelry. When the fuel shortages eased, tourists flocked to the Southwest, precipitating another "Indian craze." The jewelry craze peaked in the late 1970s, and the rug craze continued for several more years.

During the early 1980s, articles on the healthy markets for both historic and contemporary Navajo weaving appeared with some frequency. A long article appeared in the November issue of *The Indian Trader* and concluded that the market for rugs seemed stronger than that for jewelry and pottery. Rug sales were expected not to "peak for quite some time. . . . it should stay 'very healthy' for a long time" (Link 1980, 3). Retail prices appeared to have doubled from 1975 to 1980 or, in some cases, within two years. One long-time reservation trader remarked on the increase in foreign tourists who "appreciate the craft involved in weaving a rug . . . [as] the world is losing our traditional art forms" (Link 1980, 3). A dealer remarked that he could sell three to four times as many rugs if he could find them. Those halcyon days were short-lived.

Prices for contemporary Navajo textiles stalled and then decreased in 1984. Arnold (1988) queried antique textile dealer Joshua Baer about the market for contemporary Navajo weaving. He admitted that contemporary textiles "fluctuated in value" (41). According to Baer, the market peaked in 1982–83 and dropped 25 to 30 percent after 1984. Another dealer, active since 1972, said he had never seen the historic rugs drop in value while he has been in the business. He remarked that rugs woven between 1900 and 1940 were still available "at good prices . . . between $500 to $1,200" (Arnold 1988, 41). The individuals interviewed agreed that it did not matter whether a buyer invests in a new or an old rug; the important thing is quality. Another dealer claimed that the current market for classics is a "fine art market" (Johnson 1980–99). The nineteenth-century classics are now available only through auctions or private dealers. Most traders and dealers admit that it may take from twenty to thirty years for a contemporary rug to appreciate in value, and the market for contemporary weaving has declined precipitously over the past fifteen years.

WORRIED WEAVERS' VOICES

The drop in demand for contemporary weaving in the late 1980s is borne out in other articles published in *The Indian Trader* and in stories related to me by Navajo weavers. One woman, whose rugs are depicted in a popular publication, was deeply concerned about the devaluation of her work by an active collector-dealer who previously paid her more than $1,100 per rug. Within the last five years, he not only purchased her rugs less frequently, but refused to pay her more than $700 for a textile of equivalent quality. Because her daughter and son-in-law had to move to Phoenix to find jobs, she has to raise three of her grandchildren and worries how she will support them. The dealer has also become increasingly active in the investment market for historic Navajo weaving. He and his counterparts in other areas of the Southwest can keep prices low because the market for contemporary Navajo weaving is oversaturated. Consequently, weavers continue to have a difficult time finding dealers who will purchase their weavings at equitable prices.

A Navajo woman temporarily residing in Phoenix provides a sobering example of the economic squeeze endured by weavers. This woman comes from a family of relatively well-known weavers and jewelers. In 1991, she accompanied her sister to one of the largest off-reservation dealers of Navajo rugs. Her sister had woven a two-by-three-foot fine rug of her own handspun yarn with an intricate pattern. The gallery owner inquired as to how much she thought her rug was worth. The woman replied, "Six hundred dollars." He answered, "You've got to be kidding; I'll give you twenty-five dollars." Shocked, they turned to leave, and he said, "Well, I'll give you fifty dollars."

Unfortunately, such stories are not rare. I have documented several other situations in which weavers were offered the equivalent of "a nickel an hour" for their handspun textiles. Weavers also admitted that traders and dealers compared their rugs to the work of other weavers and commented on the continual need for "improvement" to perfect their weaving. This type of comment is repeated in examples given by weavers interviewed as part of an oral history project in the Ganado area (Begay 1986, Brugge 1970). It appears to be a standard refrain used by traders and dealers to pressure women to accept less cash or goods in exchange for their textiles (see also Milgram in press). Although weavers resent it when traders make derogatory comments about their work in comparison to textiles woven by other Navajo, there is little they can do about it.

In conversations with weavers on several occasions, I was told stories of how their mother's weavings were placed on the wool scale to assess the selling price. In one story, a woman acknowledged as a "master weaver," who raised her eleven children by her weaving, related how she needed cash when her husband required medical attention. She had spent nearly a year spinning wool from her own sheep, then dyeing the wool, and weaving a room-size rug. Several traders refused to pay her cash, insisting on trade. In 1968, the trader at Black Hat paid her $250 for the rug. Today a similar rug of superb quality woven of handspun wool would sell for more than $40,000 in a gallery. Several weavers related how they have told Anglos about "pound blankets and rugs" woven by themselves or by their relatives, but the Anglos do not believe them!

RUG AUCTIONS ON THE RESERVATION

Periodically, rug auctions are held on the Navajo Reservation at various "chapter houses." The best-known auction, formerly held quarterly, is the Crownpoint rug auction, now held monthly in a school gymnasium in northwestern New Mexico. The auction is currently the only nonprofit Navajo-run market for textiles held on a regular basis. It was begun during the 1960s by the trader at Crownpoint who was discouraged by the six to eight dollars that local weavers averaged for their rugs (Conner 1991, 46). For a time, the Bureau of Indian Affairs superintendent and the trader supervised the auction.

During the 1970s, as market conditions improved, the auction grew in popularity, and it continues to be popular today. As many as three hundred to six hundred rugs may be brought to each auction. Weavers suggest the minimum acceptable bid, and receive 85 percent of the proceeds. The woven products range from single saddle blankets (thirty-six inches square) to room-size rugs. Depending on weather and time of year, several hundred people crowd into the gym to watch or participate in the bidding. Ed Chamberlain, curator at Hubbell Trading Post, Ganado, Arizona, has tracked sales at Crownpoint. The average price of a Navajo textile has increased from $225 in 1991 to $256 in 1998. Only a small percentage of rugs elicit volatile bidding. Rugs that do not meet opening bids are retrieved by their makers at the end of the evening. Clearly, weavers are not benefitting from brisk sales of their work.

Evidence from varying sources reveals the drop in demand from dealers and the public at large for contemporary Navajo weaving. My interviews with weavers, traders, and off-reservation dealers corroborate the downturn in the market. One southern Colorado dealer who was part of a panel at a Heard Museum conference in 1994 admitted that "the market is no longer there." In the recent past, he frequently had to decline fine textiles brought to him by excellent weavers because their previous creations still remained in his stockroom.

CONTINUED APPROPRIATIONS OF PATTERNS

Navajo weavers have faced dual threats affecting the market for their work for more than a century. Their loss of control over the marketing of their textile production is similar to the constraints faced by indigenous producers described by some of the other contributing authors of this volume. For example, by 1885, researchers and curio dealers were avidly collecting historic Navajo textiles acquired from traders such as Lorenzo Hubbell. Correspondence between Lorenzo Hubbell and Herman Schweizer of the Fred Harvey Company in 1910 reveals that the latter was importing "well-woven greys" from Mexico that were much cheaper than Navajo weaving (Hubbell Papers, box 37, June 6, 1910).

Today, copy or imitation knockoffs of Navajo weaving are imported from Guatemala, Peru, Hong Kong, India, Pakistan, Japan, northern Thailand, Romania, and, in particular, Mexico. David Brugge (1971) surveyed six stores on the Interstate Highway in New Mexico and five stores in Gallup, a town just east of the Navajo Reservation. Most stores carried the "copy" weaving. Some of the copies were mixed in with the genuine rugs. Brugge (1971) found that the imitations sold at prices well below the prices for Navajo textiles, which gives Navajo weavers "unfair competition and undermines the public's confidence in the craft" (3). The Mexican rugs are also woven of handspun wool yarn, with designs that are quite similar (Dockstader 1976, 475). Most copies are single and double saddle blanket sizes, up to four by six feet. Currently, the Zapotec are weaving variants of the Yei patterns, taken from the Navajo ceremonials. There are differences between the techniques utilized in making the side cords and the top and bottom selvages that a knowledgeable individual can spot. However, by simply looking through a pile of rugs without carefully checking, buyers can be easily fooled into thinking they are purchasing a genuine Navajo rug. Noel Bennett (1973) provides information on how to determine if a rug is a Navajo textile or a knockoff.

More recently, far more sophisticated copies, including the earlier Chief's Blanket styles have been imported from Mexico. These carefully dyed and woven rugs are created by thousands of Zapotec weavers active in "cottage industries" (see Cohen, this volume). Weaving traditions in this region of Mexico date from pre-Columbian times. Zapotec weavers have their own rich repertoire of patterns. However, due to the popularity of the southwestern look, entrepreneurs have provided Zapotec weavers with patterns appropriated from coffee table books on the topic. They import and retail the finished products in the United States and earn profits from 200 to 1,000 percent (Stephen 1993, 47). By law, all woven imports must have a label attached when checked at customs, noting country of origin and materials. Tags sometimes conveniently "fall off" between the customs office and the shops, however. Retail outlets in the Southwest frequently display large signs advertising "Navajo rugs" or "Indian rugs," but only a portion of the shop's stock is the genuine Navajo product. These rugs provide a real threat to the contemporary Navajo textile market because they are priced well below those woven by Navajo weavers.

My recent survey of Taos, New Mexico, retail outlets revealed only two stores carrying contemporary Navajo weaving. Eighteen shops carried only knockoffs (featured as "Native American rugs"), and three galleries had extensive collections of historic Navajo weaving. For example, the nineteenth-century "child's blanket" was priced between eighteen thousand and thirty thousand dollars. Similar ratios exist in other southwestern towns and cities attracting tourists (Brugge 1996). Retailers who own one store in Taos have choreographed the production of Navajo knockoffs from beginning to end. They have appropriated geometric elements frequently incorporated in authentic Navajo textiles, and the designs are universalized as "pan-Indian." Other entrepreneurs oversee the production of high-quality identical copies of nineteenth-century Navajo patterns in sizes ranging from pillow covers to room-size rugs. Anglo entrepreneurs and designers periodically reside with the Zapotec weavers and work to improve the quality of the knockoffs, drawing on an amalgam of New Age and collective unconscious rhetoric to justify their actions (Goin Papers 1996). Such appropriations are not an example of cultural intermingling, but a forced marriage brokered by entrepreneurs.

The poor market for Navajo weavers' creations is evidenced by the low values they receive at auctions and by the decline in the number of retailers who handle contemporary rugs. Both the entrepreneurs selling the knockoffs and the dealers high-lighting historic textiles are well organized and well advertised. Dealers who carry the copy weaving maintain well-stocked booths at nationally advertised home shows cater-ing to interior decorators. Their counterparts advertise in publications such as *Archi-tectural Digest* and send salespeople out to drum up new clients. Some dealers adver-tise on the Internet. Although thousands of weavers currently reside on the Navajo Reservation, they lack access to markets because there are no market towns and no agencies or other infrastructure support, such as the alternative trade organizations described by Grimes, Lynd, MacHenry, and Rosenbaum (this volume). Navajo weav-ers also experience constraints similar to those endured by their third world counter-parts, as demonstrated by both Cohen and Milgram (this volume). The following sec-tion highlights how the "aesthetics of appropriation" have been addressed in the anthropological literature and surveys the repercussions for Navajo weavers.

THE PRODUCTION OF WOVEN COLLECTIBLES BY WOMEN

Prior to the 1970s, anthropologists most often neglected gender as an analytic cat-egory. Navajo weaving has lacked adequate contextualization within Navajo culture because much of the ethnography of the craft was done by previous generations of anthropologists during the heyday of cultural particularism and acculturation (Frazier 1993, Reichard 1968, Underhill 1983). A high percentage of the literature reflects the asymmetry of gender relations as constituted historically in the West because weaving is perceived as women's domestic activity engaged in for practical purposes, nonsacred because materials were borrowed from non-Navajo sources, and dominated by a hand-ful of traders who fathered styles catering to consumer preferences (Amsden 1975, Bailey and Bailey 1986, Kent 1985, Rodee 1996). In contrast, the effects of globaliza-tion and free trade on indigenous third world producers have met with rigorous analy-ses and critiques strengthened by feminist perspectives. Many indigenous groups main-tain vital linkages with nongovernmental organizations (NGOs) and fair trade associations (Nash 1993a, 1994a).

The marked shift in discourse from women as victims of patriarchy and ex-ternal market factors to women as active negotiators demonstrating agency expresses the importance of textiles as a form of cultural identity (Milgram, Eber, this volume). Clifford (1988) has remarked on the accelerating pace of the postmodern world, signified by increasing eclecticism and bricolage: "art collecting and culture collecting now take place within the changing field of counterdiscourses, syncretisms, and re-appropriations, originated both outside and inside 'the West'" (236). With regard to contemporary Latin American textile production, Berlo (1996) similarly argues, "American and European textile designers freely take from native sources. . . . this is part of a long artistic tradition in the West. . . . the contemporary indigenous textile aesthetic is, in many regions, an aesthetic of appropriation and accumulation" (452).

In her research with Zapotec weavers in Teotitlán del Valle, Stephen (1996, 1993) confirms the magnitude of Navajo pattern appropriation. For the past twenty years, entrepreneurs have taken popular Navajo patterns appropriated from ubiquitous books on the subject to Mexico and other parts of the world for local artisans to copy. Stephen (1996) documents the exponential increase in orders for Navajo-style patterns, which kept thousands of Zapotec weavers working overtime during the 1980s. She describes the four levels of production engaged in by Zapotec weavers. The third level comprises "mass produced pieces," up to five by seven feet, that feature several popular designs; Navajo designs currently dominate. These pieces are bought by smaller-scale Mexican and US distributors who run their own businesses. This is the largest sector of the market in Teotitlán. The 1980s were marked by a surge of orders for Navajo designs (1996, 384).

Stephen remarks that because of demand, there is a shortage of weaving labor. Zapotec weavers often have more work than they can handle. She comments that Zapotec weavers do not understand U.S. American taste, but they want to produce what sells. Thousands of weavers effectively produce a technically high-quality product by incorporating elements of foreign design, color, and content into their work. As avid weavers, the Zapotec are able to sustain ritual and kinship obligations within their communities. Stephen (1993) visited the Hubbell Trading Post at Ganado in 1989 and spotted a pamphlet titled "How to Distinguish a Mexican from a Genuine Navajo Rug." She commented that the Navajo weavers present were familiar with Zapotec textiles and "resented the intrusion on their market and the 'stealing' of their designs" (51).

Several recently published texts highlight the effects of globalization on indigenous Latin American weavers (Ehlers 1990, Nash 1993a, Stephen 1996, Tice 1995). Within the last several years, Zapotec weavers have encountered competition from Dhuri rugs woven in India and imported into North America by retail chains, such as Pier One. This recent development graphically demonstrates how appropriated patterns can be appropriated once more by entrepreneurs attempting to fill new market niches and increase their profits (Stephen 1993, 48).

Documentation and confirmation of this appropriative activity without critique sanction an activity that threatens the Navajo lifeways. They also provide an intellectual rationale for equating the symbols of consumerism with emergent types of communal identity. Such commentary evokes the image of anthropologist as neutral observer and reporter of commoditized cultural formation. Such a stance gives intellectual support to acts of appropriation. Harries-Jones (1993) provokes reconsideration of this postmodern position. Noting that neoconservatives require free markets on a global scale to permit the spread of consumerism, he cautions,

> this gives rise to numerous epistemic problems in anthropology especially where there is a spatial divorce of cultural expression from the intimacies of a defined local space in which cultural forms were hitherto socially reproduced . . . to continue to treat culture as epistemological object within a defined space; and to insist that anthropologists remain neutral observers of this context is, in fact, to take an intellectual position about globalization. Such a position allows little room for critique of the process in which commoditized forms of culture are disembedded from active collectivity and marketed through simulations of cultural performance. . . . we need to stand as witnesses, uncovering [such] sets of relations. (9)

The appropriation of popular Navajo patterns is not just a pilfering of pretty designs. It is theft of a way of life. Such appropriation on a massive scale threatens the destruction of activities vital to Navajo culture and perpetuates processes that began more than a century ago.

CONCLUSION

The popularity of the Navajo rug as a collectible continues to obscure the importance of weaving for Navajo people. First-person accounts of weaving have only recently appeared in publications (Begay 1996, Keams 1996, Thomas 1996). Several weavers have expressed reservations about writing down their thoughts about weaving because weaving is not about words; it is about *k'e* or kin relations. The weavers' reticence has left a vacuum that has been quickly filled with publications focusing on Navajo weaving as "art." However, classifying an object as either art or craft becomes a political act because such labeling shapes the object's subsequent history (M'Closkey 1996a). Although historic Navajo weaving has recently been promoted from lowly craft to high art, neither category adequately describes the context of weaving in Navajo society itself, mainly because the Western concept of art and its basic tenet maintains that the essential value of material culture lies outside the context of its meaning and use (M'Closkey 1996b).

Complex patterns of Navajo relations were occluded through the epistemological lens of the colonizers and, later, the ethnographers. The narrative of the origin of the loom and weaving tools as revealed in the Creation Story is frequently referenced at the beginning of texts on Navajo weaving. Authors then describe the facts and relate how everything was borrowed: the loom from the Pueblos, sheep from the Spaniards, dyes and patterns from the traders. Because none of the ingredients are deemed indigenous, most authors disclaim any symbolism or sacred associations attached to the woven textiles. What is suppressed, overtly or covertly, is the acknowledgment of women's provisioning as a core component of k'e. The bifurcation of sacred and profane thrusts Navajo weaving into an alien field. It has become completely disassociated from what ethnographers have designated as Navajo religion (Reichard 1950).

Had weaving been adequately historicized by previous generations of researchers, the investment market may not have enjoyed the success that it has (or at least scholars of southwestern textiles may have thought twice about producing books for collectors and dealers). Instead, narratives relating the quixotic relations between traders and weavers continue to be recycled in the extant literature (Kaufman and Selser 1985, Rodee 1996). The extensive literature on reservation traders contains a treasure trove of information for the nostalgically inclined. Had weaving been appropriately contextualized within Navajo culture, the multiple appropriations of Navajo patterns over the past century—first by trade blanket manufacturers and then by the recent escalation of entrepreneurs wishing to cash in on the southwestern look—would have met with critique. Not only has textile production by Navajo women fallen between the paradigmatic cleavages in anthropology, it has been left vulnerable because geometric patterns are considered part of the "public domain" and not amenable to copyright protection.[5]

Postmodernist readings of cultural reformulations through appropriations demonstrate an attenuated understanding of aesthetics. In order to reconceptualize an alternative interpretation of Navajo weaving, it is necessary to reconfigure the concept of aesthetics that continues to influence Western discourses on forms of material culture. Aesthetic evaluation is perceived to be an individual action exercised in relation to the beauty contained in the isomorphic object, and, as such, it dovetails nicely with Lockean theories of private property undergirding possessive individualism (Coombe 1993, Handler 1997, Tsosie 1997). Only by reformulating outmoded concepts of aesthetics can readers surmise the threat to Navajo lifeways. Because weaving fell between the cleavages in the discipline (the bifurcation between political economy and symbolic spheres), it is impossible to acknowledge adequately, much less critique, the multiple appropriations through referencing most of the extant literature on the subject.

In order to counter the inimical effects of pattern appropriation, I have provided several southwestern politicians with information demonstrating the importance of Navajo textile production to regional merchants historically and have discussed the feasibility of legislation to protect Navajo communal property rights. In 1997, I was interviewed on KTNN, Navajo Nation Radio, and in 1996, I curated "First Nations/ Fine Weavers," funded by Burlington Art Centre, Burlington, Ontario, in collaboration with the Arizona Commission of the Arts. The exhibition toured in the Southwest United States and in southern Ontario. The initial two-year tour was extended until summer 2000. To date, twenty of the initial thirty-three weavings have been sold, and replacements were acquired from individual weavers or Hubbell Trading Post, Ganado. The exhibition documentation and small catalog emphasize how weavings are material manifestations of relationships, and they critique the twin threats posed by the collectors' and knockoff markets. Thus, I continue to make public the linkages between the roots of Navajo impoverishment and the current circumstances of Navajo life.

NOTES

[1] I wish to thank editors Kimberly Grimes and Lynne Milgram, and acknowledge financial support from the Social Science Research Council of Canada; the Zdenka Volavka Fellowship in Art History, York University; and the Newberry Library, Chicago, in the form of a National Endowment for the Humanities postdoctoral award.

[2] See also Cohen (this volume) for more discussion on how Teotitlán weavers achieve their success.

[3] The 1890s figure represents only the value of weaving shipped from the reservation. The Navajo were at that time still weaving for themselves and for intertribal trade to a limited extent. In addition, unlicensed traders operating posts adjacent to the reservation and trading with off-reservation Navajo were not required to file reports; thus, the figures quoted are conservative.

[4] Currently, there are two active weavers' organizations located in the New Mexico portion of the reservation: the Ramah Navajo Weavers' Organization, begun in 1984, and the recently formed Eastern Navajo Weavers' Association, Crownpoint.

5   Recent publications by Coombe (1993), Greaves (1994), Handler (1997), Pask (1993), and Tsosie (1997) provide the context to critique the magnitude of the problem and gauge the consequences of multiple appropriations.

ANDREW CAUSEY

10. THE HARD SELL

ANTHROPOLOGISTS AS BROKERS OF CRAFTS IN THE GLOBAL MARKETPLACE

In 1994, I traveled to North Sumatra, Indonesia, to study the ways that Toba Batak wood-carvers are responding to tastes and desires of souvenir-buying Western tourists.[1] During the fifteen months I lived in the village Huta Mungkap[2] on Samosir Island close to the shore of Lake Toba, I developed a desire to help the carvers find ways to reach a larger audience and thus improve their welfare. Although this motivation to support the Toba Batak wood-carvers was straightforward, the actual implementation of the assistance was both challenging and confusing. Using my own fieldwork interactions with Toba Batak wood-carvers on Samosir Island as a case study, this chapter investigates the sometimes unforeseen difficulties associated with mediating between Western consumers' tastes and desires and artisans' traditions as well as their capacities for change and innovation. My research focuses on touristic sales, but the marketplace I am referring to extends beyond this context and can include venues such as import stores and mail-order catalogs. The opportunity to write this essay also permits me to investigate the work of other anthropologist-brokers working in the Pacific Rim,[3] but I should mention at the outset that this work is an exploration of the problems and possibilities related to the mediation issue rather than a thorough review of the literature. Because this area of investigation is not yet well defined, existing research is often difficult to locate. How can anthropologists successfully broker the crafts of the people with whom they work? In addressing my own experiences, I hope that this short work helps to open up a space for honest and critical examinations of this topic in the future.

WOOD CARVING ON SAMOSIR ISLAND

Lake Toba, in the center of the province of North Sumatra, is one of Indonesia's premier tourist locales. Both domestic and international tourists come to the huge crater lake to escape from the heat of the lowlands and to experience the natural beauty of the surrounding mountains and Samosir Island, which rises up from the middle of the lake. Much of the land surrounding the lake is the ancient homeland of the Toba Batak, one of Indonesia's most numerous ethnic groups. The majority of Toba Batak are subsistence farmers living at or above Indonesia's poverty level. For those fortunate enough to live in one of the few coastal areas frequented by tourists, life can be slightly easier. Many Toba Batak living in these areas open restaurants and guesthouses or supplement their agricultural activities by making souvenir wood carvings for tourists.

Despite the seeming prosperity of Lake Toba's larger towns, the past decade has been difficult for Toba Batak who depend on tourism for their livelihoods. In the late 1970s and early 1980s, their homeland was a favorite haunt of backpack travelers from Europe, North America, and Australia.[4] The situation changed in the mid-1980s, for at the same time that adjacent areas were beginning to attract tourist attention, some unscrupulous Toba Batak hotel owners and vendors tried to take advantage of Western travelers by charging for services not rendered or by selling them inferior merchandise. As often happens in such cases, the news sped down the informal travelers' grapevine. Soon, published guidebooks began warning readers of swindlers and thieves in the Batak area.[5] When I arrived on Samosir in 1994, local people informed me that these problems had been eradicated and that those now doing business were intent on improving their services and the crafts they sold. Tourism again seemed to be on the upswing.

That was before the uncontrollable forest fires on Borneo and Sumatra began to choke lowland cities and mountainous rural areas alike in the summer and fall of 1997; the horrific crash of Garuda Flight GA-152 outside North Sumatra's largest city, Medan, which killed all 238 people on board, was blamed in part on the dense smoke.[6] Despite its high elevation, Lake Toba was not immune from the noxious smoke, and like many areas in Southeast Asia, tourism on Samosir dropped off dramatically (*Waspada* 1998a, 1998b).[7] Although the tumultuous changes that have taken place in Indonesia throughout 1998, such as the economic crisis and the political revolution, may result in future benefits to the people, they have incapacitated tourism throughout the country.[8] Among those hardest hit economically by these dramatic transformations are the Toba Batak wood-carvers of Samosir Island, whose subsistence is derived almost entirely from sales to Western tourists.

Wood carvings are among the most ubiquitous of the souvenirs offered for sale in the tourist marketplaces on Samosir Island, but carving operations remain a household production: all steps of the manufacturing process are performed within a nuclear family, and at the time of my research, there were no village or area cooperatives (as discussed in many of the chapters in this volume). Many Toba Batak males—including adults, teenagers, and adolescents—and even a few females have some knowledge of carving and may produce carvings part-time as a supplement to their family incomes, but actually only a few individuals spend the majority of their time and energy carving. I identified three main carving neighborhoods on the island that are the home to approximately fifteen to twenty full-time carvers and perhaps one hundred part-time carvers.[9] Of this number, at most only ten to fifteen possess the technical expertise and the knowledge of the repertoire of traditional forms necessary to be locally recognized as *tukang ukir* (master carvers). I was very fortunate to locate myself in the village Huta Mungkap, which is home to three master carvers.

Although the wood-carving industry is localized and its workforce limited, it is not inconsequential to the economy and to social relations of the larger community. The artistry of a Toba Batak carver often benefits not only his or her immediate family, but also the hundreds of sales representatives, intermediaries, and vendors who offer the carvings for sale in the local tourist marketplaces and in urban curio shops. When tourism is thriving, a master carver might see his success (and his profits) aiding a number of extended relatives who live outside the main tourist sphere.

In addition, the carvers' work has cultural ramifications. Because the majority of Toba Batak converted to Christianity by the early decades of the twentieth century (Pedersen 1970, 69), much of the impetus was lost for creating carvings such as ancestor figures, water buffalo horn medicine containers, and the shaman's magic staffs. In addition, metal, glass, and plastic household items imported from outside the local area supplanted the bamboo, wood, and pottery implements the people had used earlier. By the 1950s, such changes, exacerbated by deforestation in the Toba Batak homeland, forced wood carving into a severe decline (see Cunningham 1958, 47). According to the carvers with whom I spoke, the only thing that kept the art from becoming extinct was the appearance of tourism in the late 1960s. Westerners wanted souvenirs of their trips to Lake Toba, and, luckily, there were still a few older men who knew how to carve some of the ancestral forms. These days, although it is true that only tourist, not local, interest sustains the carving tradition,[10] it is also true that many Toba Batak are proud of their carved wood patrimony. They appreciate the pre-Christian forms not as evidence of a pagan past, but as examples of their own distinct cultural aesthetic.

When the first wave of tourists came to Samosir in the late 1960s, the business of re-creating traditional objects was far from easy. The experiences of the senior carver in Huta Mungkap, Nalom, is representative. Nalom explains that the early days of the new business were confusing and stressful. He was the only one in his village who knew the characteristics of traditional carvings because as a child he had watched his father carve. The majority of older carvings had been sold or cast off years earlier, so he had very few prototypes to copy. This forced him to depend primarily on his memories of earlier forms. Over time and with practice, he was able to improve the quality of his carvings. Lately, with the help of a Toba Batak merchant on the mainland who has European connections, he has been able to examine antique carvings pictured in Western museum catalogs and books, thus expanding his repertoire of forms. In the thirty years he has been carving, Nalom has served as the sole mentor of a dozen carvers in Huta Mungkap.

To revitalize the art of carving in the early years of tourism, Nalom and other Toba Batak carvers faced a number of problems. Not only did they have to rediscover traditional techniques and forms, but they had to anticipate what Westerners would buy and how to communicate with them. Currently these two problems—what things to make and how to sell them—continue to plague most Toba Batak carvers. When deciding what to make, some carvers limit the variety of forms they make and focus on producing a quantity of moderately priced objects to attract travelers on tight budgets. Others make a wide repertoire of objects, trusting that at least one of the number will find a buyer. Still others restrict their production to copies of antique forms, whereas some carvers create innovative items with the expectation that novelty will catch the eye of a customer (Causey 1999a).

The methods Toba Batak carvers use to market their crafts are also varied. Some carvers expect their wives to sell their handiwork because the marketplace is traditionally considered to be a female realm (Sherman 1990)[11] and because they choose to focus on the production of their crafts; yet a woman who has only an elementary school education or who has difficulty learning the English language independently puts the family economy at a disadvantage because English is the de facto language of commerce in the tourist markets.[12] Consequently, these carving families may decide to sell their items to local middlemen or wholesalers. Although they get less money for their work, they are not forced to engage with Western tourists. If language is not considered to be a problem, the wife of a carver (in some cases the carver himself) displays the crafts in a rented marketplace stall or in a home showroom, bargaining directly with buyers. Many vendors limit their communication to price information, but there are others who try to cater to Westerners' interest in authenticity by providing stories or histories with the works they sell. This sales technique can be effective but is not always predictable (Causey 1999b).

Despite the variety of possibilities for creating and selling wood carvings, few (if any) carvers on Samosir Island have discovered a combination that is successful and dependable, and most remain living in conditions that are close to poverty.[13] Frustrated and desperate, two of the carvers from Huta Mungkap (Nalom and his brother-in-law Partoho) asked me to help them market their products. They wanted insight into the buying habits and preferences of other Westerners; they also wanted information about how they could sell their wares outside the local and highly competitive tourist marketplaces. They knew that my research put me in daily contact with travelers from Europe, North America, and Australia, and surmised that I would be an ideal informant—someone who might understand the visitors' tastes and who could communicate consumer preferences to the carvers using the Indonesian language.

At first, I was conflicted about this arrangement because I felt it would compromise my desire to study their culture without actively changing it. As I considered the situation at greater length, however, I began to question my motives for not wanting to assist the carvers. At one point, I realized that if I were actually interested in their welfare (rather than some preconceived image of their culture as a pristine entity that could be protected), I should address their questions and concerns as honestly as I could, making clear to them nonetheless that I was no more or less an ideal representative of my culture than they were of theirs. As it turns out, I was unable to help them in the ways they wanted, and my cautious efforts often only complicated an already confused situation.[14] Nevertheless, when it came time to leave Samosir, I promised to do whatever I could to help them promote their carvings once I arrived back in Texas. The following story shows how unpredictable and intricate such an intermediary position can be. Although the details of my story are unique, the situation surely resonates with the experiences of other craft-oriented anthropologists. I hope this story helps to illuminate the complexity of consumer tastes and preferences as well as the logistical difficulties of marketing and selling craft items outside the context of a particular culture.

"THE DANCING DOLL IS HIS FORTUNE"

Three months after I had settled down in Huta Mungkap, I checked around for a way to study wood carving. I was not a little surprised when two of the master carvers in the village referred me to a man named Partoho. Although I had chatted with Partoho many times on the road, and his wife Ito was one of the vendors most friendly to me in the marketplace, I did not realize that Partoho was a tukang ukir. The two carvers told me that he was the one who had both the talent and the temperament to teach a Westerner; they told me that he was the one who knew most of the old forms and could also create new ones. "Also," they continued, "he is the one who knows all the stories, all the *ways* to carve." I went down the cobbled road to his house the next day.

I found Partoho putting elaborate *gorga*[15] designs on a dozen powder horns he had made in the antique style. The twelve of them lay on a workbench jumbled with tools, wood shavings, cigarette packs crumpled and torn, and cast-off plastic buckets filled with drill bits and coping-saw blades. The morning sun was already up and burning, so he moved a slab of tree trunk into the shade of the house eaves for me to sit on, which put me in the midst of his buffalo horn shavings and wood scraps, and also at his feet while he worked. He carved, and we talked—buzzing the same sorts of stories as usual, humorous and serious, often peppered with some stray gossip heard last night along the road or at the *kedai* (a roadside stall where coffee, tea, and other refreshments are sold). Thin tendrils of grey buffalo horn floated down on my arms as I sat there aching to create something. Finally, I picked up a heavy shaving of wood, found my Swiss army knife, and began carving, doing what I could to make a human face and body out of it.

Partoho, seeing me work, took a cigarette break and hunkered down on his haunches, quietly watching me. He puffed hard on his *kretek* (a clove-tobacco cigarette) without taking it from his lips and, squinting his eyes from the sting of smoke, said, "Here, this is how you do it." He gently took the wood from my hands and began fine-tuning my coarse work. The long carving knife he had been using to shape the water buffalo horn was obviously too large to be doing the kind of whittling he was doing on my figure, but he handled it as if it were a weightless scalpel. Narrow slips of wood were pared off the figure one after another, methodically, his thumb pressing the wood into shape. By the time his kretek had smoldered to a dull black, he had transformed the figure's awkwardness into elegance. The elephantine legs now had a dancer's lilt, and the bulbous head was now oval and smiling. He reached up to the worktable from where he was squatting and fumbled around until he found a short-handled knife and finished the little figure, now removing thin shavings of wood more judiciously. He knew I was following his knife's every slice with my eyes, so he dared not make a false cut. The tiny human was a comical mix of both Toba Batak and Western elements. She had a large flip hairdo and collared blouse but held her hands up as if dancing a serious *tortor* (a traditional formal dance). For some reason, Partoho cut notches in the bottom of her pleated skirt, then carved delicate little legs to fit in them so that when the figure was jiggled, her legs kicked back and forth furiously. He gave the little creature one last look front and back, then handed it and the knife back to me. "Now you just need to scrape the small hairs off the surface," he instructed me.

Later on, when his wife and two oldest sons returned from the field, he had me pull the figure out of my bag and said to them, "Look at this. He already knows how to carve! He has been pretending he knows nothing, and suddenly he produces this. This is already the work of a master carver!" Ito looked at me in frowning surprise and examined the workmanship, her sons peering over her shoulder. She was laughing as she bobbled the tiny puppet on its string, making its feet kick. "Ha!" she finally erupted, slapping my shoulder and smiling, "You didn't make this, did you? Ha! I know my husband's work." Partoho smirked and refused to look at her as she tried to get him to admit that he was teasing her once again.

I tried making two more small figures from large wood chips, but with each one Partoho made a few deft cuts, changing my ostensibly Toba Batak figures into hilarious caricatures of Westerners: one a fierce man with a crewcut and muscular arms, the other a scrawny woman in a voluminous skirt. Although Partoho took great delight in making these charming little parodies of the outsiders with whom he interacted every day, he also seemed to be testing how serious I was about being taught to carve in the traditional style. Although they were very funny, not only to me but to Ito and the children, I was getting frustrated by seeing another day pass with no real instruction about how to carve traditional objects.

The next day, he told me to stop making these "dolls" because they were both too small and not traditional. "Here," he said, thrusting a wedge of black in my hands, "You make heads okay, so maybe you'd be interested in making this into a small head. Bodies are probably too hard for you to make, so just stick to the head. You can copy that mask I have in the *kios* [a stall or small shop from which carvings (or other commodities) are sold] . . . make it Batak style." I took the piece of water buffalo horn that he had fished out of the venomously black water in the old oil drum lying on its side by the kitchen door. Partoho had all kinds of strange bits and pieces soaking in the oil drum—antlers and horns of all sorts pickling and softening for weeks or months. The piece he gave me was still damp.

In the twelve months I worked with him, Partoho taught me the way to carve a few basic forms; the fact that I never learned to carve any of them very well did not seem to bother him. He seemed to be satisfied to show me some of the intricacies of his work and to learn whatever he could from me about Westerners and their buying habits. He especially wanted to know what kinds of things Western travelers wanted to buy.

What could he sell to the visitors who entered his shop, examined each of his many and various carvings with care, but then left empty-handed? I was at a loss to try to explain the capriciousness of individuals laconically browsing and making impulse purchases.

As I prepared to return home to Texas, Partoho asked me one favor: "Try to find someone who can sell my carvings in America." Like both Milgram and Eber (this volume), I felt this was a small thing to ask considering the amount of time and kindness he and his family had offered to me. I told him that I would look for a buyer, confident that the superior workmanship and artistry of Toba Batak traditional carvings would find an eager clientele in the United States among people with a taste for the "exotic," the handmade, and the elegant.

Once I had returned home and unpacked the carvings from my study collection, I checked with friends to see who might be interested in handling such works and was told that there were two men in particular to contact. The first was a former anthropology student who had gone on to establish a successful import store in town; the other was a connoisseur of the rare and unusual who owned a store that combined an amalgam of antiques, curiosities, and crafts from around the world. Once contacted, both agreed to come to my house to see Partoho's carvings.

The former anthropologist was very businesslike and quickly glanced over the two shelves I had devoted to the carvings, giving me this succinct appraisal: despite their meticulous craftsmanship, the carvings probably would not sell well. He told me that they did not fit a known niche—that is, "primitive" or "folk"—and were not from an area of the world that is well known in Texas. He predicted that if he were able to sell anything, it would be entirely serendipitous. He felt it was a financial risk to buy them outright, so he did not even consider my suggestion to place an order directly with Partoho. Nevertheless, he kindly agreed to take a few carvings as consignments, reminding me that I must be prepared to supply more if indeed they did sell. His offer to display Partoho's work in his already crowded shop was a generous one, but his plan meant that I would have to display my own study collection and would have to order duplicates from Partoho (prepaid, including shipping costs, of course) in the event that they sold. This arrangement was unsuitable for me because I needed to work with my collection of objects and did not have the finances to place an order with Partoho.

The second store owner was a more affable man and studied me earnestly as I told him about the carvings and the Toba Batak culture. He continued nodding his head long after I had finished talking, then winced and said, "Nope. They just don't . . . fit

... somehow. Sorry." That was it. He was very nice about it and kept complimenting them as he inched toward the door. Then something caught his eye. On the shelf adjacent to my study collection, he saw a pile of cheap souvenir pens and brooches bought in Bali and behind them the three small tourist caricatures that Partoho had "fixed" for me. "Now, these I can sell!" he said with excitement. I told him the story about the figures and explained how "inauthentic" they were, how completely without meaning they were to Toba Batak traditional culture, but he would not be swayed. If he were to buy anything I had in the room, he told me, it would be these. "Tell your friend to make a hundred ... no, make it two hundred of these little characters, and I can probably get him eight bucks a piece for them," he said and continued out the door saying, "Be sure to get back to me when you hear from him, OK?" This plan again required me to front the money, but this time the initial costs for wood and shipping were so low that I might be able to afford it, forwarding the actual profits as they came rolling in.

I closed the door excited at the new prospect and began composing the letter in my head: "Dear Partoho, a store owner here in Texas is really interested in your carvings! Not the ones passed down from your revered ancestors, but the small funny ones with the wobbly legs." No. How about: "Dear Partoho, a clever businessman told me that Texas collectors prefer carved spoofs of themselves to your traditional artwork." The letter was very difficult to write. Not only would I have to find a way to present this business prospect in such a way that respected Partoho's expertise and dignity, I would also have to find the words to remind him what it was I wanted him to make—such was the fleeting moment in which the tourist figures were originally made. "Dear Partoho, Do you remember how we sat around after dinner making fun of the tourists? If you can make two-inch dolls as funny as our jokes, you'll be rich!"

The first return letter I received made no mention of my request, so I wrote another, explaining in more detail what I was looking for (including drawings of the three figures) and verifying the price they would fetch, a price I was sure would need further description because it was comparable with one he might receive on Samosir for a covered box completely ornamented with gorga. The second return letter made a feeble mention of the figures, only to say that he was looking for appropriate wood to make them. Finally, the third letter explained the situation in full. He had no clear remembrance of the figures except that they were puppets that made the children laugh, and thus he had no idea what it was I wanted; he was busy at work making ancestor figures and a king's staff in case I wanted to order some of them. I made mention of the caricature figures only once more (at the behest of the shop owner, who was still very keen on the project), but Partoho politely informed me that he could not make what I was requesting and that he had no idea why anyone would want such things.

BROKERING CRAFTS: A CAUTIONARY TALE

The story presented above raises issues that can be problematic for anthropologists working with craftworkers. How will the researcher's role as advisor or broker to craftworkers change the previous social relationships between them? What personal limitations might influence whether or not a researcher is able to help craftworkers? Does the researcher have the expertise or qualifications necessary to assist the artisans in marketing and selling their work? If one decides to act as an agent for the artisans, what are the best avenues to ensure success of the endeavor? As demonstrated in other chapters in this volume (e.g., Grimes, Milgram, Eber), each individual researcher will make his or her own decisions about how best to address these questions based on personal proclivities and abilities, the needs and requirements of the artisans, and extenuating circumstances. A brief exploration of these questions, however, can help clarify the issues and can provide a foundation on which future considerations and decisions might be made.

In a circumstance like the one I described, the researcher quickly realizes that changes in her or his relationships with craftworkers, both as a group and as individuals, are unavoidable. The researcher may work hard to develop a particular rapport with artisans over a period of months or years only to see temporary (sometimes permanent) disruptions in the relationships unfolding as soon as he or she opts to take the role of advisor or broker. When originally deciding whether to help Partoho, I was concerned that there would be animosity from the other carvers in Huta Mungkap, who might feel jealous that my assistance was not being given equally. Fortunately, everyone seemed to accept the situation because it was natural that I would have a closer relationship with my teacher than with other carvers. The change in my personal relationship with Partoho is more complex. Over the period of two months, my casual friendship with him had eventually developed into an asymmetrical *abang-adik* (older brother, younger brother) relationship, with him as the abang. It was this transformation that enabled him to take on the superior position of teacher.[16] A year later, when he asked for aid in selling his work and I responded, our relationship was inverted: now I was the older brother. The long-term implications of this inversion are as yet unclear.

In addition to concerns about changing the nature of his or her relationships with artisans, a researcher must also consider whether there are personal limitations that will affect the decision to act as an agent. Giving occasional reasoned advice to a craftworker does not necessarily disrupt a research timetable, but acting as a regular interpreter or helping to facilitate the formation of a cooperative can unintentionally disrupt carefully constructed fieldwork plans. The possible problems are not limited to activities in the field. Trying to fulfill a blithe promise to broker craftworks at home can consume vast blocks of time as the researcher attempts to locate sales venues and develop marketing strategies. I gave up trying to sell Partoho's carvings in Texas after only a month's time, but I had already devoted days of work to the plan. I do not begrudge the time spent on Partoho's behalf because it came nowhere near compensating him for his teaching me how to carve, but the very real fact is that the many hours spent pursuing this project were taken from the limited time I had to write my dissertation and grade papers.

This leads me to the next issue. Does the researcher have the necessary expertise and qualifications to assist the artisans in marketing and selling their work? As Milgram (this volume) also notes, anthropologists choosing or being requested by informant friends to act as agents of craft sales will come upon two substantial (and now familiar) problems: knowing what Westerners want and knowing how to tap the global market in order to sell the wares successfully.

The complexity of Western consumers' desires and tastes, plus their effect on the marketplace, is well documented and theorized in the social science literature. One need only look at the work of Csikzentmihalyi and Rochberg-Halton (1981), Bourdieu (1984), McCracken (1990), Belk (1995), Marcus and Myers (1995), and Pearce (1995), among others, to see broad overviews of how the West's economic wealth and political control has created an ever-expanding need for more arcane or more exotic commodities. The work of Jules-Rosette (1984), Price (1989), Thomas (1991), and Steiner (1994), among others, provide more detailed and localized examples of ways that tourists and collectors are implicated in the transformation of indigenous crafts. For an anthropologist wanting to help craftworkers but untrained in market analysis, these works show how the incredible variety of Western consumer needs and preferences can turn hope into despair. As shown in my example, good intentions and faith in the workmanship of the craftspeople are not sufficient to succeed in the highly competitive and often fickle market of craft items.

Even if the anthropologist as agent is confident about locating a market niche, there is a question of whether the artisans are able or willing to use their expertise and talents to transmute their arts into forms that are saleable to a wide audience. Are consumers looking for "traditional" or simply "handmade" crafts (Nash 1993a, 10)? Do they want to consider their purchase to be "art" or "craft"? Are they seeking something familiar or something unusual, something useful or something decorative? Researchers working with Australian Aboriginal artists describe situations in which oversupply causes prices to plummet (Altman 1990) and in which a decline in quality tarnishes the reputation of a group's work (Scott-Mundine 1990). Unless one is able to understand the needs of the buyer, providing help to the craftworker may depend wholly on fortuitous circumstances.

Quality crafts that are also well conceived with respect to buyers' interests and needs may still fail if the appropriate venue for selling them is not found. Although the global marketplace offers incredible potential to sell, the buyers may be geographically dispersed. There may be any number of individuals interested in buying Partoho's traditional carvings, but clearly they do not all live in Austin, Texas. The notion of a global bazaar with goods from around the world changing hands via hundreds of currencies and barters may not be a dream exactly,[17] but neither is it a reality for many people in the world.

The foregoing discussion might give the impression that my own efforts to help Partoho were completely abandoned under a pall of dejection and that anthropologists acting as agents for craftworkers are generally doomed to failure. It is true that much of what I have written is of a cautionary nature, but I hope it does not dissuade anyone who decides to assist the artisans with whom they work from following through with their plans.[18] As the chapters in this volume show, there are success stories. Alternative trading organizations (ATOs), in particular, are providing artisans who are otherwise disenfranchised from the global market with effective and equitable ways to sell their wares (Grimes, this volume). In this last section, I would like to review a few additional examples of researchers who are working effectively as brokers for artisans.

Jon Altman and Luke Taylor's (1990) edited volume *Marketing Aboriginal Art in the 1990s* brings together essays that describe the various ways that Australian Aboriginal artists (primarily painters) sell their work. Although the current popularity of Aboriginal art means that these artists do not have to seek out a niche for their wares, their experiences indicate they must still keep a close watch on their place in the market. So far, it seems, many of the Aboriginal groups that produce paintings and tourist art have developed strong enterprises, usually in the form of artist cooperatives or other intermediary community-based organizations, which act to broker the artists' work as well as to provide them with discounted art supplies. Working closely with outsiders— such as gallery owners, museum professionals, marketing specialists, and financial managers—not only have the Aboriginal artists integrated new technologies into their work, helping to keep quality high, they have also discovered ways to begin resolving complex cultural questions concerning who may produce and view certain images (see also Morphy 1991, 24). In this way, they have found a way to tread the fine line between being savvy about the international art market and staying honest to their traditions.

Lawrence Rinder's (1998) work with Maisin (Papua New Guinea) fabric artists shows that well-planned museum exhibitions can provide a way to popularize a relatively unknown group's art, while also creating a venue for future sales. Rinder worked closely with the Maisin community's council of clan elders to organize an exhibition of *tapa* paintings in Berkeley, California. This initiative also included plans to send a handful of artists to the United States to learn new technologies (such as silk-screening) with which to innovate their traditional forms.[19] As a result of the Berkeley exhibition, the Maisin group formed a business that set standards for quality, pricing, and distributed profits. There are still problems to be sorted out when it comes to considering the possible mass production of Maisin tapa designs (some of which are sacred), but it appears that the community is committed to finding ways to negotiate these issues as a collective.

Other work has been done in Papua New Guinea, and although it does not involve craftwork per se, it may provide a model for anthropologists' future efforts in working with artisans.[20] Ethnomusicologist Steven Feld (1990, 1995) has worked for many years to make the music and environmental sounds of the Kaluli people from Bosavi, Papua New Guinea accessible to a wide audience. With the help of Mickey Hart and using an innovative format and state-of-the-art audio technology, he compiled songs and sounds for a CD intended for popular (not specifically academic) consumption. Sales of the CD have been good and have served not only to popularize Kaluli sounds, but also to provide much-needed finances for a community fund. In a similar case, Keila Diehl (1998) assisted in the development and overseas marketing of a cassette tape for a Tibetan rock band (241). Although sales of the cassette were lower than expected, the project may serve to motivate other Tibetan musicians to reach beyond local audiences. The successes of anthropologists involved in helping to popularize a particular group's music may not, of course, be translated exactly into success for an anthropologist assisting craftworkers, but they can serve as inspirations. Perhaps anthropologists working as agents for artisans might begin to consider the possibilities of current technologies (such as the Internet and computer CDs) when considering not only how to sell craftworks but also how to market them.

CONCLUSIONS

Toward the end of my stay in Huta Mungkap, a formal gathering was held by the village carvers, to which I was invited as an observer. The main point to be discussed was whether everyone could agree to put old disagreements and selfish desires aside in order to form a carving cooperative. After several hours of talk, no consensus was reached, partly because no one at the meeting had accurate information about how a cooperative actually worked, but also because many carvers feared the loss of their autonomy. The man who called the meeting asked all carvers present to continue thinking about the proposal, suggesting that another meeting could be held in the future, and then ended the session by addressing me. In short, he said that a cooperative would have success only if it was properly represented and promoted in the world marketplace. "That is how you, Andro, can help everyone in this village," he went on. "You can promote the work we do."

The responsibility of promoting, mediating, brokering, or otherwise representing the work of craftspeople can be an onerous task for underinformed and busy anthropologists to accept, especially if they proceed in their efforts unaware of the challenges they may face. Nevertheless, as many authors in this volume show, there are numerous ways for anthropologists to act successfully as agents for artisans (whether working by themselves or with the assistance of ATOs). With sufficient preparation and knowledge of the market, of the artisans' abilities, and of their own limitations, both anthropologist agents and the craftworkers with whom they work can enjoy the benefits of the global marketplace.

NOTES

[1] This research, which took place between January 1994 and August 1995, was funded by a grant from Institute of International Education (IIE Fulbright and from the Joint Committee on Southeast Asia of the Social Science Research Council and the American Council of Learned Societies, with funds provided by the Andrew Mellon Foundation, the Ford Foundation, and the Henry Luce Foundation. Additional funding came from a Mellon Foreign Area Fellowship at the Library of Congress.

2 To protect the privacy of the inhabitants of my field site, the village name and the names of individuals are pseudonyms.

3 "Broker" may imply a level of involvement deeper than most researchers would admit, yet I use the term as defined by Steiner (1994, citing Robert Paine 1971): "the broker is someone who manipulates, mediates, or 'processes' the information which is being transmitted between . . . two groups . . . [and] is one who interprets, modifies, or comments on the knowledge which is being communicated" (155).

4 Western backpacking travelers are the predominant international visitors to Samosir Island, although occasionally groups from Malaysia and Singapore also visit; on certain holidays, groups of Chinese Indonesians from Medan spend time at the lakeside.

5 Compare, for example, Tony Wheeler's 1977 edition of *South-East Asia on a Shoestring* (89) with his 1989 edition (240).

6 There is no proof of a direct connection between the crash and the smoke, but the pilot complained of low visibility because of the haze moments before the accident (*CNN Interactive* 1997b).

7 A decrease in the number of tourists arriving was felt in Singapore, Indonesia, Brunei, the Philippines, southern Thailand, and Malaysia (Seattle P-I Plus Getaways 1997). In fact, Malaysia's prime minister was so concerned about the smoke that he "barred teachers and scientists in state universities . . . from speaking publicly on the haze because it said those comments were hurting tourism, Malaysia's big foreign exchange earner" (*CNN Interactive* 1997a).

8 Except, it seems, in Bali, where tourism has remained fairly stable.

9 The three areas actually extend for a mile or so in all directions and may include several hamlets in their environs; all are in a very limited area on the east coast of the island, very close to the other tourist venues such as hotels, restaurants, and markets. They are Tomok or Sosor Tolong, Tuk-tuk, and Siallagan.

10 The objects made by carvers ordinarily replicate traditional pre-Christian forms that have no practical use in the lives of local rural Christian Toba Batak. Aside from a two-stringed lute *(hasapi)* and desk nameplates, I never saw traditional carvings in the homes or offices of the people with whom I spoke. The carvings are made strictly for sale to outsiders (although it is possible that they are used to decorate the homes of urban Toba Batak).

11 Janet Rodenburg (1997) gives evidence that this may not have been the case in the nineteenth and early twentieth centuries (45, 49–50).

12 In Indonesian public schools, foreign-language instruction usually begins in secondary school.

13 Their situation is not helped by the fact that Indonesian government-sponsored brochures rarely promote Toba Batak carvings, preferring instead to highlight the traditional weavings called *ulos* (Causey 1998).

14 For a more complete description of the misunderstandings associated with my attempts to help Partoho by suggesting what Westerners might want to buy, see Causey (1999a).

15 Gorga is an intricate surface intaglio work that is distinctive of Toba Batak wood carving; it often has the form of sinuous and symmetrical foliates and meanders.

16 At the start of our interactions, it was clear that Partoho was not comfortable with the idea of being my teacher because I have more education than he. When we discovered that he was several months older than I, he was able to take a superior position.

17 This sort of exchange might be said to be happening in mail-order sales, but it is perhaps more clearly evident in on-line ATO sales networks such as Peoplink (see Grimes, this volume).

[18] See Lynd's essay (this volume) for practical information and suggestions on planning a brokering project.

[19] Artists also consulted with apparel manufacturer Patagonia to create a hypothetical line of outerwear using the tapa designs (Rinder 1998, 68).

[20] There are important differences between the Kaluli situation and that being discussed in this essay. Despite the fact that a substantial percentage of the profits from the sale of the CD go to the Kaluli people, their sounds are not, strictly speaking, commodities, which may make them less susceptible than crafts to change stemming from consumer desires and pressures.

J u n e   N a s h

P O S T S C R I P T
T o   M a r k e t ,   T o   M a r k e t

For Ricardo, the market linked producers and consumers in an equation that maximized satisfactions on both ends. For Marx, the cash nexus binds the commodity and the consumer in a spectral dance of skeletal figures that fetishizes social relations. In the global marketplace, where any remnant of social contact between producer and consumer seems doomed to annihilation, from the multiple production sites where goods are assembled to the faceless malls where they are purchased, a new mediator has stepped in to rescue the moral encounter. This is the alternative trading organization (ATO) that mediates between the impoverished, often female artisans-cultivators of third world countries and the well-heeled and politically conscious consumers of first world countries.

The mission of these new sales mediators goes far beyond that of their entrepreneurial predecessors. They bring the faces and narrative conditions of the producers to a marketplace of jaded consumers who are seeking not only exotic tokens of distant cultures but also the satisfaction of pursuing a moral crusade. These consumers' concern with the plight of the producers extends to a willingness to pay a fair price for the objects they buy that will take into account the needs of the producers and their families. These attitudes are often paired with a concern for the environment and a willingness to subsidize additional costs for keeping the environment free of toxic wastes and the polluting by-products of production. The anthropologists who write about their experiences with third world producers in the course of this volume are participants in these new mediations, either by interpreting the symbols carried in the commodities or by evoking the cultural context in which the goods are produced. They often exert a strong impact on the prices of producers' work by cultivating an appreciation of the artistry that goes into the making of that work. Some may even go on to convey information to the producers as to what first world consumers are likely to prefer.

As the authors in this volume show, these formal ATOs united in the Fair Trade Federation (FTF), along with the less formal mediations of anthropologists and/or traders, are contributing to the hybridization of cultures in the global ecumene. By serving as go-betweens in annual exchanges of more than a billion dollars, they are sustaining the life chances of traditional producers in the very globalized circuits that have upset the balances on which the artisans once relied. Kimberly Grimes, as coeditor and contributor, summarizes the context in which these mediations arose after World War II, when Mennonite- and Brethren-affiliated businesses addressed issues of social justice and thus stimulated increasing numbers of fair trade stores of a nonreligious nature in the 1970s and early 1980s. These were the decades of increasing inequality in the distribution of rewards, when neoliberal rhetoric cultivated the amorality of market-dominated trading relations among nations as well as corporations. The major trade agreements that have been signed—from the General Agreements on Tariffs and Trade right after World War II to the recent North American Free Trade Agreement (NAFTA) that went into effect in 1994—benefit the major players in global exchange. With the weakening of the nation-state, the small producers have little recourse to defend their position in the market. Thus, the ATOs play a critical role not only in sustaining producer organizations but also in ensuring the survival of the producers' families.

It is in this context that we can appreciate the efforts of nongovernmental organizations (NGOs) and their anthropological collaborators. With varying degrees of success, they carry out the delicate balancing act between a cooperative ideology and its practice. The broader the stated goals of the cooperative organization, the greater the potential it has for success. In her comparative study of two Ifugao Philippine weavers' cooperatives, coeditor Lynne Milgram indicates that the cooperative that has a stronger grassroots base tends to enhance the women's awareness of their own potential, thus ensuring the greater viability of their organization. By engaging in educational pursuits and consciousness raising, as well as in production and sales, cooperatives often address issues of gender equality that are essential for the very survival of the organization.

The importance of broadly based programs in ensuring the success of the cooperative enterprise is also borne out in Brenda Rosenbaum's and Christine Eber's activist research with the Mayas. The Guatemalan group of resettled Mayan urban migrants with whom Rosenbaum works, Unidas para Vivir Mejor (United to Live Better), addresses the concerns of women cut off from their subsistence base in rural villages. Like the Mayas of Guatemala, the Chiapas Mayas studied by Eber share a similar history of military intervention and political repression. The disruption of their economy by government troops living in their presence prevents them from meeting their needs through subsistence cultivation. Artisan products, sold through a grassroots cooperative, are one of the most important means of obtaining much needed cash.

The selling of artisan products for needed cash is also seen in Rachel MacHenry's investigation of cooperatives with women of different cultural backgrounds in Nepal. The first cooperative she studied was an association of craft producers of Nepal comprising more than eight hundred low-caste Hindu women producers from a variety of ethnic groups. The second group of Buddhist Tibetan refugees enjoyed a higher level of social services in exile than did the Nepalese, who resented the special privileges the Tibetans had gained. This situation is replicated in many countries where the international aid available for refugees gives them more opportunities than producers enjoy in their host country.

The FTF might well address the issue these authors raise of invidious comparisons between indigenous and exile populations that they assist and those that have to survive by their own wits. Anthropologists can provide many such examples of how such conflicts arise and how they can be overcome. I became familiar with the problem in the context of the Lacandon jungle in Chiapas, Mexico, where Guatemalan Mayas in exile were able to gain farmlands through the rental paid by international refugee organizations and to find assistance from religious groups that marketed their artisan products. This occurred in the 1980s, when Mexican Mayas were unable to gain title to lands promised to them by their own government and when women artisans suffered harassment trying to sell their products in the streets of San Cristóbal. Then, too, the Guatemalans had funding for schools in areas where Mexican Mayas lacked teachers and had rudimentary thatched huts for their schools. The sharp contrasts, which made Mexican Mayas feel like outlaws in their own lands, added fuel to the rebellion of the Zapatistas. Coordination of the efforts of relief agencies and trade organizations is crucial in avoiding such conflicts.

Cooperatives are clearly a potential basis for mobilizing the political energies of women as a disenfranchised group in much of the world. As yet, the impetus for such intervention is based on religious and political morality, countervailing the amorality of market exchanges. In order to build these concerns into an international order, the ATO movement might consider ways of introducing issues of social justice into international trade agreements. The growing reaction to NAFTA or to regional exchanges such as Southern Cone Common Market (MERCOSUR) is building in third world countries. The Zapatista uprising in Mexico is a prime example of a social movement that sparked protest among other sectors of the population that suffered from the fast-track approach of NAFTA. In protesting their country's neglect of its own citizens, the Zapatistas, who lost their protected markets for corn and coffee, found an ally in the debtors' group of entrepreneurs who lost their businesses because of soaring interest rates. The Fair Trade Association (FTA) might well become a hearing ground for such injuries in the global market because it alerts consumers to the imbalances in the global exchange of goods. Indigenous producers of organic crops in Chiapas, for example, are beginning to develop contacts with trading associations that enable them to weather the extreme cycles in demand as they expand consumer knowledge of the health hazards of chemicals used in most food production.

Another important alliance can be forged between the FTA and environmental groups. Precisely because cooperatives link first world countries through the exchange of products in a global market, they can promote awareness of environmental degradation in the context of the fair trade movement. Paradoxically, the very mobility of capital that allows first world capitalists to escape the consequences of the conditions they foster in third world industrial sites can promote this new confrontation. Germans who sponsored the weaving cooperative studied by Rachel MacHenry in Nepal helped the women develop innovative closed systems of treating the waste from dyeing solutions to avoid the diffusion of the toxic materials.

The intervention by anthropologists in the process of craft promotion is a potentially beneficial sideline to investigation. Brenda Rosenbaum and Christine Eber show how essential their intervention in the retailing of artisan products was during critical periods in the countries in which they worked. Yet advice is not always welcome, as Jeffrey Cohen's caveats suggest. He describes how jealousy among the households whom he patronized as a buyer resulted in the alienation of good informants. He also discovered that his field contacts could become very annoyed when customers he directed to their houses did not buy any goods. On the other hand, he points out that working with the local museum in Santa Ana, Oaxaca, was less problematic. He provided photographs, which became part of the museum's displays, and he frequently played the role of an impromptu guide. Andrew Causey was more ingenuous in his discussion of the Toba Batak wood-carvers he was studying. Although they urged him to advise them how to market their carvings, they were unwilling to accept the advice he gave on what figures to carve based on his questioning of retailers in the United States. The carvers were especially reluctant to produce the caricatures of tourists that Causey had himself produced with the aid of one of the Toba Batak artisans and that Causey himself feared would debase their artistic tradition! Martha Lynd found that the artisans who produced textiles for her fair trade organization developed such a dependency on her outlets in the United States that she decided to work full-time as a facilitator for the groups in Guatemala.

The least problematic and clearly one of the most fruitful roles for anthropologists is that of cultural property arbiter. The responsibilities range from delving into the history and even prehistory of the artisan products, as Kathy M'Closky has done for Navajo weaving, to engaging in cultural properties research, as she and increasing numbers of anthropologists are doing (see especially Tom Greaves 1994). Copyrights on designs and even trade names to avoid undercutting the prices with debased products claiming to be part of a cultural tradition have become important means of advancing the rights of artisans to their patrimony. The current outsourcing of the production of "Navajo rugs" in Zapotec workshops where weavers carry out the designs of Navajos is a cost-cutting "solution" that injures producers in both cultures.

The void that the fair trade movement fills in the lives of producers is distinct from interventions promoted in the global market. The movement creates a sense of community, as Kimberly Grimes indicates in her discussion of ATOs. In a world where indigenous communities are threatened by the predatory invasion of capitalist markets, it is an interim measure promoting the survival of peoples and their cultures. By introducing producers to consumers via the products as they are exchanged, it has the potential to overcome the fetishizing of social relations in commodity exchange. But as these authors have so keenly shown, it is not a panacea for all the injustices in global exchange.

REFERENCES CITED

Acheson, James. 1972. "Accounting Concepts and Economic Opportunities in a Tarascan Village: Emic and Etic Views." *Human Organization* 31(1): 83–91.

Agarwal, Anil, and Narin Sunita. 1989. *Towards Green Villages: A Strategy for Environmentally Sound and Participatory Rural Development.* New Delhi: Centre for Science And Environment.

Aguilar, Filomeno V., and Virginia A. Miralao. 1984. *Handicrafts, Development and Dilemmas over Definition (the Philippines as a Case in Point).* Handicraft Project Paper Series, no. 1. Manila: Ramon Magsaysay Foundation.

Alarcón, Rafael. 1992. "Norteñización: Self Perpetuating Migration from a Mexican Town." In *U.S.-Mexico Relations: Labor Market Interdependence,* edited by J. Bustamante, R. Hinojosa, and C. Reynolds, 302–18. Stanford: Stanford University Press.

Altman, Jon. 1990. "Selling Aboriginal Art." In *Marketing Aboriginal Art in the 1900s: Papers Presented to a Workshop in Canberra,* edited by J. Altman and L. Taylor, 1–18. Canberra: Aboriginal Studies.

Altman, Jon, and Luke Taylor, eds. 1990. *Marketing Aboriginal Art in the 1900s: Papers Presented to a Workshop in Canberra.* Canberra: Aboriginal Studies.

American Indian Art Magazine. 1972–98. Scottsdale, Arizona.

Amsden, Charles Avery. 1975 [1934]. *Navajo Weaving, Its Technique and History.* Salt Lake City: Peregrine Smith.

Anderson, Marilyn, and Jonathan Garlock. 1988. *Granddaughters of Corn: Portraits of Guatemalan Women.* Willimantic, Conn.: Curbstone.

Angotti, Thomas. 1995. "The Latin American Metropolis and the Growth of Inequality." *NACLA Report on the Americas* 28(4): 13–18.

Appadurai, Arjun. 1996. *Modernity at Large: Cultural Dimensions of Globalization.* Minneapolis: University of Minnesota Press.

Appleton, Helen, ed. 1995. *Do It Herself: Women and Technical Innovation.* London: Intermediate Technology Publications.

Arizona Highways. 1974. Special Issue on Southwest Indian Weaving, 50: 7.

Arnold, Judith. 1988. "An Investment in Beauty." *Southwest Profile* (fall): 38–41.

Asian Women in Co-operative Development Forum (AWCF) and National Confederation of Co-operatives (NATCCO). 1995. *Liberating Co-ops: Stories of Women-Friendly and Gender-Responsive Co-operatives in the Philippines.* Manila, Philippines: AWCF and NATCCO.

Attwood, Donald. 1989. "Does Competition Help Cooperation?" *Journal of Development Studies* 26(1): 5–27.

Attwood, Donald, and B. S. Baviskar, eds. 1988. *Who Shares? Cooperatives and Rural Development.* New Delhi: Oxford University Press.

Attwood, Donald, and Jill Hanley, eds. 1996. *Cooperative Values in a Changing World: A Cooperative Critique.* CASC 1993 Yearbook. Saskatoon: University of Saskatchewan, Centre for the Study of Cooperatives.

Bacdayan, Albert. 1977. "Mechanistic Cooperation and Sexual Equality among the Western Bontoc." In *Sexual Stratification: A Cross-Cultural View,* edited by Alice Schlegel, 271–91. New York: Columbia University Press.

Bailey, Garrick, and Roberta Bailey. 1986. *A History of the Navajo: The Reservation Years.* Santa Fe: School of American Research Press.

Bailón Corres, Moisés Jaime. 1979. "Articulación de modes de producción: Producción mercantil simple y sistema comercial en los valles centrales de Oaxaca." Ph.D. diss., Universidad Autónoma Benito Juárez de Oaxaca, Oaxaca Instituto de Investigaciones Sociológicas, Oaxaca City.

Baizerman, Suzanne. 1987. "Textiles, Traditions, and Tourist Art: Hispanic Weaving in Northern New Mexico." Ph.D. diss., Department of Clothing and Textiles, University of Minnesota, Minneapolis.

Barlow, Maude, and Tony Clarke. 1998. *The Multilateral Agreement on Investment and the Threat to American Freedom.* New York: Stoddart.

Barry, Tom. 1992. *Inside Guatemala: The Essential Guide to Its Politics, Economy and Society, and the Environment.* Albuquerque: Interhemispheric Research Center.

Begay, Clarenda. 1986. "Rug Study Interviews." Hubbell Trading Post National Historic Site, Ganado, Arizona.

Begay, D. Y. 1996. "Shi'Sha'Hane' (My Story)." In *Woven by the Grandmothers,* edited by Eulalie Bonar, 13–27. Washington, D.C.: Smithsonian Institution Press.

Belk, Russell. 1995. *Collecting in a Consumer Society.* London: Routledge.

Benería, Lourdes, and Martha Roldán. 1987. *The Crossroads of Class and Gender: Industrial Homework, Subcontracting, and Household Dynamics in Mexico City.* Chicago: University of Chicago Press.

Bennett, Noel. 1973. *Genuine Navajo Rug—Are You Sure?* Window Rock, Ariz.: Museum of Navajo Ceremonial Art and the Navajo Tribe.

Berger, Margherite, and Mayra Buvinic, eds. 1988. *La Mujer en el sector informal: Trabajo femenino y microempresa en América Latina.* Caracas: Editorial Nueva Sociedad.

Berlo, Janet. 1996. "Beyond Bricolage: Women and Aesthetic Strategies in Latin American Textiles." In *Textile Traditions in Mesoamerica and the Andes: An Anthology,* edited by Margo Schevill, Janet Berlo, and Edward Dwyer, 437–79. Austin: University of Texas Press.

Bhanti, Raj. 1998. "Development Plans and the Plight of Tribal Women." Paper presented at the 14th Congress of the International Anthropological and Ethnological Sciences Union, Williamsburg, Virginia, July.

Black, Jan Knippers. 1991. *Development in Theory and Practice: Bridging the Gap.* Boulder, Colo.: Westview.

Bourdieu, Pierre. 1984. *Distinction: a Social Critique of the Judgment of Taste.* Translated by R. Nice. Cambridge: Harvard University Press.

Brown, Michael. 1993. *Fair Trade: Reform and Realities in the International Trading System.* London: Zed.

Brugge, David. 1970–72. *Hubbell Trading Post Ethnohistoric Project.* Ganado, Ariz.: Hubbell Trading Post National Historic Site.

———. 1971. "Imitation Navajo Rugs." *The Call of the Plateau* 10(3): 3–4.

———. 1996. Telephone conversation with Kathy M'Closkey. December 30.

Bunolna, Jacinto N. 1993. *Medium and Short Term Trade and Industry Plans, Province of Ifugao, 1993–1998 Report.* Lagawe, Ifugao, Philippines: Department of Trade and Industry.

Burkert, Claire. 1994. *Janakpur Art: A Living Tradition.* Nepal: Janakpur Women's Development Center.

Casteñeda, Quetzil. 1997. "On the Correct Training of Indios in the Handicraft Market at Chichen Itza: Tactics and Tactility of Gender, Class, Race, and State." *Journal of Latin American Anthropology* 2(2): 106–43.

Causey, Andrew. 1998. "*Ulos* or *Saham?:* Presentations of Toba Batak Material Culture in Official Tourism Promotions." *Indonesia and the Malay World* 26(75): 97–106.

———. 1999a. "The *Singasinga* Table Lamp and the Toba Batak's Art of Conflation." *Journal of American Folklore* 112 (445): 424–36.

———. 1999b. "Making a Man Malu: Western Tourist and Toba Bataks in the Souvenir Marketplace." In *Converging Interests: Traders, Travelers and Tourists in Southeast Asia,* edited by Jill Forshee, 279–91. Berkeley: University of California Press.

Central Cordillera Agricultural Programme (CECAP). 1995. *Annual Report.* Banaue, Ifugao, Philippines: CECAP.

Cerigua Weekly Briefs. 1998. "Development." 36 (September 17). On-line at www-personal.engin.umich.edu/~pavr/harbury/archive/cerigua.

Cetina, Gabriela. 1998. "Flexible Looms: Weavers' Organizations in Chiapas." Paper presented at the 97th Annual Meeting of the American Anthropological Association, Philadelphia, December.

Chamberlain, Ed. 1998. "Navajo Weaving Today." Paper presented at the 11th Annual Navajo Studies Conference, Window Rock, Arizona, October 24.

Chen, Tsuh Yin. n.d. "Counting Threads or Counting Money: A Study of Informal Education among Traditional Weavers and Weaving Cooperative Members in San Pedro Chenalhó, Chiapas, Mexico." Unpublished paper.

Cherneff, Jill. 1982. "Gender Roles, Economic Relations, and Cultural Change among the Bontoc Igorot of Northern Luzon, Philippines." Ph.D. diss., Department of Anthropology, New School for Social Research, New York.

Clements, Helen Peeler. 1990. "La historia de una comunidad artesana: Santo Tomás Jalieza, 1857–1940." In *Lecturas históricas del Estado de Oaxaca, 1877–1930*, vol. 4. Oaxaca: INAH, Colección Regiones de México.

Clifford, James. 1988. *The Predicament of Culture*. Cambridge, Mass.: Harvard University Press.

CNN Interactive. 1997a. "Malaysian Opposition Criticizes Ban on Comments about Haze." www.cnn.co.fp/EARTH/971108/malaysia.haze/. November 8.

———. 1997b. "Moments Before Indonesian Crash, Jet Pilot Blinded by Haze." September 26. www3.cnn.com/WORLD/970926/indonesia.crash.pm/index.html.

Cohen, Jeffrey H. 1990. "Markets, Museums, and Modes of Production: Economic Strategies in Two Zapotec Weaving Communities of Oaxaca, Mexico." *Society for Economic Anthropology Newsletter, 1990,* 12–29.

———. 1997. "Popular Participation and Civil Society: The Shan-Dany Museum and the Construction of Community in Mexico." *Practicing Anthropology* 19(3): 36–40.

———. 1998. "Craft Production and the Challenge of the Global Market: An Artisans' Cooperative in Oaxaca, Mexico." *Human Organization* 57(1): 74–82.

———. 1999. *Cooperation and Community: Economy and Social Change in Rural Mexico.* Austin: University of Texas Press.

Comite del Museo Shan-Dany (CMSD). 1992. *Foleto del Mueso Shan-Dany.* Santa Ana del Valle, Tlacolula, Oaxaca: Comite del Museo Shan-Dany, Instituto Nacional de Antropología e Historia, y Gobierno Constitucional de Santa Ana del Valle, Tlacolula, Oaxaca.

Community Crafts Association of the Philippines (CCAP). 1997. *Fair Trader.* Manila, Philippines: CCAP.

Conner, Deborah. 1991. "An Ethnography of the Crownpoint Navajo Rug Auction." M.A. thesis, Department of Anthropology, New Mexico State University, Las Cruces.

Cook, Scott. 1984. "Peasant Economy, Rural Industry, and Capitalist Development in the Oaxaca Valley, Mexico." *Journal of Peasant Studies* 12(1): 3–40.

———. 1986. "The Managerial versus the Labor Function: Capital Accumulation and the Dynamics of Simple Commodity Production in Rural Oaxaca, Mexico." In *Entrepreneurship and Social Change,* Monographs in Economic Anthropology, edited by S. M. Greenfield and A. Strickon, 54–95. Lanham, Md.: University Press of America.

———. 1993. "Craft Commodity Production, Market Diversity, and Differential Rewards in Mexican Capitalism Today." In *Crafts in the World Market: The Impact of Global Exchange on Middle American Artisans,* edited by June Nash, 59–83. Albany: State University of New York Press.

Cook, Scott, and Leigh Binford. 1990. *Obliging Need: Rural Petty Industry in Mexican Capitalism.* Austin: University of Texas Press.

Coombe, Rosemary. 1993. "The Properties of Culture and the Politics of Possessing Identity: Native Claims in the Cultural Appropriation Controversy." *Canadian Journal of Law and Jurisprudence* 6(2): 249–85.

Csikzentmihalyi, M., and E. Rochberg-Halton. 1981. *The Meaning of Things: Domestic Symbols and the Self.* Cambridge: Cambridge University Press.

Cunningham, Clark E. 1958. *The Postwar Migration of the Toba-Bataks to East Sumatra.* Yale University Southeast Asia Studies Cultural Report Series. New Haven: Yale University Press.

DeCesare, Donna. 1998. "The Children of War: Street Gangs in El Salvador." *NACLA Report on the Americas* 32(1): 21–29.

Deere, Carmen Diana, and Magdalena León de Leal. 1981. "Peasant Production, Proletarianization and the Sexual Division of Labor in the Andes." *Signs* 7(2): 338–60.

Derks, Scott, ed. 1990. *The Value of a Dollar, 1860–1989.* Detroit: Gale Research.

Diehl, Keila. 1998. "Echoes from Dharamsala: Music in the Lives of Tibetan Refugees in North India." Ph.D. diss., Department of Anthropology, University of Texas, Austin.

di Leonardo, Micaela. 1991. "Introduction: Gender, Culture, and Political Economy: Feminist Anthropology in Historical Perspective." In *Gender at the Crossroads of Knowledge: Feminist Anthropology in the Postmodern Era,* edited by M. di Leonardo, 1–48. Los Angeles: University of California Press.

Dockstader, Frederick J. 1976. "The Marketing of Southwestern Indian Textiles." In *Irene Emery Roundtable on Museum Textiles,* edited by Irene Emery and Patricia Fiske, 467–76. Proceedings of Ethnographic Textiles of the Western Hemisphere. Washington, D.C.: Textile Museum.

Downer, Alan, and Al Klesert. 1990. "Preservation on the Reservation." In *Navajo Nation Papers in Anthropology*, vol. 26, edited by Alan Downer and Al Klesert, 201–6. Window Rock, Ariz.: Navajo Nation Historic Preservation Department.

Driscoll-Engelstad, Bernadette. 1998. "Contested Values: Inuit Art and Craft Production in the Canadian Arctic." Paper presented at the 14th International Congress of Anthropological and Ethnological Sciences, Williamsburg, Virginia, July 26– August 1.

Drummond, William. 1998. "Forced Out." National Public Radio Broadcast, September 21.

Dunsmore, John. 1997. "The Nettle Knitters of Nepal." *Eco Design Journal* 5(3): 37.

Dunsmore, Susi. 1993. *Nepalese Textiles.* London: British Museum Press.

Duus, Gloria. 1987. *Navajo Weavers and Wool Growers' Market Study.* Window Rock, Ariz.: Office of Navajo Women and Families.

Eber, Christine. 1995. *Women and Alcohol in a Highland Maya Town: Water of Hope, Water of Sorrow.* Austin: University of Texas Press.

———. 1998. *Seeking Justice, Valuing Community: Two Women's Paths in the Wake of the Zapatista Rebellion.* Women in International Development Working Paper Series, no. 265. East Lansing: Michigan State University Center for Women in International Development.

———. 1999. "Seeking Our Own Food: Indigenous Women's Power and Autonomy in San Pedro Chenalhó, Chiapas (1980–1996)." *Latin American Perspectives* 106: 6–36.

———. n.d. "Buscando una nueva vida (Looking for a New Life): Liberation through Autonomy in San Pedro Chenalhó, 1974–1998."

Eber, Christine, and Brenda Rosenbaum. 1993. "That We May Serve beneath Your Hands and Feet: Women Weavers in Highland Chiapas, Mexico." In *Crafts in the World Market: The Impact of Global Exchange on Middle American Artisans,* edited by June Nash, 154–80. Albany: State University of New York Press.

———. n.d. "Making Souls Arrive: Enculturation and Identity in Two Highland Chiapas Towns." Unpublished paper.

Ehlers, Tracy Bachrach. 1990. *Silent Looms: Women and Production in a Guatemala Town.* Boulder, Colo.: Westview.

———. 1993. "Belts, Business, and Bloomingdale's: An Alternative Model for Guatemalan Artisan Development." In *Crafts in the World Market: The Impact of Global Exchange on Middle American Artisans,* edited by June Nash, 181–98. Albany: State University of New York Press.

El-Guindi, Fadwa, and H. A. Selby. 1976. "Dialectics in Zapotec Thinking." In *Meaning in Anthropology,* edited by K. H. Basso and H. A. Selby, 181–96. Albuquerque: University of New Mexico Press.

El Periódico. 1997a. "La pobreza se afianza en Guatemala." December 19, 8.
————. 1997b. "Vivir en el filo." August 24, 13.

————. 1998. "Derrumbe cobra la vida de ocho personas." October 10, 3.

Esman, Milton J., and Norman T. Uphoff. 1984. *Local Organizations: Intermediaries in Rural Development*. Ithaca: Cornell University Press.

Espinosa, Lair, and Edgar Hidalgo. 1994. *Una experiencia de participación comunitaria en las Areas Precarias de la Guatemala*. Guatemala: UNICEF.

Etienne, Mona. 1980. "Women and Men, Cloth and Colonization: The Transformation of Production-Distribution Relations among the Baule (Ivory Coast)." In *Women and Colonization*, edited by M. Etienne and E. Leacock, 214–39. New York: J. F. Bergin.

Feld, Steven. 1990. *Sound and Sentiment: Birds, Weeping, Poetics, and Song in Kaluli Expression*. Philadelphia: University of Pennsylvania Press.

————. 1995. "From Schizophonia to Schismogenesis: On the Discourses and Commodification Practices of World Music and World Beat." In *The Traffic in Culture: Refiguring Art and Anthropology*, edited by G. E. Marcus and F. R. Myers, 96–126. Berkeley and Los Angeles: University of California Press.

Facultad Latino Americana de Ciencias Sociales (FLASCO). n.d. "La Brigada: Una colonia popular del Area Metropolitana de Guatemala." Unpublished research report.

Frazier, Lessie Jo. 1993. "Genre, Methodology, and Feminist Practice: Gladys Reichard's Ethnographic Voice." *Critique of Anthropology* 13(4): 363–78.

Fry, Howard T. 1983. *A History of the Mountain Province*. Quezon City, Philippines: New Day.

Gailey, Christine Ward. 1987. *Kinship to Kingship: Gender Hierarchy and State Formation in the Tongon Islands*. Austin: University of Texas Press.

Gaither, Edmund Barry. 1992. "Hey! That's Mine": Thoughts on Pluralism and American Museums." In *Museums and Communities: The Politics of Public Culture,* edited by I. Karp, C. M. Kreamer, and S. D. Lavine, 56–64. Washington, D.C.: Smithsonian Institution Press.

Gallin, Rita S., and Anne Ferguson. 1991. "Conceptualizing Difference: Gender, Class, and Action." In *The Women and International Development Annual*, vol. 2, edited by Rita S. Gallin and Anne Ferguson, 1–30. Boulder, Colo.: Westview.

García Canclini, Néstor. 1993. *Transforming Modernity: Popular Culture in Mexico*. Austin: University of Texas Press.

————. 1996. "North Americans or Latin Americans? The Redefinition of Mexican Identity and the Free Trade Agreements." In *Mass Media and Free Trade: NAFTA and the Cultural Industries,* edited by Emile McAnany and Kenton Wilkinson, 142–56. Austin: University of Texas Press.

Gay, José Antonio. 1986. *Historia de Oaxaca.* Mexico City: Editorial Porrúa, SA.

George, Susan. 1988. *A Fate Worse Than Debt.* New York: Grove Weidenfeld.

Ghimere, Durga. 1994. "Girl-Trafficking in Nepal: A Situation Analysis." In *Red Light Traffic: The Trade in Nepalese Girls,* edited by Priscilla Annamanthodo, 4–7. Kathmandu: ABC.

Gilbert, Alan. 1998. *The Latin American City.* 2d ed. London: Latin America Bureau.

Gleason, Judith. 1999. *Chiapas: Prayer for the Weavers.* New York: Filmmakers Library. Videocassette.

Global Exchange. 1998. *On the Offensive: Intensified Military Occupation in Chiapas Six Months Since the Massacre at Acteal, a Special Investigative Report, June.* San Francisco: Global Exchange.

Goin Papers. 1996. Museum of Northern Arizona, Flagstaff.

Greaves, Tom. 1994. *Intellectual Property Rights for Indigenous Peoples: A Sourcebook.* Oklahoma City: Society for Applied Anthropology.

Grimes, Kimberly. 1998. *Crossing Borders: Changing Social Identities in Southern Mexico.* Tucson: University of Arizona Press.

Handler, Richard. 1997. "Cultural Property, Culture Theory, and Museum Anthropology." *Museum Anthropology* 21(3): 3–4.

Harries-Jones, Peter. 1993. "Affirmative Theory: Reflections on the ASA Decennial." Paper presented in the Department of Anthropology, York University, Toronto, Ontario, October.

Hecht, Susanna, and Alexander Cockburn. 1990. *The Fate of the Forest: Developers, Destroyers, and Defenders of the Amazon.* New York: HarperCollins.

Hedstrom, Edward. 1997. "New Peace, Old Problems in Guatemala: Racial, Economic Divisions Remain." *San Francisco Chronicle,* January 6, A4.

Hellman, Judith. 1997. "Social Movements: Revolution, Reform, and Reaction." *NACLA* 30(6): 13–18.

Hendrickson, Carol. 1995. *Weaving Identities: Construction of Dress and Self in a Highland Guatemalan Town.* Austin: University of Texas Press.

Hernández Castillo, Rosalva Aída. 1998. "Construyendo la utopía esperanzas y desafíos de las mujeres Chiapanecas de frente al siglo XXI." In *La otra palabra: Las mujeres y violencia en Chiapas, antes y despues de Acteal,* edited by Rosalva Aída Hernández Castillo, 1–24. Mexico City: CIESAS, COLEM, and CIAM.

Hubbell Papers. 1875–1965. Documents, personal correspondence, journals, ledgers, and day books. Special Collections Library, University of Arizona, Tucson.

James, George Wharton. 1974 [1914]. *Indian Blankets and Their Makers.* New York: Dover.

Jefremovas, Villia. 1994. "Maids, Money, and Material: Class, Gender, and Textiles in Northern Luzon, Philippines." In *The Transformative Power of Cloth in Southeast Asia,* edited by Lynne Milgram and Penny Van Esterik, 102–14. Montreal: Canadian Asian Studies Association.

Jenista, Frank Lawrence. 1987. *The White Apos: American Governors on the Cordillera Central.* Quezon City, Philippines: New Day.

Jensen, Kurt Morck. 1987. *Non-Agricultural Occupations in a Peasant Society: Weavers and Fishermen in Noakhali, Bangladesh.* Center for Development Research Report, no. 12. Copenhagen: CDR.

Johnson, Harmer. 1980–99. "Auction Block." *American Indian Art Magazine.* Scottsdale, Arizona.

Johnston, Denis. 1966. *An Analysis of the Sources of Information on the Population of the Navajo.* Smithsonian Bulletin, no. 197. Washington, D.C.: Smithsonian Institution Press.

Jones, Marilyn. 1994. "Making a Difference: We Each Have Our Part to Play." *Taos Magazine* (August): 20–22.

Jules-Rosette, Bennetta. 1984. *The Messages of Tourist Art: An African Semiotic System in Comparative Perspective.* New York: Plenum.

———. 1986. "Aesthetics and Market Demand: The Structure of the Tourist Art Market in Three African Settings." *African Studies Review* 29(1): 41–59.

Kabeer, Nailar. 1994. *Reversed Realities: Gender Hierarchies in Development.* New York: Verso.

Kahlenberg, Mary Hunt, and Tony Berlant. 1972. *The Navajo Blanket.* New York: Praeger.

Kaplan, Flora. 1993. "Mexican Museums in the Creation of a National Image in World Tourism." In *Crafts in the World Market: The Impact of Global Exchange on Middle American Artisans,* edited by June Nash, 103–25. Albany: State University of New York Press.

Kapoun, Robert. 1992. *The Language of the Robe.* Salt Lake City: Peregrine Smith.

Karim, Wazir Jahan. 1995. "Introduction: Genderising Anthropology in Southeast Asia." In *'Male' and 'Female' in Developing Southeast Asia,* edited by Wazir J. Karim, 11–34. Oxford: Berg.

Kaufman, Alice, and Christopher Selser. 1985. *The Navajo Weaving Tradition 1650 to the Present.* New York: E. P. Dutton.

Keams, Kalley. 1996. "Beeldléí Bah Hane' (The Blanket Story)." In *Woven by the Grand-*

mothers, edited by Eulalie Bonar, 43–45. Washington, D.C.: Smithsonian Institution Press.

Kent, Kate Peck. 1985. *Navajo Weaving: Three Centuries of Change.* Santa Fe: School of American Research Press.

Kerkvliet, Benedict J. 1980. "Classes and Class Relations in a Philippine Village." *Philippine Sociological Review* 28: 31–50.

Kleymeyer, Charles, ed. 1994. *Cultural Expression and Grassroots Development.* Boulder, Colo.: Lynne Reinner.

Lavine, Steven. 1992. "Audience, Ownership, and Authority: Designing Relations between Museums and Communities." In *Museums and Communities: The Politics of Public Culture,* edited by I. Karp, C. M. Kreamer, and S. D. Lavine, 137–57. Washington, D.C.: Smithsonian Institution Press.

Leacock, Eleanor. 1981. "History, Development, and the Division of Labor by Sex: Implications for Organization." *Signs* 7(2): 474–91.

Link, Marty, ed. 1980. "The Growing Navajo Rug Market." *The Indian Trader* (November): 3–12.

Littlefield, Alice. 1978. "Exploitation and the Expansion of Capitalism: The Case of the Hammock Industry of Yucatan." *American Ethnologist* 5(3): 495–508.

Littrell, Mary, and Marsha Dickson. 1997. "Alternative Trading Organizations: Shifting Paradigm in a Culture of Social Responsibility." *Human Organization* 56(3): 344–52.

—————. 1999. *Social Responsibility in the Global Market: Fair Trade of Cultural Products.* Thousand Oaks, Calif.: Sage.

Lockwood, Victoria S. 1993. *Tahitian Transformations: Gender and Capitalist Development in a Rural Society.* Boulder, Colo.: Lynne Rienner.

Lundberg, Lea. 1981. "Threads of Tradition." *Arizona Living* 12(19): 16–18.

Lury, Celia. 1996. *Consumer Culture.* New Brunswick, N.J.: Rutgers University Press.

MacHenry, Rachel. 1998. "Women, Textiles, and Development." M.A. thesis, Central Saint Martins College of Art and Design, London.

Madeley, John. 1996 [1992]. *Trade and the Poor: The Impact of International Trade on Developing Countries.* 2d ed. London: Intermediate Technology.

Marcus, George, and Michael Fischer. 1986. *Anthropology as Cultural Critique: An Experimental Moment in the Human Sciences.* Chicago: University of Chicago Press.

Marcus, George, and Fred Myers. 1995. "The Traffic in Art and Culture: An Introduction."

In *The Traffic in Culture: Refiguring Art and Anthropology,* edited by G. E. Marcus and F. R. Myers, 1–54. Berkeley and Los Angeles: University of California Press.

Marín, Carlos. 1998. "Plan del ejército en Chiapas, desde 1994: Crear bandas paramilitares, desplazar a la población, destruir las bases de apoyo del EZLN." *Proceso* 1105 (January 4): 6–11.

May, Karen, and Sabrina Craig. 1994. "Women for Economic Justice Support J'Pas Joloviletik." *Gandhicrafts Journal* 4 (fall): 10–12.

Mazumdar, V. 1989. *Peasant Women Organise for Empowerment: The Bankura Experiment.* Occasional Paper, no. 13. New Delhi: Centre for Women's Development Studies.

McCracken, Grant. 1990. *Culture and Consumption: New Approaches to the Symbolic Character of Consumer Goods and Activities.* Bloomington: Indiana University Press.

M'Closkey, Kathy. 1996a. "Art or Craft?: The Paradox of the Pangnirtung Weave Shop." In *Women of the First Nations: Power, Wisdom, and Strength,* edited by Pat Chuchryk and Cristine Miller, 113–26. Winnipeg: University of Manitoba Press.

———. 1996b. "Myths, Markets, and Metaphors: Navajo Weaving as Commodity and Communicative Form." Ph.D. diss., Department of Anthropology, York University, Ontario, Canada.

McNitt, Frank. 1962. *The Indian Traders.* Norman: University of Oklahoma Press.

Mies, Maria. 1982. *The Lacemakers of Narsapur: Indian Housewives Produce for the World Market.* London: Zed.

Mies, Maria, and Vandana Shiva. 1993. *Ecofeminism.* London: Zed.

Milgram, B. Lynne. 1997. "Crossover, Continuity, and Change: Women's Production and Marketing of Crafts in the Upland Philippines." Ph.D. diss., Department of Anthropology, York University, Toronto, Canada.

———. 1998. "Craft Production and Household Practices in the Rural Philippines." In *Transgressing Borders: Critical Perspectives on Household, Gender, and Culture,* edited by Lynne Phillips and Suzan Ilcan, 169–88. Westport, Conn.: Bergin and Garvey.

———. 1999. "Locating 'Tradition' in the Striped Textiles of Banaue, Ifugao." *Museum Anthropology* 23(1): 3–20.

———. In press. "Situating Handicraft Market Women in Ifugao, Upland Philippines: A Case for Multiplicity." In *Women Traders in Cross-Cultural Perspective: Mediating Identities, Marketing Wares,* edited by Linda J. Seligmann. Stanford: Stanford University Press.

Mohanty, Chandra Talpade. 1991. "Under Western Eyes: Feminist Scholarship and Colonial Discourses." In *Third World Women and the Politics of Feminism,* edited by Chandra Mohanty, Ann Russo, and Lourdes Torres, 51–80. Bloomington: Indiana University Press.

Montoya, Alex. 1996. "Letter on Behalf of Navajo Health Foundation." Sage Memorial Hospital, Ganado, Arizona, November.

Moore, Henrietta. 1988. *Feminism and Anthropology.* Minneapolis: University of Minnesota Press.

Morales Lersch, Teresa, and C. Camarena Ocampo. 1987. "La experiencia de Constitución de Museo 'Shan-Dany,' de Santa Ana del Valle, Tlacolula, Oaxaca." *Boletín Oficial de Instituto Nacional de Antropología e Historia* 14: 9–11.

———. 1991. "La participación social en los museos." In *Etnia y Sociedad en Oaxaca,* edited by A. Castellanos Guerrero and G. López y Rivas, 181–90. Mexico City: Instituto Nacional de Antropología e Historia, y la Universidad Autónoma Metropolitana.

Morphy, Howard. 1991. *Ancestral Connections: Art and an Aboriginal System of Knowledge.* Chicago: University of Chicago Press.

Morris, Walter F. 1988. *Living Maya.* New York: Harry Abrams.

———. 1991. "The Marketing of Maya Textiles in Highland Chiapas, Mexico." In *Textile Traditions of Mesoamerica and the Andes: An Anthology,* edited by M. B. Schevill, Janet C. Berlo, and Edward B. Dwyer, 403–33. New York: Garland.

———. 1996. *Handmade Money: Latin American Artisans in the Marketplace.* Washington, D.C.: Organization of American States.

Nafziger, E. Wayne. 1978. *Class, Caste, and Entrepreneurship: A Study of Indian Industrialists.* Honolulu: University of Hawaii Press.

Nash, June. 1993a. "Introduction: Traditional Arts and Changing Markets in Middle America." In *Crafts in the World Market: The Impact of Global Exchange on Middle American Artisans,* edited by June Nash, 1–22. Albany: State University of New York Press.

———. 1993b. "Maya Household Production in the World Market: The Potters of Amatenango del Valle, Chiapas, Mexico." In *Crafts in the World Market: The Impact of Global Exchange on Middle American Artisans,* edited by June Nash, 127–53. Albany: State University of New York Press.

———. 1994a. "Global Integration and Subsistence Insecurity." *American Anthropology* 96(1): 7–30.

———. 1994b. "Producción artesanal y el desarrollo de la industria: Cambios en la transmisión cultural por medio de las mercancías." In *Semillas de industria: Transformaciones de la tecnología indígena en las Américas,* edited by M. Humberto Ruz, 99–122. Mexico City and Washington, D.C.: Centro de Investigaciones y Estudios Superiores and the Smithsonian Institution Press.

————. 1997. "When Isms Become Wasms: Structural Functionalism, Marxism, Feminism, and Postmodernism." *Critique of Anthropology* 17(1): 11–32.

Nash, June, and María Patricia Fernandez-Kelly, eds. 1983. *Women, Men, and the International Division of Labor.* Albany: State University of New York Press.

Nestor, Sarah. 1987. "The Woven Spirit." In *Harmony by Hand: Art of the Southwest Indians,* edited by Patrick Houlihan, 51–58. San Francisco: Chronicle Books.

North American Congress on Latin America (NACLA). 1994. "Disposable Children: The Hazards of Growing Up Poor in Latin America." *NACLA Report on the Americas* 27(6): 19.

Northern Luzon Federation of Cooperatives and Development Center (NORLU). 1992. *Capital Build-Up Strategies for Cooperatives/Credit Unions.* Baguio City: NORLU.

————. 1998. *The NORLU Education Training Unit Services.* Baguio City: NORLU.

O'Brian, Robin. 1997. *Maya Market Women's Sales Strategies in a Stationary Artisan Market and Response to Changing Gender Relations in Highland Chiapas, Mexico.* Women in International Development Working Paper Series, no. 261. East Lansing: Michigan State University Center for Women in International Development.

Otzoy, Irma. 1992. "Identidad y trajes Mayas." *Mesoamérica* 12(93): 95–112.

Page-Reeves, Janet. 1998. "Alpaca Sweater Design and Marketing: Problems and Prospects for Cooperative Knitting Organizations in Bolivia." *Human Organization* 57(1): 83–93.

Papanek, Victor. 1995. *The Green Imperative: Natural Design for the Real World.* London: Thames and Hudson.

Parpart, Jane L. 1995. "Deconstructing the Development 'Expert': Gender, Development and the 'Vulnerable Groups.'" In *Feminism, Postmodernism, and Development,* edited by Marianne Marchand and Jane Parpart, 221–43. New York: Routledge.

Par Yaxon, Julia. 1998. Personal communication to Martha Lynd. Panajachel, Sololá, Guatemala.

Pask, Amanda. 1993. "Cultural Appropriation and the Law: An Analysis of the Legal Regimes Concerning Culture." *Intellectual Property Journal* 8 (December): 57–86.

Pearce, Susan. 1995. *On Collecting: An Investigation into Collecting in the European Tradition.* London: Routledge.

Pedersen, Paul Bodholdt. 1970. *Batak Blood and Protestant Soul: The Development of National Batak Churches in North Sumatra.* Grand Rapids: Eerdmans.

Peiris, Kamala. 1997. *Weaving a Future Together: Women and Participatory Development.* Utrecht, Netherlands: International Books.

Pérez Sáinz, Juan Pablo. 1990. *Ciudad, subsistencia, e informalidad: Tres estudios sobre el Area Metropolitana de Guatemala.* Guatemala: FLASCO.

Phillips, Ruth, and Christopher Steiner, eds. 1999. *Unpacking Culture: Art and Commodity in Colonial and Postcolonial Worlds.* Berkeley and Los Angeles: University of California Press.

Picton, John. 1995. "Technology, Tradition, and Lurex: The Art of Textiles in Africa." In *The Art of African Textiles: Technology, Tradition, and Lurex,* edited by John Picton, 6–30. London: Lund Humphries.

Pradhan, Gauri. 1993. *Misery behind the Looms: Child Labourers in the Carpet Factories in Nepal.* Kathmandu: Child Workers in Nepal Concerned Center.

Prensa Libre. 1998. "Sumidos en la pobreza." October 13, 2.

Price, Sally. 1989. *Primitive Art in Civilized Places.* Chicago: University of Chicago Press.

Pye, Elwood. 1988. *Artisans in Economic Development: Evidence from Asia.* Ottawa, Canada: IDRC.

Rahnema, Majid. 1997. "Development and the People's Immune System." In *The Post-Development Reader,* edited by Majid Rahnema and Victoria Bawtree, 111–29. London: Zed.

Reichard, Gladys. 1950. *Navajo Religion: A Study in Symbolism.* Bollingen Series, no. 18. New York: Pantheon.

———. 1968 [1936]. *Navajo Shepherd and Weaver.* Glorieta, N.Mex.: Rio Grande Press.

Rinder, Lawrence. 1998. "Painting around the Fire: Maisin Culture and Collectivity." *Art Journal* 57(2): 61–72.

Rodee, Marian. 1996. *One Hundred Years of Navajo Rugs.* Albuquerque: University of New Mexico Press.

Rodenburg, Janet. 1997. *In the Shadow of Migration: Rural Women and Their Households in North Tapanuli, Indonesia.* Leiden: KITLV.

Rodman, Margaret C. 1987. "Constraining Capitalism? Contradictions of Self-Reliance in Vanuatu Fisheries Development." *American Ethnologist* 14(4): 712–26.

Roseberry, William. 1988. "Political Economy." *Annual Review in Anthropology* 17: 161–85.

Rosenbaum, Brenda. 1992. "Mujer Maya, tejido e identidad etnica: Un ensayo histórico." In *La indumentaria y el tejido Mayas a través del tiempo,* edited by L. Asturias de Barrios and D. Fernández, 57–69. Guatemala City: Museo Ichel del Traje Indígena de Guatemala.

———. 1993. *With Our Heads Bowed: The Dynamics of Gender in a Maya Community.* Austin: University of Texas Press.

Rosenbaum, Brenda, and Liliana Goldin. 1997. "New Exchange Processes in the International Market: The Re-Making of Maya Artisan Production in Guatemala." *Museum Anthropology* 21(2): 71–82.

Roth, Gabriel. 1997. "NAFTA on Crack." *San Francisco Bay Guardian,* October 15, 25.

Rovira, Guiomar. 1997. *Mujeres de maíz: La voz de las indígenas de Chiapas y la rebelión Zapatista.* Barcelona: Ediciones La Letra SCCL.

Rus, Diane. 1990. *La crisis económica y la mujer indígena: El caso de Chamula, Chiapas.* San Cristóbal de Las Casas: Instituto de Asesoría Antropológica para la Región Maya.

Rus, Jan. 1995. "Local Adaptation to Global Exchange: The Reordering of Native Society in Highland Chiapas, Mexico, 1974–1994." *European Review of Latin American and Caribbean Studies* 58: 71–89.

Russell, Susan D. 1987. "Middlemen and Moneylending: Relations of Exchange in a Highland Philippine Economy." *Journal of Anthropological Research* 43(2): 139–61.

Rutten, Rosanne. 1993. *Artisans and Entrepreneurs in the Rural Philippines: Making a Living and Gaining Wealth in Two Commercialized Crafts.* Quezon City, Philippines: New Day.

Sánchez Otero, Germán. 1993. "Neoliberalism and Its Discontents." *NACLA Report on the Americas* 26(4): 18–21.

Sattaur, Omar. 1996. *Nepal: New Horizons?* Oxford: Oxfam.

Schevill, Margot, and Jeffrey Foxx. 1997. *The Maya Textile Tradition.* New York: Harry N. Abrams.

Scott-Mundine, Djon. 1990. "Cultural Sustainability and the Market." In *Marketing Aboriginal Art in the 1990s: Papers Presented to a Workshop in Canberra,* edited by J. Altman and L. Taylor, 53–59. Canberra: Aboriginal Studies.

Seattle P-I Plus Getaways. 1997. "Smog from Forest Fires Leaves Much of SE Asia in the Shade." www.seattle-pi.com/pi/getaways/110697/smog06.html.

Sells, Cato. 1913. *Annual Report of the Commission of Indian Affairs.* Washington, D.C.: U.S. Government Printing Office.

SERRV International. 1999. *SERRV International 1998–1999 Catalog.* Bensonville, Ill.: World Color.

Sherman, D. George. 1990. *Rice, Rupees, and Ritual: Economy and Society among the Samosir Batak of Sumatra.* Stanford: Stanford University Press.

Smith, Lawrence. 1989. *North American Indian Arts: An Index of Prices and Auctions, 1985, 1986, 1987.* Albuquerque: Artlist.

Stamp, Patricia. 1989. *Technology, Gender, and Power in Africa.* Ottawa, Ontario: IDRC.

Steiner, Christopher B. 1994. *African Art in Transit.* Cambridge: Cambridge University Press.

Stephen, Lynn. 1987. "Zapotec Weavers of Oaxaca: Development and Community Control." *Cultural Survival Quarterly* 11(1): 46–48.

———. 1991a. "Culture as a Resource: Four Cases of Self-managed Indigenous Craft Production in Latin America." *Economic Development and Cultural Change* 40(1): 101–30.

———. 1991b. *Zapotec Women.* Austin: University of Texas Press.

———. 1993. "Weaving in the Fast Lane: Class, Ethnicity, and Gender in Zapotec Craft Commercialization." In *Crafts in the World Market: The Impact of Global Exchange on Middle American Artisans,* edited by June Nash, 25–57. Albany: State University of New York Press.

———. 1996 [1991]. "Export Markets and Their Effects on Indigenous Craft Production: The Case of the Weavers of Teotitlán del Valle, Mexico." In *Textile Traditions of Mesoamerica and the Andes: An Anthology,* edited by Margot Blum Schevill, Janet C. Berlo, and Edward B. Dwyer, 381–402. Austin: University of Texas Press.

Stromberg-Pellizi, Gobi. 1993. "*Coyotes* and Culture Brokers: The Production and Marketing of Taxco Silverwork." In *Crafts in the World Market: The Impact of Global Exchange on Middle American Artisans,* edited by June Nash, 85–100. Albany: State University of New York Press.

Swedish, Margaret. 1998. "Poverty: Guatemala's Other Peace Time Challenge." *Central America/Mexico Report* 18(5): 8.

Thakar, Prabha. 1995. "Carpet Making in Nepal." In *Do It Herself: Women and Technical Innovation,* edited by Helen Appleton, 231–48. London: Intermediate Technology.

Thomas, Nicholas. 1991. *Entangled Objects: Exchange, Material Culture, and Colonialism in the Pacific.* Cambridge, Mass.: Harvard University Press.

Thomas, Wesley. 1996. "Shil Yool T'ool: Personification of Navajo Weaving." In *Woven by the Grandmothers,* edited by Eulalie Bonar, 33–42. Washington, D.C.: Smithsonian Institution Press.

Tice, Karen. 1995. *Kuna Crafts, Gender, and the Global Economy.* Austin: University of Texas Press.

Tsosie, Rebecca. 1997. "Indigenous Peoples' Claims to Cultural Property: A Legal Perspective." *Museum Anthropology* 21(3): 5–27.

Tyabji, Laila. 1998. "A Designer in Development." In *Handmade in India,* edited by B. Page and L. Taylor, 30–39. London: Crafts Council Exhibition Catalogue.

Ujpan Pérez, Teresa. 1998. Personal communication to Martha Lynd. Panajachel, Solalá, Guatemala.

Underhill Ruth. 1983 [1956]. *The Navajo.* Norman: University of Oklahoma Press.

UNICEF. 1996. *Children and Women of Nepal: A Situation Analysis.* Kathmandu: UNICEF.

Vander Ryn, Sim. 1996. *Ecological Design.* Washington, D.C.: Stuart Cowan, Island Books.

Van Esterik, Penny. 1995. "Rewriting Gender and Development Anthropology in Southeast Asia." In *'Male' and 'Female' in Developing Southeast Asia,* edited by Wazir Jahan Karim, 247–59. Oxford: Berg.

Van Valkenburgh, R., and J. McPhee. 1974. *A Short History of the Navajo People.* New York: Garland.

Vásquez, Marcus, and L. Vásquez Dávila. 1992. *Como hacemos tapetes en Santa Ana del Valle.* Oaxaca: Casa de la Cultura Oaxaqueña, Instituto Technológico Agropecuario de Oaxaca, Oaxaca City.

Vásquez Dávila, Luz Elena, M. A. Vásquez, and M. B. Solís. 1992. "Fitoquímica tradicional: Las plantas Tintóreas de Santa Ana del Valle, Oaxaca." In *Etnias, desarrollo, recursos, y tecnologías en Oaxaca,* edited by A. González and M. A. Vásquez, 205–36. Oaxaca: CIESAS y Gobierno del Estado de Oaxaca.

Vázquez Rojas, Gonzalo. 1991. "Definición y metodología en los museos communitarios de Oaxaca." In *Etnia y sociedad en Oaxaca,* edited by A. Castellanos Guerrero and G. López y Rivas, 177–80. Mexico City: Instituto Nacional de Antropología e Historia y la Universidad Autónoma Metropolitana.

Villatoro, Elba. 1996. "La guerra interna en Guatemala: Efectos socioculturales y psicosociales en los pueblos Mayas." *Revista del Centro de Estudios Folkloricos: Tradiciones de Guatemala* 45: 109–42.

Wali, Afaka. 1994. "Living with the Land: Ethnicity and Development in Chile." In *Cultural Expression and Grassroots Development,* edited by Charles Kleymeyer, 167–78. Boulder, Colo.: Lynne Reinner.

Waspada. 1998a. "Aktivitas pelaku pariwisata di kota turis Parapat lumpuh." November 11. www.waspada.com/111198/sumut/sumut1.htm.

————. 1998b. "Keadaan kepariwisataan Parapat memprihatinkan." October 16. www.waspada.com/ 101698/sumut/sumut5.htm.

Weiner, Annette, and Jane Schneider. 1989. *Cloth and Human Experience.* Washington, D.C.: Smithsonian Institution Press.

Wheeler, Tony. 1977. *South-East Asia on a Shoestring.* Hawthorn, Australia: Lonely Planet.

————. 1989. *South-East Asia on a Shoestring.* 6th ed. Hawthorn, Australia: Lonely Planet.

Winn, Peter. 1976. "Workers into Managers: Worker Participation in the Chilean Textile Industry." In *Popular Participation in Social Change: Cooperatives, Collective, and Nationalized Industry,* edited by J. Nash, J. Danler, and N. S. Hopkins, 577–601. The Hague: Mouton.

Witherspoon, Gary. 1987. *Navajo Weaving: Art in Its Cultural Context, Monograph 37.* Flagstaff: Museum of Northern Arizona.

Wolf, Diane. 1996. "Situating Feminist Dilemmas in Fieldwork." In *Feminist Dilemmas in Fieldwork,* edited by Diane Wolf, 1–55. Boulder, Colo.: Westview.

Wood, William W. 1995. "Zapotec Artisans: The Genealogy of an 'Other.'" Paper presented at the American Anthropological Association Annual Meeting, Washington, D.C., November.

———. 1996. "Teotitlán del Valle: A Maquiladora in Oaxaca, Mexico." Paper presented at the American Anthropological Association Annual Meeting, San Francisco, December.

Zamora Chavarría, Eugenia María. 1994. "The Precarious Situation of Latin America's Children." *NACLA Report on the Americas* 27(6): 37.

ABOUT THE CONTRIBUTORS

Andrew Causey received his Ph.D. in anthropology from the University of Texas at Austin in 1997 and recently completed research at the Library of Congress as a Mellon Foreign Area Fellow. He is currently working in the curatorial department at the Texas State Preservation Board.

Jeffrey H. Cohen received his doctorate in 1994 from Indiana University, Bloomington. His work in rural Oaxaca focuses on three areas: craft production, economic development, and transnational migration. His book, *Cooperation and Community: Economy and Society in Oaxaca,* was published by the University of Texas Press in 1999. He teaches at Pennsylvania State University, University Park, where he lives with his wife Maria and children.

Christine E. Eber is an assistant professor of anthropology at New Mexico State University. She has been conducting research on women's experiences with social change in San Pedro Chenalhó, Chiapas, since 1984 and is involved in applied work with a weaving and a bakery cooperative there. She is author of *Women and Alcohol in a Highland Maya Town: Water of Hope, Water of Sorrow* (University of Texas Press, 1995).

Kimberly Grimes is the cofounder and director of Made By Hand International Cooperative, a nonprofit organization that assists in the social and economic development of artisans and their communities worldwide through the advancement of fair trade practices. She teaches at the University of Delaware in Georgetown and is the author of *Crossing Borders: Changing Social Identities in Southern Mexico* (University of Arizona Press, 1998).

Martha Lynd works full-time with Maya backstrap weavers in Guatemala. In her work with the fair trade business Maya Traditions, she documents and helps preserve traditional weaving patterns and incorporates these patterns into high-quality products for the U.S. market. She also facilitates herbal medicine and high school scholarship programs to benefit the families of the weavers. Research interests include healing people from war trauma and the promotion of indigenous crafts and of sustainable fair trade business in the context of integral community development.

Rachel MacHenry is currently a Ph.D. candidate in the Faculty of Environmental Studies, York University, Canada. Her research examines environmental concerns facing women textile producers in Nepalese cooperatives. She received her M.A. from Central Saint Martins College of Art and Design in England, where her thesis focused on fair trade and ecological issues in relation to village-level textile production in Nepal. She has been involved for the last six years with cooperative producers in Nepal and India.

Kathy M'Closkey is an adjunct assistant professor in the Department of Sociology and Anthropology, University of Windsor, Ontario, and a research associate at the Southwest Center, University of Arizona, Tucson. She continues to research archival sources to historicize the contributions of Navajo weavers within the context of the global political economy. Recent publications include, "Weaving and Mothering: Reframing Navajo Weaving as Recursive Manifestations of K'e," in *Transgressing Borders: Critical Perspec-*

tives on Gender, Household, and Culture, edited by Suzan Ilcan and Lynne Phillips (Bergin and Garvey, 1998), and *Threads of Time: Eldon House Embroideries* (London Regional Art and Historical Museums, 1998).

Lynne Milgram is a postdoctoral fellow in the Department of Anthropology, University of Toronto, and a research associate at the Royal Ontario Museum (Near Eastern and Asian Civilizations). Her research examines the commercialization of household crafts in the northern Philippines. Recent publications include, "Locating 'Tradition' in the Striped Textiles of Banaue, Ifugao," in *Museum Anthropology* 23(1) (1999), and "Crafts, Cultivation, and Household Economies: Women's Work and Positions in Ifugao," in *Research in Economic Anthropology* 20 (1999). Her current research analyzes women's craft cooperatives as well as women and microfinance initiatives in the Philippines.

June Nash has done research with Maya of Chiapas, Mexico, for the past forty years. She has published a monograph on a pottery-production village, *In the Eyes of the Ancestors,* and has edited three anthologies: *Crafts in the World Market, Artisan Production in State Formation,* and *The Explosion of Communities in Chiapas.* She has done research on gender, editing with Helen Safa, *Sex and Class in Latin America: Women and Change in Latin America,* and with M. Patricia Fernandez Kelly, *Women, Men, and the International Division of Labor.* She has also published books and articles on Bolivia and the United States. She is Professor Emeritus at the City College and Graduate School of the City University of New York.

Brenda Rosenbaum received her Ph.D. in anthropology from the State University of New York at Albany in 1987. Currently she works with Mayan Hands, a program linking Maya artisans with global markets, aiming both at improving the living standards of the artisans and creating awareness in first world countries of the political responsibility of consumers. She is the author of *With Our Heads Bowed: The Dynamics of Gender in a Maya Community* and recent articles dealing with gender, artisan production, and globalization.

INDEX